Changing Family Dynamics and Demographic Evolution

The Family Kaleidoscope

Edited by

Dimitri Mortelmans

Centre for Longitudinal Life Course Studies (CLLS), University of Antwerp, Belgium

Koenraad Matthijs

Centre for Sociological Research, KU Leuven, Belgium

Elisabeth Alofs

Faculty of Law and Criminology, Free University of Brussels, Belgium

Barbara Segaert

University Centre Saint Ignatius Antwerp, Belgium

Edward Elgar
PUBLISHING

Cheltenham, UK • Northampton, MA, USA

Published by
Edward Elgar Publishing Limited
The Lypiatts
15 Lansdown Road
Cheltenham
Glos GL50 2JA
UK

Edward Elgar Publishing, Inc.
William Pratt House
9 Dewey Court
Northampton
Massachusetts 01060
USA

A catalogue record for this book
is available from the British Library

Library of Congress Control Number: 2016935777

This book is available electronically in the **Elgar**online
Social and Political Science subject collection
DOI 10.4337/ 9781785364983

Printed on elemental chlorine free (ECF)
recycled paper containing 30% Post-Consumer Waste

ISBN 978 1 78536 497 6 (cased)
ISBN 978 1 78536 498 3 (eBook)

Typeset by Servis Filmsetting Ltd, Stockport, Cheshire
Printed and bound in the USA

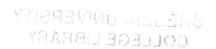

Contents

v

Contributors

Elisabeth Alofs (PhD in Law, Advanced Masters in Social Law) is Professor of Law at the Vrije Universiteit Brussel (Free University of Brussels), Belgium, where she teaches family law, matrimonial property law and inheritance law. She publishes on family law and social security law, especially about the legal status and protection of married and non-married partnerships in private and public law.

Tine Brouckaert has a PhD in Comparative Sciences of Culture at the Ghent University, Belgium and the University of Saint-Etienne, France. Her dissertation on 'Accoucher la citoyenneté. Expériences et témoignages de femmes sans-papiers à propos de leur travail maternel' (Giving birth to citizenship) addresses questions on mothering with an undocumented citizenship status. Her research interests are critical citizenship studies, mothering, anthropology of gender and diversity, postcolonial and feminist studies.

David De Wachter holds a PhD in Sociology and is a researcher at the University of Antwerp (Centre for Longitudinal and Life Course Studies, CLLS), Belgium, involved in research on socio-economic differentials in fertility and family formation in Europe and on the pension protection of first, second and subsequent generations of immigrants in Belgium.

Christine Defever holds a Master's degree in Sociology. She works as junior researcher in the Flemish Policy Research Centre on Equality Policies. She published a Gender Monitor for the Flemish Government and is currently researching lone parenthood and the transition to adulthood.

Katie Featherstone is Director of Post Graduate Research at Cardiff School of Nursing and Midwifery Studies, UK. Her expertise is in the sociology of biomedical knowledge, with particular emphasis on the social consequences of genetic technologies. She has produced a body of ethnographic work examining kinship and disclosure in the context of genetic risk information; the classification of genetic syndromes and their social consequence; the technologies of health service evaluation and clinical guidelines; and the diagnosis and classification of medical entities. The recurrent theme of this work is the production and translation of biomedical knowledge and the interaction between the laboratory, the clinic, and patient populations.

Frank F. Furstenberg is the Zellerbach Family Professor of Sociology and Research Associate in the Population Studies Center at the University of Pennsylvania, USA. His previous books and articles centre on children, youth, families and the public. His current research projects focus on the family in the context of disadvantaged urban neighbourhoods, adolescent sexual behavior, cross-national research on children's well-being and urban education.

Tine Kil holds a Master's degree in Sociology. She is currently working at the Centre for Longitudinal and Life Course Studies (CLLS) at the University of Antwerp, Belgium, where she is preparing a doctoral dissertation on the link between work, family and social policy. Her research focuses on socio-economic and ethnic differentials in family formation in Belgium.

Koenraad Matthijs is Full Professor of Sociology, and president of the Research Group Family and Population Studies at the Centre for Sociological Research, Faculty of Social Sciences, KU Leuven, Belgium.

Petra Meier is Professor at the Department of Political Science, University of Antwerp, Belgium and coordinator of the Flemish Policy Research Centre on Equality Policies. Her research and publications focus on the representation of gender in politics and policies. Her latest publication is *The Symbolic Representation of Gender. A Discursive Approach* (with Emanuela Lombardo, 2014, Ashgate).

Dimitri Mortelmans is Full Professor of Sociology at the Faculty of Social Sciences of the University of Antwerp, Belgium. He teaches qualitative research methods, applied multivariate statistics and advanced topics in family sociology, life-course sociology and demography. He is head of the Centre for Longitudinal and Life Course Studies (CLLS). His research concentrates on family sociology and sociology of labour. He has published on divorce, new constituted families, gendered labour careers and work–life balance. He is also the main author of the *Step in Statistics* book series of which six volumes have been published (in Dutch). On qualitative methodology, he published the *Handbook of Qualitative Research Methods* and *Qualitative Analysis with Nvivo*.

Lívia Murinkó holds a PhD in Sociology from the Corvinus University of Budapest, Hungary. She has been a Research Fellow at the Hungarian Demographic Research Institute (HDRI) since 2008. Her main research interests include family and household structure, fertility patterns, transition to adulthood, event history analysis and multilevel regression modelling. Her main publications in English are:

Spéder, Z., L. Murinkó and R.A. Settersten Jr. (2014), 'Are conceptions of adulthood universal and unisex? Ages and social markers in 25 European countries', *Social Forces*, 92 (3), 873–898.

Bartus, T., L. Murinkó, I. Szalma and B. Szél (2013), 'The effect of education on second births in Hungary: a test of the time-squeeze, self-selection and partner-effect hypotheses', *Demographic Research*, 28 (1), 1–32.

Karel Neels is Associate Professor of Demography and Statistics at the Centre for Longitudinal and Life Course Studies (CLLS) at the University of Antwerp, Belgium. His work focuses on patterns of family formation and the position of migrant populations in Belgium and Europe.

Jacqueline Scott is Professor of Empirical Sociology at the University of Cambridge, UK and a Fellow of Queens' College. From 2004 to 2009 she was director of a large UK research network on gender inequalities in production and reproduction, GeNet, funded by the Economic and Social Research Council. GeNet produced three edited books: *Women and Employment, Changing Lives and New Challenges* (Scott et al., 2008); *Gender Inequalities in the 21st Century* (Scott et al., 2010) and *Gendered Lives, Gender Inequalities in Production and Reproduction* (Scott et al., 2012). Her current interests include family change and life course research.

Barbara Segaert holds a Master's degree in Oriental Studies, Islamic Studies and Arab Philology from KU Leuven, Belgium and a Master's in the Social Sciences from the Open University, UK. Since 2002 she has been scientific coordinator at the University Centre Saint-Ignatius Antwerp, Belgium, where she develops academic programmes on various topics of contemporary relevance to society.

Wendy Sigle is Professor of Gender and Family Studies at the Gender Institute and the Centre for Analysis of Social Exclusion of the London School of Economics, UK. Her research applies both econometric and demographic methods to analyse questions on family issues. Her work spans a wide interdisciplinary base including sociology, economics, gender studies and demography. Thus far, the primary focus has been to gain a better understanding of the processes of family formation and the ways in which family structure is related to subsequent outcomes for children and adults in the United States and other industrialized countries.

Ivett Szalma holds a PhD in Sociology from the Corvinus University of Budapest, Hungary. She currently works as a Postdoc Researcher at the Swiss Centre of Expertise in the Social Sciences (FORS). She is the Head of the Family Sociology Section of the Hungarian Sociological Association. Her research topics include the effects of economic crises on work–life conflict, post-separation fertility, childlessness, and the measurement of homophobia and adoption by same-sex couples. Her main publications in English are:

Bartus, T., L. Murinkó, I. Szalma and B. Szél (2013), 'The effect of education on second births in Hungary: a test of the time-squeeze, self-selection and partner-effect hypotheses', *Demographic Research*, 28 (1), 1–32.

Szalma, I. and J. Takács (2013), 'Should men have more rights . . .? Gender role-related attitudes before and during the 2008 crisis', in G. Jónsson and K. Stefánsson (eds), *Retrenchment and Renewal? Welfare States in Times of Economic Crises*, Helsinki: NordWel Studies in Historical Welfare State Research 6.

Takács, J. and I. Szalma (2013), 'How to measure homophobia in an international comparison?', *Družboslovne Razprave*, 73 (1), 11–42.

Laurent Toulemon leads the Research Unit on Fertility, Family and Sexuality at the French National Institute for Demographic Studies (INED), Paris, France. His main research fields are fertility measures and determinants, including partnership behaviour and the use of contraception, migration and integration, family and children, society and solidarity, projections and forecasts. He is currently working on non-standard family forms, including multiple residence and, more precisely, the family situations related to having more than one usual residence. Together with Olivia Samuel and Anne Solaz, he is editor of the journal *Population*.

Jorik Vergauwen is currently working for the Centre for Longitudinal and Life Course Studies (CLLS) at the University of Antwerp, Belgium, where he is preparing his Doctoral dissertation. This dissertation is part of a research project on 'Socio-economic differentials in fertility and family formation in Europe: how are they related to social policies and economic context?' In the context of this project he is preparing several research papers on how transitions between living arrangements (in relation to family formation) are linked to economic context and interrelated with education. He has been presenting this work at various international conferences and some of the papers are pending publication in international peer-reviewed scientific journals.

Jonas Wood is Junior Researcher at the Centre for Longitudinal and Life Course Studies (CLLS) at the University of Antwerp, Belgium. His work focuses on socio-economic differentials in family formation, uptake of family policy, and maternal employment.

Introduction: a view through the family kaleidoscope

Dimitri Mortelmans, Koenraad Matthijs, Elisabeth Alofs and Barbara Segaert[1]

FAMILIES IN CONTEXT

Societies are always on the move, never attaining a long-term equilibrium. We shape and reshape our environment in a continuous fashion, creating the impression that we live in perpetual motion. Family life is no different from this. Even though many people find peace and quiet in their families, others see their families change at a pace they would not have thought possible. The same impressions arise when family scientists look at changes in families. On the one hand, they find stability: families are formed, children are born, and family solidarity remains one of the main pillars upon which families are built. Some of these patterns have existed for many centuries, while others may have existed since the dawn of mankind. At the same time, family forms are changing; in particular, the forms of family in which daily life is lived are subject to shifts that give the impression of acceleration and diversification. Demographic processes are known to evolve over time, but the changes witnessed in the family as a social phenomenon during the past 50 years give the impression that we have never before in history seen such speed in the evolution of family life. We know that this impression is faulty, and that we are historically blind (see, e.g., Coontz 2004, 2006; Therborn 2004): change has been continuous at all times and it is our mission as scientists to study this change and look at its consequences today.

The story of the recent demographic evolutions has, to a large extent, been documented (Sobotka and Toulemon 2008). In the late 1960s, demographic behaviour started to shift as people started marrying later and parenthood was postponed (Billari and Liefbroer 2010). Couples also had fewer children than before, leading to below replacement fertility in many countries (Billari et al. 2007; Frejka and Sobotka 2008). At the same time, divorce figures started to climb to unprecedented levels (Kalmijn 2007).

The next step was the slow abandonment of marriage, the ascent of unmarried cohabitation and the subsequent rise of births out of wedlock (Kiernan 2001, 2002). Theoretical explanations have been offered from both the economic and the demographic sides. The economic explanation draws largely upon the new home economics of Gary Becker (Becker 1981; Becker et al. 1977) and posits that the increased labour participation of women changed the opportunity costs of marriage and parenthood. Being economically independent implies having the power to make one's own choices, and having the opportunity to leave an unhappy marriage. The introduction of the contraceptive pill also meant the making of independent choices as a mother, and gave women the possibility to postpone parenthood or even reject it entirely. A more cultural explanation is given by considering values. According to the paradigm of the second demographic transition (Lesthaeghe 2010; Lesthaeghe and Van de Kaa 1986), the driving force behind the immense changes was an ideational shift. Using Inglehart's (1977) notion of postmaterialism, the theory argues that economic circumstances and increased labour participation of women are not sufficient explanations. Individualistic and anti-authoritarian values, spreading through Western societies as welfare states were maturing, gave rise to changing views on relationships and led to changes in demographic behaviour. Neither the new home economics nor the theory of second demographic transition has succeeded in explaining all evolutions occurring in Europe and beyond. Yet they are 'powerful narratives' (Sobotka 2008) serving to link transitions and to shed light on their interrelatedness across countries. A third, more recent, stream explains family dynamics by pointing to the evolution in gender equality across countries. This 'incomplete revolution', as Esping-Anderson (2009) calls it, points to the shifting behaviour and preferences of women in families. Throughout the evolution of families in the late twentieth and early twenty-first centuries, the shifting role of women, their preferences and the late adaption by men explains why countries evolve at different tempos, and to different degrees (Esping-Andersen and Billari 2015; Goldscheider et al. 2015).

THE FAMILY KALEIDOSCOPE

Although scholars struggle to agree upon a theoretical framing, the trends involving the transition of family dynamics are clear and impressive during the past four decades. Both from the American and the European perspective, the conclusion is that family life has become more diverse and more complex. This has inspired us to use the image of a kaleidoscope to look at this diversity and complexity. The word 'kaleidoscope' originates from the Greek words *kalos* (beauty), *eidos* (form) and *skopos* (examine). The kaleidoscope thus looks at the beauty of different forms. This is exactly what this book aims to do. We start with Chapters 1 and 2 by Furstenberg and Toulemon, respectively, and look at the diversity and fragmentation of present-day family life. Like the kaleidoscope, each turn generates a different view through the built-in mirrors reflecting new insights into the coloured glass and beads. With this book, we bring the reader new insights into the field of family dynamics and family diversity.

An overview of the content reveals that our particular kaleidoscope offers five different views on the matter at hand. These five perspectives connect the chapters transversally and show not only how the field of family studies investigates diversity and complexity, but also how it is composed of diverse and complex themes and angles.

A first view the kaleidoscope offers, regards the diversity of families, by taking the wide range of family forms into account. In this book, analyses are presented of childless families, young parenthood and empty-nest families. Many chapters take the perspective of children in families, a bottom-up perspective that reveals another wide variety of possible living arrangements for children. Not only do children grow up in married and unmarried families, divorced families with children also make clear that single parents, reconstituted families and re-re-constituted families cover the daily environment of children (Toulemon, Chapter 2 and Furstenberg, Chapter 1). In addition, custody arrangements go beyond the classic mother model or the 50:50 co-parenthood model. Children of divorced couples now move more frequently between their parents, and (moving) stepchildren add to the complexity of the family even further (Murinkó and Szalma, Chapter 8).

This book also captures a wide range of disciplines and theoretical perspectives. Even though family studies have a rich tradition in sociology and social demography, the range of disciplines looking at family life is much broader. This book offers perspectives from the fields of epidemiology (Featherstone, Chapter 6), anthropology (Brouckaert, Chapter 5) and gender studies (Furstenberg, Chapter 1 and Sigle, Chapter 9), all contributing ways of looking at cross disciplinary boundaries. Intersectionality invites traditional and dominant perspectives to open up their views and embrace new lines of thinking, analysing and informing policies, Siglie (Chapter 9) argues.

A third aspect of the book is that it does not centre on one methodology. Quantitative methodology, being dominant in family studies, is usually a connecting thread in books on population and family issues. Sophisticated survival analyses and multilevel models explore the complexity of processes that unfold over time. This book, however, also offers insights gained via qualitative methodologies (Brouckaert, Chapter 5). Using ethnography and living with undocumented women reveals hidden facets of their reality that no survey could ever capture. Additionally, CART analyses (classification and regression trees) (Mortelmans et al., Chapter 4 and Sigle, Chapter 9) show how new quantitative techniques can reveal populations that would remain invisible with traditional regression-style analyses. The sophistication of today's graphical representations adds to the depth of exploring data and integrating theoretical perspectives such as the intersectionality approach.

A fourth kaleidoscopic look brings us to levels of analysis. Most of this introduction thus far has focused on the complexity that arises when studying trends over time. This is certainly one of the major domains of interest, but the book also offers a unique perspective on the interplay between macro and micro perspectives. The international community has invested a lot of effort in collecting comparable survey data enriched with context indicators. This allows us to study family processes such as fertility decisions in a wider context, the most obvious of which – from a European perspective – is the nation state. De Wachter et al. (Chapter 7) and Murinkó and Szalma (Chapter 8) use international harmonized data to compare the influence of context at the state level. They empirically document what Furstenberg and Toulemon observed in the introductory chapters: context matters, and the complexity of change can be explained by taking this context into account. When society changes, and especially when change is going at a rather quick pace, stragglers find themselves in a disadvantaged position. New family compositions seem to be characterized by neutrality and free choice, but instead turn out to be factors of segregation and discrimination. One of the major inequalities that has barely changed during the family turnover is gender. We have already mentioned the plea of Sigle to bring in the feminist concept of intersectionality but Kil et al. (Chapter 3) also point at the often forgotten stagnation in the division of household labour. Gender roles have evolved tremendously, leading to a greater gender equity within couples, but when it comes down to the activities in the kitchen and laundry room, the old male breadwinner model still prevails in the daily lives of partners.

A fifth and last reality that the kaleidoscope shows us is the inertia of institutions. Most of our welfare systems are built on the idea of a breadwinner society with a clear-cut division of labour between men and women. Marriage is at the heart of the system and supports the legislation regarding property, social security, some labour market regulations, and so on. Even though our institutions have changed enormously during the past century, they often show a remarkable lag when it comes to catching up with demographic evolutions. The final chapter of the book

(Scott, Chapter 10) looks at this inertia from the point of policy makers. If institutions are not adapted to societal change, policy makers are the ones that need to change them. Family policy, and more specifically the care deficit, is debated in Scott's chapter. She shows how ideology can blur the policy discussion, and continues to fuel the inertia.

OUTLINE OF THE BOOK

The book is divided into four parts. Part I builds on this introduction, and looks back at changes in family diversity and family dynamics. From a trans-Atlantic perspective, Furstenberg (Chapter 1) and Toulemon (Chapter 2) sketch a historical and geographical overview of the major changes that have occurred in the past few decades. This is mirrored in Part IV, where Sigle (Chapter 9) and Scott (Chapter 10) cast a forward glance, focusing on new theoretical perspectives to study the kaleidoscope and the policy context that will need to respond to it. Even though all the chapters are connected in many ways, we chose to organize them thematically in the book. Besides the mentioned historical and prospective view, two guiding principles became apparent throughout the different chapters: a focus on gender, and a focus on children. These connections were taken as a guiding principle to organize Parts II and III.

The first two chapters set the scene of this book on family transitions by picturing the above-mentioned evolutions from a US and a European perspective. Furstenberg's Chapter 1 spans half a century of developments in American family life. Departing from the 1963 prediction of William Goode (1963) that family life would converge to the conjugal family, he shows how divergence was what actually took place after the 1960s. Like Esping-Andersen and Billari (2015) and Goldscheider et al. (2015), Furstenberg also considers the gender revolution as one of the major forces driving the changes behind families. He shows how a combination of economic, technological, social and cultural factors all undermined the traditional male breadwinner model of the early post-war era. The gender role revolution went hand in hand with a widening stratification in the American society. Furstenberg describes this as the two-tiered family system. The top tier consists of well-educated and rich couples who cohabit for a certain period, after which they usually marry. Children in the top tier get more resources and time from their parents and are more likely to end up in a more favourable position themselves (Carlson and England 2011). The lower tier consists of more disadvantaged couples who cohabit early and often have children within a short period of time. In this second tier, families are much more unstable, generating more complex families as time passes. Social inequality is both installed and reinforced by this two-tiered family system.

The first chapter ends with a comparison with Europe, which connects perfectly to Chapter 2 by Toulemon, who examines family change across Europe. Toulemon documents the same kind of processes as Furstenberg, but shows the European variations in these patterns. For instance, not all European countries have followed the same pace through the generations; there are clear differences marked by the North–South and West–East gradients. Toulemon maintains that the differences in pace notwithstanding, the economic, technological, social and cultural factors play a similar role in all European countries. The differentiation in family trajectories does not go uniformly hand in hand with social stratification processes, as was suggested by Furstenberg for the US; most of Europe's diversity is due to institutional, political and cultural differences among its nation-states, rather than to social stratification.

Part II of the book combines three chapters that take the analysis of gender as a starting point. Kil, Neels and Vergauwen (Chapter 3) provide us with a pan-European outlook on gender inequality in domestic work. Using data from the European Social Survey, they show that the gender balance in domestic work throughout the continent still disfavours women compared to men. The gender gap is smaller in younger families and families without children. In a multilevel analysis, both the national gender culture and the policy context interact with micro-level characteristics. Gender culture turns out to be more important for the division of unpaid labour than national policies on gender equality.

Chapter 4, by Mortelmans, Meier and Defever, uses intersectionality in an empirical study on early adulthood. Drawing on what Sigle (Chapter 9) calls an 'inter-categorical' approach, these authors examine social categories such as gender, ethnicity and social class in order to expose patterns of inequality in the transition to adulthood. Leaving the parental home is a particular moment in an adolescent's life; it is a moment of great change, but it also turns out to be a transition in the life course with a high risk of increasing inequalities between young adults. Using a cross-national, quantitative intersectionality approach, the chapter identifies groups exposed to an accumulation of risk factors. The chapter concludes with a reflection on how quantitative analysis can adopt the intersectionality approach and provide new insights that can guide policies.

Chapter 5 by Brouckaert shows how ethnographic methods can unveil gender inequality in impoverished high-risk families. Brouckaert participated in the lives of undocumented mothers surviving in the anonymity of urban areas. She focuses on the ways these mothers instil 'feelings of home'. When living in an undocumented, 'illegal' way in a country, the concept of 'home' for a mother with her children is quite problematic. The chapter shows that daily, repetitive tasks like preparing food are essential practices in establishing some notion of integration with the society they are living in. Highlighting the importance of mundane activities like preparing food for a family, Brouckaert touches on the basic elements of what can turn households into families.

Part III presents three studies that take the perspective of children. Children are important actors in families and the diversity of research focusing upon children not only illustrates this importance, but also points to the huge vulnerabilities and inequalities that exist among the variety of families with children. In Chapter 6, Featherstone links Parts II and III by focusing on both gender and children in her study on genetic risk and its place in family life. Touching upon the same basic issues of what constitutes a family, Featherstone uses genetically inherited diseases as starting point for a qualitative study on the core essence of kinship. The study explores patterns of (non-)disclosure within families affected by an inherited degenerative condition.

De Wachter, Neels, Wood and Vergauwen (Chapter 7) take another aspect of (young) households into consideration: female labour participation and childcare. More specifically, they look at the educational gradient of maternal employment patterns in 11 European countries. Using the first round of the Generations and Gender Survey, they show how more highly educated women tend to stay active on the labour market after giving birth. Low-educated women, on the other hand, tend to leave the labour market or decrease their working hours. The country comparison showing that the educational gradient is clearer for highly educated women, indicating that they receive better chances to combine work and family life compared to low-educated women. This gender inequality is partially explained by taking the differential use of childcare into account.

In the third chapter of Part III, a cross-country analysis is again used on the Gender and Generations Survey. In Chapter 8, Murinkó and Szalma focus on re-partnering from the perspective of men. The analysis not only takes a comparative perspective but also provides detailed insight into different family constellations that men end up in after a relational break-up. Not only are cohabiting and marital unions considered, but also – and more importantly – the residential arrangements of the children. This approach reveals that co-residence with children after parental separation in general makes it easier for men to re-partner. The country differences were small, indicating a parallel trend between France, Hungary and Norway.

The concluding Part IV of the book ambitiously looks into the future. In the demographic literature, this might mean that simulations give an insight into how future developments are expected to go, under well-defined conditions. We conclude our kaleidoscopic view on families by taking theory and policy prospects into account.

Chapter 9 by Sigle looks at theoretical perspectives in the field of demography and the predominance of economic theory therein. A dominance as such is not problematic, she argues, but the hegemonic refusal to use different perspectives when needed, leads to an impoverishment of the field. The chapter uses the concept of intersectionality as an example of how demographic research can be enriched by new insights from disciplines other than economics. Intersectionality, as a feminist research paradigm, points to the separability and multiplicativity of sex and race as social categories, the former dominated by white educated women and the latter by black men. Using fertility as an example, Sigle shows how intersectionality can help to gain other – more critical – insights than the current frameworks would allow.

The book concludes with a prospective outlook from Scott (Chapter 10). Policy needs scientific evidence to inform decision-making, she argues. Two crucial areas – child-centred perspectives and gender inequalities – are at the heart of this debate. The child perspective is crucial because research in sociology is too often adult-centred, leaving out the lived experiences of the children themselves. Scott illustrates this by using child poverty as an example. Gender inequality is illustrated as a major domain where the scientific body of evidence is huge. At the same time, (United Kingdom) policy deals with the work–life issue in multiple ways, leading to very different and often unexpected outcomes. The conclusions from these analyses lead to a plea not only to 'deconstruct' the literature on children and gender inequalities but also, more importantly, to give room to knowledge-based policies that go beyond ideologies that simply misuse or misinterpret scientific results.

NOTE

1. This book is based on an international workshop organized by the University Centre Saint-Ignatius Antwerp (www.ucsia.org) at the University of Antwerp, Belgium, in March 2014. During this workshop, a multidisciplinary group of experts exchanged ideas and results on the panoply of new family forms and its societal challenges (more at http://www.ucsia.org/main.aspx?c=*UCSIAENG2&n=116376).

REFERENCES

Becker, G.S. (1981), *A Treatise on the Family*, Cambridge, MA: Harvard University Press.

Becker, G.S., E.M. Landes and R.T. Michael (1977), 'An economic analysis of marital instability', *Journal of Political Economy*, 85 (6), 1141–1188.

Billari, F.C., H.P. Kohler, G. Andersson and H. Lundstrom (2007), 'Approaching the limit: long-term trends in late and very late fertility', *Population and Development Review*, 33 (1), 149–170. doi:10.1111/j.1728-4457.2007.00162.x.

Billari, F.C. and A.C. Liefbroer (2010), 'Towards a new pattern of transition to adulthood?', *Advances in Life Course Research*, 15 (2–3), 59–75. doi:j.alcr.2010.10.003.

Carlson, M. and P. England (2011), *Social Class and Changing Families in an Unequal America*, Stanford, CA: Stanford University Press.

Coontz, S. (2004), 'The world historical transformation of marriage', *Journal of Marriage and Family*, 66 (4), 974–979.

Coontz, S. (2006), *Marriage, a History: How Love Conquered Marriage*, London: Penguin.

Esping-Andersen, G. (2009), *The Incomplete Revolution. Adapting to Women's New Roles*, Cambridge: Policy Press.

Esping-Andersen, G. and F.C. Billari (2015), 'Re-theorizing family demographics', *Population and Development Review*, 41 (1), 1–31. doi:10.1111/j.1728-4457.2015.00024.x.

Frejka, T. and T. Sobotka (2008), 'Overview chapter 1: fertility in Europe: diverse, delayed and below replacement', *Demographic Research*, 19 (3), 15–46. doi:10.4054/DemRes.2008.19.3.

Goldscheider, F., E. Bernhardt and T. Lappegård (2015), 'The gender revolution: a framework for understanding changing family and demographic behavior', *Population and Development Review*, 41 (2), 207–239. doi:10.1111/j.1728-4457.2015.00045.x.

Goode, W.J. (1963), *World Revolution and Family Patterns*, New York: Free Press of Glencoe.

Inglehart, R. (1977), *The Silent Revolution: Changing Values and Political Styles among Western Publics*, Princeton, NJ: Princeton University Press.

Kalmijn, M. (2007), 'Explaining cross-national differences in marriage, cohabitation, and divorce in Europe, 1990–2000', *Population Studies*, 61 (3), 243–263. doi:10.1080/00324720701571806.

Kiernan, K. (2001), 'The rise of cohabitation and childbearing outside marriage in Western Europe', *International Journal of Law, Policy and the Family*, 15 (1), 1–21. doi: 10.1093/lawfam/15.1.1.

Kiernan, K. (2002), 'Cohabitation in Western Europe: trends, issues, and implications', in A. Booth and A.C. Crouter (eds), *Just Living Together: Implications of Cohabitation on Families, Children, and Social Policy*, Mahwah, NJ: Lawrence Erlbaum Associates Publishers, pp. 3–32.

Lesthaeghe, R. (2010), 'The unfolding story of the second demographic transition', *Population and Development Review*, 36 (2), 211–251. doi:10.1111/j.1728-4457.2010.00328.x.

Lesthaeghe, R. and D.J. Van de Kaa (1986), 'Twee demografische transities?', in D.J. Van de Kaa and R. Lesthaeghe (eds), *Bevolking: Groei en krimp*, Deventer: Van Loghum Slaterus, pp. 9–24.

Sobotka, T. (2008), 'Overview chapter 6: the diverse faces of the second demographic transition in Europe', *Demographic Research*, 19 (8), 171–224. doi:10.4054/DemRes.2008.19.8.

Sobotka, T. and L. Toulemon (2008), 'Changing family and partnership behaviour: common trends and persistent diversity across Europe', *Demographic Research*, 19 (6), 85–138. doi:10.4054/DemRes.2008.19.6.

Therborn, G. (2004), *Between Sex and Power: Family in the World 1900–2000*, New York: Routledge.

PART I

Looking back at families

1. The changing American family: an overview from 1965 to 2015

Frank F. Furstenberg

INTRODUCTION

With the United States Supreme Court ruling in *Obergefell v. Hodges* that welcomed same-sex marriage in June 2015, the concept of the American family was once again reformed. The turnabout on marriage reflects society's changing opinions, values and attitudes toward same-sex marriage; and, I might argue, the American 'family' as we know it. Indeed, the changes in marriage, childbearing and family formation have been equally dramatic (and not confined to the United States). The long-standing link between the initiation of sex and marriage has broken down. Marriage, at least as we have known it, has weakened in most nations. Cohabitation has become more widespread and acceptable in almost all Western countries. Rates of non-marital childbearing have risen; childbearing, especially in marriage, occurs much later; rates of childlessness are growing quickly; and as I will discuss, social class differences in family formation in the United States have become more pronounced with growing inequality.

Although many lament the passing of the 'traditional' family, one wonders if there ever was such a thing. Certainly from my perspective – a student of family change for the past half-century – the bedrock 'traditional' family was never really evident, save perhaps for a short-lived time in the mid-twentieth century; a time we now hold up as the 'golden era' of the family. But a closer look reveals that this golden era was not only short-lived, but perhaps an anomaly.

This chapter chronicles the rapid changes in the American family from my own particular vantage point as a sociologist and family scholar. I have witnessed and studied changes in the American family system from the time I was in graduate school in the mid-1960s to the present, and the change that has occurred over the past half-century was simply unimaginable back then. Indeed, my mentor and thesis advisor, William J. Goode, arguably the most influential family scholar of the past century, missed the mark when it came to foreseeing the future of the Western family system. When he published his landmark book on family change in 1963, it was impossible to fathom the changes that would take place. In this chapter, I provide an overview of these changes, a set of reasons why the changes occurred, and a commentary on the underlying sources of tension created by the new, more class-based family system that has emerged in the United States.

THE 'IDEAL' VANISHES

In the mid-1960s, when I began my study of teenage parenthood in Baltimore, the marriage pattern of the post-war years – romantic, almost impetuous early marriage – was still largely intact. Little did I know then, but I would have a ringside seat to the breakdown of this standard of early marriage. The changes that I was witnessing among black teens would foreshadow trends in non-marital childbearing that would soon sweep through the rest of the lower-income, less-advantaged population.

At the time, almost all the pregnant white teens in my study (about one-fifth of the sample) married before their child was born. The few that did not, gave up their children for adoption. Black pregnant teens, however, faced a different set of choices shaped by a lack of steady employment and poor prospects for finding jobs in the immediate future among the fathers of their children. At the time, well-paying, low-skilled jobs were beginning to leave American shores, a trend that would also affect white working males within just a few years. Mothers frequently counselled their daughters to postpone marriage until they and the fathers had completed their education and found employment. 'I told her not to marry him just to give the child a name', was a phrase I heard often in the interviews. 'Wait until he has something more to offer you', mothers counselled. The daughters did not always take their mothers' advice, but almost all confessed later that they wished they had (Furstenberg 1976).

It was becoming clear that the 'logic' of early marriage was beginning to no longer make sense to the most disadvantaged women and their families, and as more African Americans began to eschew early marriage, rates of non-marital childbearing among them soared. Had I begun my study 15 or 20 years later, I would have heard the same discussions among the families of the white teenagers. By then, the trade-off for pregnant women between a precipitous marriage and having a child outside of marriage had changed for the vast majority of American women, and the stigma of non-marital childbearing had all but disappeared.

So how did we get from here to there, and why did the changes unfold so rapidly? The story is complex and certainly not caused by a single event or action. A transformation in cultural norms and attitudes interacted with structural upheavals in work, wages and gender roles. But the first ripple in the changing landscape became apparent with the burgeoning women's movement that accompanied women's greater participation in the labour force.

In 1963, before I began my work in Baltimore, William J. Goode predicted a general convergence to the conjugal family of two parents and their children with well-defined gender roles. How wrong he turned out to be.[1] Elsewhere I have argued (Furstenberg 2013) that Goode simply did not see what was practically staring him in the face in the 1960s: an impending gender revolution that unsettled the seeming inevitability of the conjugal family. Even before Betty Friedan's (1963) *The Feminine Mystique* unleashed a movement, scholars (Bernard 1942; Komarovsky 1946) had detected a restlessness among women, born of a cultural contradiction in well-educated families. In such families, parents had been sending their daughters to college in growing numbers, only to expect them to go from college directly to their husband's home as a homemaker. The growing frustration with this role led many young women directly into the workforce for the first time. Meanwhile, among the less affluent and those without college degrees, women were entering the workforce as well; for other reasons, in part to supplement eroding male wages to maintain rising living standards that had characterized the post-war era. Some were also supporting children, with the rise in non-marital childbearing and divorce rates. As an indication of just how rapid a change this was, in the 1960s, 38 per cent of women were in the workforce. By 1980, more than half were in the workforce; and in 2000, six in ten women were working outside the home, and with greater frequency when they had young children.

At the same time, the availability of widespread family planning services and, especially, the advent of oral contraceptives, allowed women to exercise greater control over the timing of their children's births (Furstenberg 2007). For the first time, unmarried women could initiate sex without the fear of getting pregnant. In 1973, the Supreme Court affirmed the right to legal abortion, giving women another strategy for managing ill-timed and unwanted pregnancies. The growing practice of family planning facilitated and extended the work lives of women who increasingly were being counted on as supplementary wage earners or household heads. Increasingly, white women began to hedge their bets against dependency on men, much as African American women had long done, by becoming more economically self-sufficient.

Although demographic and historical scholars have not completely sorted out all of the precise paths of influence, what we do know is that from the late 1960s to the present, in a broadly linear fashion, women entered the labour force in growing numbers, marriage age began to rise, women began to feel more empowered and even compelled to pursue careers and full-time employment, use of contraceptives steadily increased, and the fertility of married couples declined accordingly.

THE EMERGENCE OF A TWO-TIERED FAMILY SYSTEM

As these changes took hold, a split began to appear between families in the upper- and low-income brackets, as inequality rose sharply from the 1980s to the present. As a result, the United States began to move toward a two-tiered family system. In the top tier of well-educated and affluent Americans, couples typically do not marry until late in their twenties or early thirties. There is now usually an extended period of cohabitation where the relationship is time-tested before they marry and before having children.

This delay occurred for a number of reasons. The time it takes to complete education has increased as children from privileged families, (financially) supported by their families, now expect not only to complete college but also to gain experience in the labour market and then return to university to receive further graduate training. They have come to regard early adulthood as a staging period for launching a career and family, but they are in less of a hurry to do so than they once were. Marriage itself is no longer the signal event that used to be, the mainspring in the transition to adulthood. If anything, it has been relegated to a second stage that occurs once education has been completed and economic autonomy is established.

As I have written elsewhere (Furstenberg 2011), marriage is increasingly regarded as less of a pledge to commitment than a celebration of commitment that has already been demonstrated. Marriage is also a transition, signalling that the couple is ready to have a family. They have acquired, in the words of some, 'the marriage mentality' (Kefalas et al. 2011). In other words, they are ready and able to settle into family life because the couple have deemed that they are emotionally well suited to each other and have sufficient resources to support a family, even if they have not decided that they want children immediately or, for that matter, ever. Under these conditions, it is not surprising that when marriages occur, their prospects of surviving are greater than they were 50 years ago (Goldstein and Kenney 2001).

In the second tier, couples generally begin forming unions – though rarely marriages – earlier than their well-educated counterparts; almost as swiftly as happened 50 years ago (Manning et al. 2013).[2] Often a pregnancy is involved. Although in the past an impending pregnancy typically meant marriage, today that is less likely to occur among those with less education. Forty per cent of women with only a high school degree have a child before marrying. And it is here that we see another divergence from their better-off peers: only 10 per cent of those with a college degree have a child before marrying (Cherlin 2009).

These higher rates of non-marital births arise for several reasons. Lower-income and less-educated couples are far more likely to have an unintended birth because they are less adept at practising contraception and have less access to abortion in the event that they become pregnant (Guzzo and Payne 2012). Arguably, they are less motivated to avoid a birth, too, if only because they have less to lose if an early birth occurs. Elsewhere, I have argued that the political culture in the United States provides less support for pregnancy prevention than in many European nations (Furstenberg 2007). Whatever the explanations, many lower-income couples are more likely than their better-off counterparts to enter partnerships facing impending parenthood. Although the new partnership is often viewed as a prelude to an eventual marriage, their hopes usually go unrealized. Most of these unions do not survive the test of time; indeed, they frequently end before children even enter school (Carlson et al. 2011).

Why has the family system of poor Americans diverged so sharply from that of their better-off counterparts? Often this debate splits into two camps: the cultural explanations and the structural explanations (see, for example, the debate generated by Charles Murray's book *Coming Apart*; Murray 2012). In my view, this debate is crudely constructed. Individuals and the family systems that they build must adapt to changing circumstances. Doing so often involves altering time-honoured practices that no longer work or have become unattainable. Both these behavioural adaptations and the accounts that people provide to explain their behaviour are likely to change over time more or less simultaneously. Cultural change usually accompanies – sometimes preceding and sometimes lagging – changes in economic circumstances (see Small et al. 2010). This adaptive process usually feeds itself as cultural norms adapt to current structural realities, and vice versa. This is surely part of the reason of why cohabitation in the United States became so prevalent over such a short span of time and is quickly becoming an alternative to formal marriage among couples with limited means and prospects.

The larger backdrop under which the two-tiered family has emerged is the growth of economic inequality. Though much of this growth has been driven by the rapid increase at the very top of the income distribution, it has also been fed by the economic stagnation of incomes in the bottom two-thirds of the income distribution. The median earnings (inflation-adjusted) of all working-age men, including those who are not currently working, have declined by 19 per cent since 1970, despite sharp productivity growth and rising gross domestic product (GDP). Men with less education saw even sharper declines: 41 per cent between 1970 and 2010 for those with just a high school education.[3]

The growth in inequality has made the family system that was in place 50 years ago far more difficult to sustain for lower-income and less well-educated couples; in other words, they are compelled to settle for cohabitation because they believe that a successful marriage has become something that is out of their reach (Edin and Kefalas 2005). This, in turn, leads young adults to question the wisdom of marrying before they are 'settled'. In a recent paper that examined the process of settling into permanent relationships, young couples told of the difficulties of becoming committed when they are still trying to complete their schooling and enter a job with some future prospects (Kefalas et al. 2011). The problem for many couples in the bottom and even the middle one-third of the socio-economic distribution is that they may never enjoy the level of security that their counterparts expected or had 50 years ago.

Young adults facing financial insecurity today face considerable churn in their relationships; the relationships are less likely to survive because of the very reason that leads couples to cohabit rather than marry: the absence of resources. Lower-income couples are under constant economic pressure, a source of guilt and resentment that not infrequently leads to conflict and recrimination. Often, these recriminations take the form of 'gender mistrust'. Women complain that men are not ready to stop running around and settle down; men, in turn, complain that their partners expect too much from them (Furstenberg 1995; Waller 2002). As the cultural norms began to erode, problematic marriages were less likely to survive because community and religious disapproval softened. At the same time, cohabitations became a route to marriage, an alternative to marriage, or merely a temporary arrangement. The strong American propensity for 'choice' largely eclipsed the ideal of 'till death us do part'.

Communication, problem-solving skills, the development of trust – particularly when these attributes are not cultivated in childhood – are in short supply in families where parental education is low, work is unstable and life is stressful. These interpersonal skills can be acquired in later life through education, work life and experience in relationships, but lower-income couples do not easily develop them, especially when they enter relationships early in life and especially with offspring on the way, as is amply demonstrated in both the Fragile Families Study and the Baltimore Study. The result of this churn is a growing complexity in family forms, including 'blended' families and children from multiple partners. What this holds for the American family is as yet unclear.

THE GROWTH OF COMPLEX FAMILIES

In the Baltimore Study, I saw the beginning of a new form of family: children from multiple partners. There, both men and women who had children from an early relationship often moved on quickly to have additional child in a new partnership (which typically occurred soon after the earlier relationship dissolved). Whether they did so deliberately or not, they appeared to regard another child as a means of securing this new union; hoping that parenthood a second (or third) time would generate a sense of commitment to the new family on the part of their current partner (Furstenberg and King 1998; Furstenberg et al. 1987).

This effort frequently fails. If anything, having children with their new partners only reduces their prospects of forming a stable second union. Multi-partnered fertility brings a series of new challenges to couples who are often ill-suited to manage them by dint of their limited resources and interpersonal skills. Of course, college-educated couples also have children with more than one partner (usually after divorce and remarriage), but far less frequently than among those with less education and income (Carlson and Furstenberg 2006; Evenhouse and Reilly 2010; Guzzo and Furstenberg 2007; Qian et al. 2005).

The impact on children is still debated. There is little evidence that household complexity per se creates greater problems for children's development and welfare. However, cross-cultural studies show that characteristic strains exist in families created by plural marriages or joint families. As far as I know, there is no evidence that children growing up in complex households in family systems across the globe experience more problems in later life; indeed, there are reasons to expect just the opposite if multiple caregivers (parents, grandparents, uncles and aunts) provide more attention and care to children in the household. The greater the number of parent figures, one might hypothesize, the greater the investment in children so long as the attention and care is stable and coordinated. There are institutionalized patterns of authority, control and caring in joint families and in households with plural marriages in parts of Africa and Asian countries, where these family systems are common (Altman and Ginat 1996; Hill and König 1970; LeVine and New 2008). Moreover, complex family systems are generally associated with the presence of greater – not fewer – resources, in stark contrast to the pattern of multi-partnered fertility that characterizes the family formation patterns of lower-income

Americans. But this is all still speculation, as very little is known about how such families in the United States function: whether and how biological parents and step-parents or social parents (parents formed by cohabitation) collaborate, how they relate to biological and non-biological children, and the practices of extended kin in family systems created by multi-partnered fertility.

However, there is a great deal of research on the complex family systems created by divorce and remarriage (Cherlin and Furstenberg 1994; Furstenberg and Cherlin 1991; Ryan et al. 2008; Sweeney 2010). And much of it points to distinctive problems in terms of conflict for couples and negative behaviour among their children (Smock and Greenland 2010).

One reason for these poorer outcomes is greater competition for fewer resources in these families. Parents (mostly fathers) must allocate money, time and emotional support to biological children with whom they may not be living, and stepchildren who may be part of their current household but with whom they have tenuous relationships. Given the limited supply of these resources, the average investment in children is likely to be lower than it is in a comparable nuclear family, if only because of the greater number of obligations that must be managed across different households (Thomson and McLanahan 2012). Similarly, organizing time and establishing regular routines across households is difficult, especially among parents who may harbour misgivings or jealousy. Parenting responsibilities are complicated to work out when ex-partners feel aggrieved and supplanted. Divorce and remarriage also frequently disrupt intergenerational exchange. Grandparents may not see their biological grandchildren (especially if they reside with the other parent). They may be reluctant to treat their step-grandchildren equally to their biological grandchildren. This can produce tensions across the generations.

All of these issues arise in a much more acute form among unmarried couples who have children in successive partnerships for a variety of reasons. For example, bonds between cohabiting couples are often weaker than they are for married couples. The lack of institutionalization among cohabiting couples suggests that parenting problems surrounding authority and control in the family could be more common. For example, social parents might be inclined to defer to biological parents even when the latter are uninvolved in childrearing. Or, conversely, they might find themselves competing with biological parents living apart from their children. They may expect their partner's ex to help out in supporting his children and resent the financial burdens imposed if he does not. The unclear boundaries of parental responsibilities may create conflicts that undermine the relations in both new and former partnerships.

Children may receive even less investment from social parents than they do from stepparents. In addition, extended kin may withhold support that they would otherwise provide in the event of a marriage. The parents of the surrogate partner may invest as much in the grandparent role as they would if the couple were married. Finally, we know relatively little about the ties that develop between full and half siblings in childhood and beyond.

Possibly, as legal and social conventions respond to the new realities of provisional families, relationships across households and the obligations they entail may become more institutionalized. In the meantime, they constitute both a less stable and a less well-established form of the family. Although many developmental researchers, not to mention social critics, think that the complexities of multi-partnered fertility contribute to poorer prospects of children's success in later life (Brown 2010; Sassler 2010), at this stage, our speculations outrun the data required to test them.

INEQUALITY AND THE TWO-TIERED FAMILY SYSTEM IN COMPARATIVE PERSPECTIVE

The changes in the family system that have occurred in the United States, notably the weakening of marriage and the increase of non-marital childbearing, are widespread throughout Europe and other Anglo-speaking nations. However, it is not as clear whether the two-tier family system that has emerged in the United States is as evident elsewhere. Nor is it clear that the emergence of multi-partner fertility is as common in Europe. Thomson (2012) finds that the rate of multi-partnered fertility is far lower in Sweden and several other European nations, for example, though she suggests that multi-partnered fertility may be more prevalent in some Eastern European nations that have very high rates of union instability.

It is entirely possible that local conditions such as culture and public policy, the strength of religious institutions, and the quality and openness of the educational and employment systems, will and do moderate the impact of family change in Europe. In the United States, the volatility of relationships occurs in part because young adults, especially those who are more economically disadvantaged, are far less adept at practising contraception and preventing unwanted pregnancies than their counterparts in Canada, Australia and most of Europe (Mosher and Jones 2010). In addition, Americans' greater geographic mobility, which can dilute family authority, and the higher levels of poverty and economic disadvantage in the United States, may weaken commitment to existing partnerships (Cherlin 2009). Yet how long this US distinction will prevail is uncertain.

CONCLUSION

Since my early years in Baltimore observing young women on the cusp of adulthood, I have been witness to an unprecedented change in the American family. The most recent manifestation – the validation of same-sex marriage – is a capstone of sorts, symbolizing the rapid changes in the family. More change is no doubt ahead, as inequality continues to widen and in many respects solidify the trajectories of the more and less affluent young adults. The path to family formation reflects and has different consequences for young adults from families in different economic brackets. Among the affluent, the family system has become more stable; while just the opposite has occurred among young adults from more disadvantaged circumstances.

In large measure, the timing and conditions of first births (the age of the parents and the level of resources that they possess) create the diverging pathways. When births are delayed until first unions have been tested by cohabitation (often leading to marriage), the likelihood that parents will have children by two or more partners declines greatly. If first births are unplanned and occur before the partners have much experience of living together, the union is much less likely to survive and the chances of having a child with another person grows. We still know far too little about the consequences of more complex families for children. For the time being, it makes good sense not to rush into a judgement on the question of whether or how family complexity affects child well-being. Nonetheless, both for theoretical and structural reasons, the chances for children who grow up in complex families may be hindered, because they receive not only less (not more) attention from the parents who assume responsibility for them, but also less material support: resources are often slim in families where child-bearing across partnerships is common.

NOTES

1. In his defence, Goode was correct about many things. Paradoxically, he was able to foresee the global changes in the developing world far more clearly than he did in assuming stability in the West (see also Cherlin 2012).
2. As a signal to declining marriage rates among the less-educated, the Pew Research Center reported in 2010 that for the first time, college-educated young adults were more likely than young adults lacking a bachelor's degree to have married by the age of 30 (Pew Research Center 2010). Although marriage rates are delayed among young adults with college degrees, marriage is more often sidestepped completely by those with less education.
3. Though it may come as a surprise to many, the majority of Americans do not have a college degree. Among those aged 25–34 today, (only) 47 per cent had a post-secondary degree (associate, BA, or graduate) in 2013 (White House 2014).

REFERENCES

Altman, I. and J. Ginat (1996), *Polygamous Families in Contemporary Society*, New York: Cambridge University Press.

Bernard, J. (1942), *American Family Behavior*, New York: Harper & Brothers.

Brown, S.L. (2010), 'Marriage and child well-being: research and policy perspectives', *Journal of Marriage and Family*, 72 (5), 1059–1077.

Carlson, M.J. and F.F. Furstenberg (2006), 'The prevalence and correlates of multipartnered fertility among urban US parents', *Journal of Marriage and Family*, 68 (3), 809–821.

Carlson, M.J., N.V. Pilkauskas, S.S. McLanahan and J. Brooks-Gunn (2011), 'Couples as partners and parents over children's early years', *Journal of Marriage and Family*, 73 (2), 317–334.

Cherlin, A.J. (2009), *The Marriage-go-round: The State of Marriage and the Family in America Today*, New York: Alfred A. Knopf.

Cherlin, A.J. (2012), 'Goode's world revolution and family patterns: a reconsideration at fifty years', *Population and Development Review*, 38 (4), 577–607.

Cherlin, A.J. and F.F. Furstenberg (1994), 'Stepfamilies in the United States: a reconsideration', *Annual Review of Sociology*, 20, 359–381.

Edin, K. and M. Kefalas (2005), *Promises I Can Keep: Why Poor Women Put Motherhood before Marriage*, Berkeley, CA: University of California Press.

Evenhouse, E. and S. Reilly (2010), 'Women's multiple-partner fertility in the United States: prevalence, correlates and trends, 1985–2008', MPRA Paper 26867, Munich: Munich University Library.

Friedan, B. (1963), *The Feminine Mystique*, New York: W.W. Norton & Company.

Furstenberg, F.F. (1976), *Unplanned Parenthood: The Social Consequences of Teenage Childbearing*, New York: Free Press.

Furstenberg, F.F. (1995), 'Fathering in the inner-city: paternal participation and public policy', in W. Marsiglio (ed.), *Fatherhood: Contemporary Theory, Research, and Social Policy*, Thousand Oaks, CA: Sage Publications, pp. 119–147.

Furstenberg, F.F. (2007), *Destinies of the Disadvantaged: The Politics of Teen Childbearing*, New York: Russell Sage Foundation.

Furstenberg, F.F. (2011), 'The recent transformation of the American family: witnessing and exploring social change', in P. England and M. Carlson (eds), *Social Class and Changing Families in an Unequal America*, Stanford, CA: Stanford University Press, pp. 192–220.

Furstenberg, F.F. (2013), 'Transitions to adulthood: what we can learn from the west', *Annals*, 646, 28–41.

Furstenberg, F.F., J. Brooks-Gunn and S.P. Morgan (1987), *Adolescent Mothers in Later Life*, New York: Cambridge University Press.

Furstenberg, F.F. and A.J. Cherlin (1991), *Divided Families: What Happens to Children When Parents Part*, Cambridge, MA: Harvard University Press.

Furstenberg, F.F. and R.B. King (1998), 'Multi-partnered fertility sequences: documenting an alternative family form', paper presented at the Biennial Meetings of the Society for Research on Adolescence, San Diego, CA, April.

Goldstein, J.R. and C.T. Kenney (2001), 'Marriage delayed or marriage forgone? New cohort forecasts of first marriage for US women', *American Sociological Review*, 66, 506–519.

Goode, W.J. (1963), *World Revolution and Family Patterns*, New York: Free Press.

Guzzo, K.B. and F.F. Furstenberg (2007), 'Multipartnered fertility among young women with a non-marital first birth: prevalence and risk factors', *Perspectives on Sexual and Reproductive Health*, 39 (1), 29–38.

Guzzo, K. and K.K. Payne (2012), 'Intentions and planning status of births: 2000–2010', NCFMR Family Profiles, FP-12-24, Bowling Green State University, KY: National Center for Family & Marriage Research.

Hill, R. and R. König (eds) (1970), *Families in East and West*, The Hague: Mouton & Co.

Kefalas, M., P. Carr, L. Napolitano and F.F. Furstenberg (2011), 'Marriage is more than being together: the meaning of marriage for young adults', *Journal of Family Issues*, 32 (7), 845–875.

Komarovsky, M. (1946), 'Cultural contradictions and sex roles', *American Journal of Sociology*, 52 (3), 184–189.

LeVine, R.A. and R.S. New (eds) (2008), *Anthropology and Child Development: A Cross-cultural Reader*, New York: Blackwell Publishing.

Manning, W.D., S.L. Brown and K.K. Payne (2013), 'Two decades of stability and change in age at first union formation', paper presented at the annual meeting of the Population Association of America, New Orleans, 11–13 April.

Mosher, W.D. and J. Jones (2010), 'Use of contraception in the United States: 1982–2008', National Center for Health Statistics, *Vital and Health Statistics*, 23 (29), 1–54.

Murray, C. (2012), *Coming Apart: The State of White America, 1960–2010*, New York: Crown Forum.

Pew Research Center (2010), 'The reversal of the college marriage gap', 7 October, accessed 22 October 2015 at http://www.pewresearch.org/2010/10/07/the-reversal-of-the-college-marriage-gap/.

Qian, Z., D.T. Lichter and L.M. Mellott (2005), 'Out-of-wedlock childbearing: marital prospects and mate selection', *Social Forces*, 84 (1), 473–491.

Ryan, R., A. Kalil and K.M. Ziol-Guest (2008), 'Longitudinal patterns of non-resident fathers' involvement: the role of resources and relations', *Journal of Marriage and Family*, 70 (4), 962–977.

Sassler, S. (2010), 'Partnering across the life course: sex, relationships, and mate selection', *Journal of Marriage and Family*, 72 (3), 557–575.

Small, M.L., D.J. Harding and M. Lamont (2010), 'Reconsidering culture and poverty', *ANNALS*, 629, 6–27.

Smock, P.J. and F.R. Greenland (2010), 'Diversity in pathways to parenthood: patterns, implications, and emerging research', *Journal of Marriage and Family*, 72 (3), 576–593.

Sweeney, M.M. (2010), 'Remarriage and stepfamilies: strategic sites for family scholarship in the 21st century', *Journal of Marriage and Family*, 72 (3), 667–684.

Thomson, E. (2012), 'Childrearing across Partnerships in the US, Australia and Scandinavia', Stockholm Research Reports in Demography 2012:2, Stockholm.

Thomson, E. and S.S. McLanahan (2012), 'Reflections on family structure and child well-being: economic resources vs. parental socialization', *Social Forces*, 91 (1), 45–53.

Waller, M.R. (2002), 'Expectations about marriage among unmarried parents: new evidence from the Fragile Families Study', *Focus*, 22 (2), 13–18.

White House Council of Economic Advisors (2014), '15 economic facts about Millennials', October, Washington, DC: White House.

2. Fifty years of family change in Europe: diversifying partnerships

Laurent Toulemon[*]

INTRODUCTION

Marriage is the traditional living arrangement for couples. While the baby boom period which took place after the Second World War in most European countries was related to a 'golden age' of marriage, with early and universal recourse to marriage, all European countries have experienced a dramatic decline in marriage frequencies, as well as an increase in divorce, since the early 1970s. This retreat of marriage in the last 50 years had many consequences on partnerships and fertility. I will first describe this trend in Europe and examine the drivers of this change, which appear to be very homogenous in Europe, even if the timing of the trends were different. The decline in marriage frequencies could lead to a corresponding decline in unions, or to an increase in other forms of union, such as unmarried cohabitations, and other legally recognized partnerships. The consequences on fertility are also very diverse, depending on whether unmarried couples have children or not. I will thus examine the numerous consequences of this decline in marriage and how diverse they are in different European countries.

THE DECLINE OF MARRIAGE IN EUROPE

The baby boom that took place in most European countries was not only a period of high fertility, but also a time of universal and early marriage in Europe. Over the last 50 years, there has been a dramatic change in marriage behaviour in most European countries, and new forms of union are now competing with marriage.

Trends in Marriage and Divorce in Europe

During the 1950s and 1960s, the crude marriage rate (number of marriages per 1000 inhabitants) was close to eight per 1000 per year (Figure 2.1): one

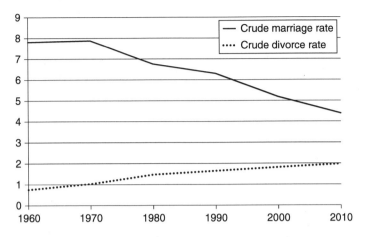

Note: European Union 27 member states before 2013.

Source: Eurostat database.

Figure 2.1   *Crude marriage rate and crude divorce rate in Europe, 1960–*
              2010 (per 1000)

marriage and thus two newly-weds per 130 inhabitants per year, one newly-wed per 65 inhabitants, at a time when life expectancy was around 70 years of age. This means that marriage was almost universal. In the 1970s, the crude marriage rate began to fall and has almost halved in 40 years, reaching the low level of 4.4 per 1000, while the crude divorce rate doubled, from 1 to 2.0 per 1000. In 2010 the number of divorces was nearly half the number of marriages, meaning that around 50 per cent of current marriages are destined to end in divorce, and not by the death of a spouse.

More refined demographic indices such as total first marriage rates (TFMR) and the mean age at first marriage can be estimated by country or group of countries, in order to get a concrete hint of the consequence of this trend. During the 1960s, almost all women got married: the TFMR were close to one first marriage per woman and even sometimes higher. The TFMRs were inflated by the decline in age at marriage, which implied that many cohorts were getting married simultaneously, but the norm towards universal and early marriage was prevalent all around Europe (Figure 2.2). From 1965, TFMRs began to decline dramatically, but the decline in marriage was far from uniform. It first took place in Northern Europe, with Sweden as a forerunner, and then the decline was gradual, in the 1970s in Western Europe, the 1980s in Southern Europe and the 1990s in Eastern Europe. In the 2000s, the TFMR range was between 0.5 and 0.7

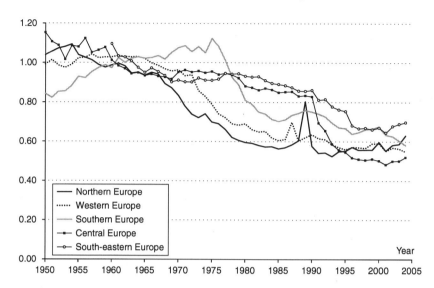

Note: Countries are grouped into regions as follows:
Western Europe: Austria, France, Western Germany, the Netherlands, Switzerland and the United Kingdom.
Northern Europe: Denmark (data available from 1955), Finland (from 1955), Norway and Sweden.
Southern Europe: Italy, Portugal and Spain.
Central Europe: Croatia (from 1960), Czech Republic, Eastern Germany (from 1960), Estonia (from 1970), Hungary, Latvia (from 1970), Lithuania (from 1970), Poland, Slovakia (from 1960) and Slovenia (from 1970).
South-Eastern Europe: Bulgaria and Romania.

Sources: Council of Europe; Eurostat. From Sobotka, Toulemon (2008).

Figure 2.2   Total period first marriage rate by region of Europe (first marriages per woman)

first marriage per woman, meaning that 30 to 50 per cent of women born in the 1980s remained unmarried.

This decline in marriage intensity was linked to a large increase in the mean age at marriage. In the 1960s the mean age was around 23. It declined in almost all countries up to the early 1970s, except in Sweden where the reversal took place in the mid-1960s. The large decline in marriage rates at young ages, starting in the 1970s in Western Europe, in the 1980s in Southern Europe and the 1990s in Eastern Europe, led to both an increase in the mean age at marriage and a decline in total first marriage rates (Figure 2.3). In the mid-2000s, the mean age at marriage was on the increase everywhere in Europe, but the continent had become more

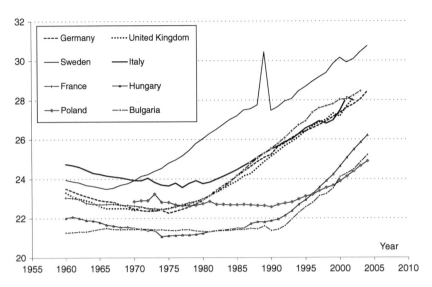

Sources: Council of Europe; Eurostat. From Sobotka, Toulemon (2008).

Figure 2.3   *Period mean age of women at first marriage in some European countries*

heterogeneous: women's first marriages took place at ages higher than 30 years of age in Sweden, at around 28 in Western and Southern Europe (France, Germany, United Kingdom, Italy) and between 23 and 26 in Eastern and Southern countries (Bulgaria, Hungary, Poland).

As a consequence, increasingly fewer women have ever married by age 50 (Figure 2.4). Among women born in the 1940s more than 90 per cent of women got married, while in Western European countries 20 to 30 per cent of women born in the 1960s are still unmarried at age 50. The decline is general in Europe and all countries seem to follow the same trend, with a 20-year lag for Eastern European countries compared to Western and Northern countries. The change is not already prominent because the proportion of women born in 1965 ever married at age 50 is the consequence of first marriage rates at ages 20 in 1985, 30 in 1995, and so on. The decline will thus surely continue among more recent birth cohorts.

Taking the example of France, one can see how great the change in marriage rates has been since 1970, and why the decline in the proportion of women ever married at age 50 will continue. The 'golden age' of universal and early marriage was replaced by late and non-universal marriage (Figures 2.5 and 2.6). In 1970, more than one French unmarried woman out of five aged 21–24 got married within the year; in 2010

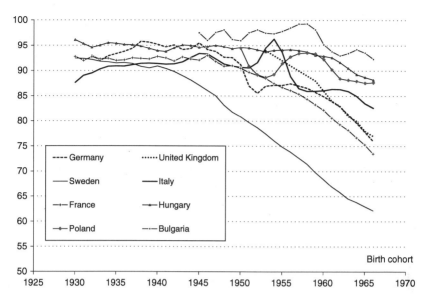

Sources: Council of Europe; Eurostat. From Sobotka, Toulemon (2008).

Figure 2.4 Proportion of women ever married at age 50, by cohort (%)

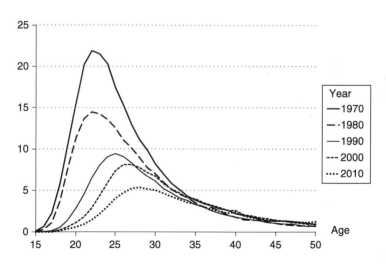

Source: Beaumel and Pla (2012).

Figure 2.5 First marriage probabilities by age and year, France, women (%)

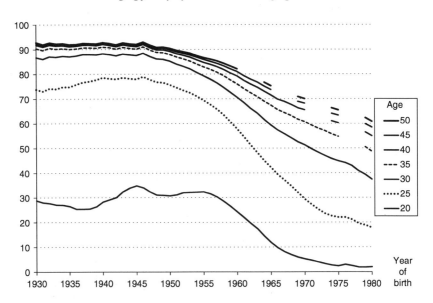

Note: The probabilities are assumed to remain constant after 2010.

Source: Beaumel and Pla (2012).

Figure 2.6   Proportion of women ever married at different ages, by birth cohort, France

marriage probabilities before age 25 fell: at age 22 it was divided by 15, from 22 per cent to 1.4 per cent. The peak in first marriage probabilities has moved to 28 and no more than 5.4 per cent of unmarried women of that age enter their first marriage. This dramatic decline of first marriages at young ages does not occur at older ages: at ages after 35, the probabilities have been more or less constant for the past 40 years. Marriage has thus completely disappeared from the process of transition to adulthood.

The downward trends in marriage probabilities before age 35 led to a large decline in the proportion of women ever married at different ages, from one cohort to the other (Figure 2.6): while more than 75 per cent of women born in the 1940s were married at age 25, it is less than 25 per cent among women born in the 1970s (the generation of their daughters): for women aged 25, the marriage norm has moved from being married to being unmarried. This decline of marriage probabilities at young ages is not compensated for at higher ages, and 30 per cent of women born in 1970 will still be unmarried at age 50, versus 8 per cent for women born in 1940. The trends shown in Figures 2.5 and 2.6 for France are very similar in

European countries where marriage crude rates have declined: a fall in first marriage probabilities at young ages and stability at higher ages, leading to fewer and later marriages (see Figures 2.3 and 2.4).

Divorce rates have increased later in the Southern European countries
In the 1960s, not only was marriage early and universal, but divorce was highly stigmatized, forbidden or difficult to obtain, and very rare in Europe. During the end of the twentieth century, divorce rates first increased rapidly in Northern, Eastern and Western Europe during the 1960s and 1970s and stabilized during the 1990s. In Southern Europe, the increase took place later, but was very large during the 1990s and the 2000s, while divorce rates leveled off in other regions since 2000, so that divorce rates are becoming more homogenous: the number of divorces is now more than one divorce for three marriages in all European regions (Figure 2.7).

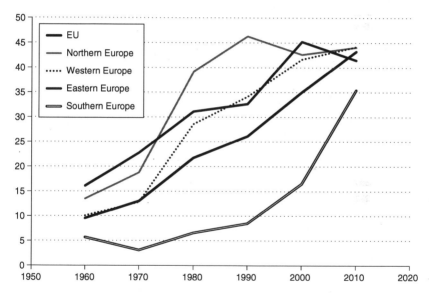

Note: Data are unweighted means by region. Northern Europe: Denmark, Finland, Sweden. Southern Europe: Cyprus, Greece, Italy, Malta, Portugal, Spain. Western Europe: Austria, Belgium, France, Germany, Ireland, Luxembourg, the Netherlands, United Kingdom. Eastern Europe: Bulgaria, Croatia, Czech Republic, Estonia, Hungary, Latvia, Lithuania, Poland, Romania, Slovakia, Slovenia.

Source: Eurostat database.

Figure 2.7   Trends in divorce rates (divorces per 100 marriages) by European regions

The period total divorce rate (sum of duration-specific divorce rates, estimating the proportion of marriages ending with a divorce), is close to 50 per cent (one divorce per two married couples) in the Nordic countries, Belgium, the United Kingdom, France, the Czech Republic, Hungary, Portugal. It remains much lower in some countries from the Eastern and Southern parts of Europe (Italy, Spain, Greece, Poland, Romania, Bulgaria) (Sobotka and Toulemon 2008) with a rapid increase in the recent years.

Unmarried cohabitation has become a long-lasting couple situation

The increase in the mean age at first marriage in Europe does not mean that first unions have also been delayed. Unmarried cohabitation has become an option for young adults since the 1960s in Northern Europe and 1970s in Western Europe. The path to the first union in Europe across cohorts has changed for cohorts born in the 1950s and 1960s (who reached age 20 between 1970 and 1990), so that three models emerge from the retrospective data collected in the international round of the Fertility and Family surveys which took place in many European countries (Macura and Beets 2002, esp. pp. 27–56 and 57–76). In Northern and Western Europe, the decline in marriage probabilities at young ages was almost entirely compensated for by an increase in unmarried cohabitation (Sweden, Finland, Estonia, France, the Netherlands, Austria, Switzerland) and the proportion of women entering their first union before age 25 remained stable. In Southern Europe (Italy, Spain and Portugal), cohabitation remained rare among young adults and the decline in marriage probabilities was reflected in lower proportions of young adults living in a union. In Central and Eastern Europe (Poland, Hungary, Czech Republic), marriage rates did not change much and marriage remained early and frequent until the 1990s, so that first marriages did not decline among women born before 1970 (Prioux 2006).

As a consequence, the prevalence of unmarried cohabitation was very diverse in Europe at the turn of the twenty-first century (Figure 2.8): around half of young couples (where the woman was aged 34 or less) were unmarried in Northern Europe, to be compared to a third in Western Europe and only 10 per cent in Southern Europe. The Eastern part of the continent was highly heterogeneous, with unmarried cohabitation remaining very uncommon in Poland and Slovakia, but widespread in Hungary and Slovenia, except for Estonia, which resembles the Northern countries.

The choice between married or unmarried cohabitation is part of a wider set of possible living arrangements for young adults. Those not living as a couple may still be in the parental home, or live single on their own, or

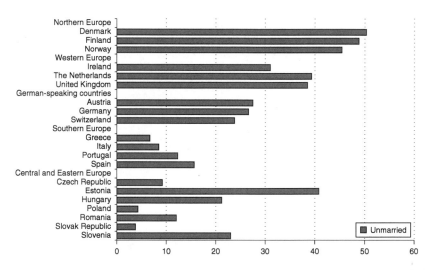

Sources: Council of Europe; Eurostat. From Sobotka, Toulemon (2008).

Figure 2.8 Proportion of unmarried couples among all couples, women aged 20–34, around 2000

share a home with co-tenants. When European countries are compared, based on 2000 census data, unmarried cohabitation appears as an alternative to staying in the parental home more than an alternative to marriage: in countries where young adults leave the parental home early, they enter their first union earlier, without getting married. This is the case especially in Northern (and Western) Europe, as opposed to countries of Southern (and Eastern) Europe where young adults stay longer with their parents and do not live as a couple before getting married. Unmarried cohabitation is common in Western Europe, but much less among couples with children, especially in German-speaking countries (Germany, Austria, Switzerland), the Netherlands and Ireland. In these countries, cohabitation often ends in the event of a pregnancy, so that the proportion of births out of marriage is low, despite the spread of unmarried cohabitation (Sobotka and Toulemon 2008).

Taking into account the mean duration of unmarried cohabitation and the causes of their termination (birth of a child, marriage, disruption), data show that cohabitation is very diverse in Europe (Heuveline and Timberlake 2004). Cohabitation may be considered as a stage in the marriage process, but it becomes an alternative to marriage when the occurrence of a pregnancy no longer leads to a marriage. Unmarried cohabitation is a substitute for marriage, based on different relationships between partners. In particular, the risk of union disruption is much higher among unmarried couples than among married couples. The occurrence of a marriage in the event of a pregnancy is a key factor limiting the duration of cohabitation. Around 2000, the proportion of unmarried pregnant women who got married before the birth was as low as 10 per cent in France and the United Kingdom, to be compared to 20 per cent in Austria and 60 per cent in Poland (Avdeev et al. 2011). In all European countries this 'nuptiality of pregnant women' is on the decline. This change opens the door to long-lasting unmarried cohabitation and leads to an increase in the proportion of births out of marriage, most of them being born to unmarried couples (Perelli-Harris et al. 2010a).

Unmarried couples are having children

The large increase in the proportion of births out of marriage is thus the consequence of two trends: first, more and more couples begin without a marriage and decide to continue that way; and second, pregnancy is less and less an incentive for getting married. In many European countries, more than 50 per cent of all births are to unmarried mothers and the proportion is increasing rapidly in countries where the proportion is still low (Figure 2.9). Most births out of marriage are to unmarried cohabiting

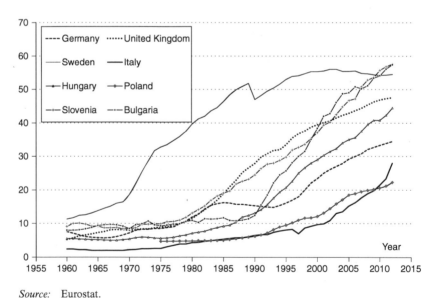

Source: Eurostat.

Figure 2.9 Proportion of births out of marriage in some European countries (%)

women, so that the proportion of births 'out of a union', to parents not living together at birth, has remained low. The proportion of children from parents who did not already live as a couple at the time of the conception is even decreasing in most European countries, hopefully due to the more widespread use of efficient contraception and recourse to abortion by young women. As a consequence, more and more children are conceived by parents who have already lived as a childless couple before envisioning having children, marriage no longer being a preliminary step for entering the union and for having children.

In some European countries, the legal relation between children and their parents does not depend on the legal status of the couple. In Sweden, recognition by both parents is compulsory. In France, there is no difference between married and unmarried parents, as long as the child is legally recognized by the father; however, a non-negligible proportion of children are not recognized by their father. The increase in the proportion of births out of marriage was associated with an increase in the proportion of children born with no official father during the 1980s, but this proportion is currently declining (Figure 2.10), indicating that cohabiting parents are as committed to their children as married parents. The proportion of children who are not recognized at birth or in the following months is very

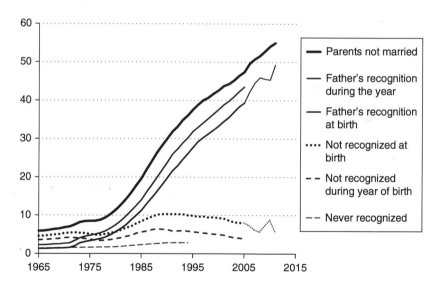

Sources: Insee, civil registration data. From Toulemon (2013).

Figure 2.10 Proportion of births out of marriage and father's recognition of the child, France, 1965–2011 (%)

close to the proportion of young mothers living by themselves: 7 per cent (Blondel and Kermarrec 2011). The proportion of children born to a single mother is around 7 per cent of all births in France (14 per cent of births to an unmarried mother), compared to 15 per cent in the United Kingdom (37 per cent among children from an unmarried mother, according to the Millenium cohort). The proportion of first births born out of a union in 2000–2004 is as low as 3 per cent in the Netherlands and 5 per cent in France and Norway, while it reaches 16 per cent in the United Kingdom (Perelli-Harris et al. 2010b).

HOW AND WHY DID MARRIAGE LOSE ITS SUPREMACY?

Before discussing the consequences on partnership and family life in Europe, I will first discuss how and why these changes took place. The decline in marriage and increase in divorce are the consequence of an overall change in partnership behaviour, with new forms of unions appearing as long-term alternatives, while the decline of unions remains very limited.

Changes in Union Status

Marriage regimes, unmarried cohabitation and new forms of partnership
In the 1970s in Western and Northern Europe, marriage first lost its role as the institution within which couples were formed. On the other hand, the legalization of divorce weakened the marriage as a lifelong commitment, and the increase in second unions, more often unmarried, added to the increasing acceptance of unmarried cohabitation as a long-lasting status for couples. Countries in Southern and Eastern Europe did not experience these trends in the 1970s and 1980s, but are now following a similar pattern.

In addition to this competing family arrangement, new forms of registered partnerships have been established, primarily because of a political wish to provide legal recognition to same-sex couples, but also based on the increasing proportion of unmarried couples who did not want to get married but nevertheless wanted their union to be socially recognized and organized. In countries where the same partnership is allowed to all couples, like France and the Netherlands, different-sex couples rapidly outnumbered same-sex couples among registered partnerships. The legal status of cohabiting couples is very diverse in Europe, some countries considering unmarried cohabitation as 'implicit marriages', being marriage-like in terms of rights and duties; while in others, cohabiting partners are considered related adults without any 'conjugal' definition of the relation. In Belgium, the legal status given by the cohabitation contract (*cohabitation légale*) established in 2000, is not restricted to couples and can also be a means to reinforce family ties (parent and child, brother and sister) as well as other friendship ties (Waaldijk 2005).

Countries that adopted a specific legal framework for same-sex couples subsequently opened marriage to same-sex couples (Baiocco et al. 2014; Pailhé et al. 2013). Simultaneously, the specific framework may remain. The retreat of marriage thus goes with an increasing diversity of union statuses, outside but as well as within marriage. In France, for instance, the *Pacte civil de solidarité* (Pacs), which was first established in order to fight against discrimination towards same-sex couples (especially in case of death of a partner), is now most often chosen by different-sex couples: in 2010 the number of Pacs reached 200 000, to be compared to less than 250 000 marriages (Mazuy et al. 2013). A recent change in the income tax law led to a large decrease in the number of Pacs (150 000 in 2011), which still remains a competing living arrangement to unregistered unmarried cohabitation or marriage: in 2013, 42 per cent of new registered unions were Pacs and 58 per cent were marriages. There are different marriage regimes in France and the status of married couples is also changing: the proportion of married couples declined from 89 per cent in 1992 to 76 per cent in 2008. The decline is larger for couples without any specific contract (equal division of property acquired during marriage as a default property regime) while the proportion of couples married with a specific contract ('separation as to property' regime) increased from 5 to 8 per cent (Frémeaux and Leturcq 2013). Economic features of marriages are thus becoming more diverse; the same could be said for religious forms of unions: fewer marriages are religious marriages in countries where different forms of marriage are possible.

A limited decline of the propensity to live as a couple

This growing heterogeneity of union forms is not related to a large decline in the proportion of people living within a union. The decline of marriage rates at young ages did not lead, except in Southern European countries, to a corresponding delay in first unions. The delay in first unions, related to longer enrolment in education, has been much more limited than the delay in marriage. The proportion of people living as a couple is nevertheless currently declining in most European countries; at young ages because of a (limited and stalled in many countries) delay in first unions, and at median ages because of union disruptions, not always and not immediately followed by a new union. Union disruptions are becoming frequent because divorce rates have increased and because unmarried cohabitations are more fragile than marriages. At higher ages the mortality decline compensates for the increase in union disruptions, and living together as a couple is becoming more frequent.

Not only are unions more diverse, but some couples may live apart together (LAT) without living in the same household. The frontier between a 'non-co-resident couple' and a 'stable intimate relationship' is not straightforward, especially at young ages, before any co-resident union. This situation may be voluntary; a LAT relationship may be preferred in the case of a late union, especially among old parents (de Jong Gierveld 2004). It may also be due to professional constraints (Levin 2004). These new forms of relationships between partners who do not share the same household are accepted more and more as a form of relationship and they frame the limits of a 'union-like' relation: based on an intimate commitment, the relation is most often sexually exclusive, but long-term commitments like having children or getting married may be raised in very different terms than within a co-resident union or a marriage.

The Drivers of the Change

Since the end of the 'golden era' of marriage, many things have changed in Europe. Three drivers can be identified as having played a major role. The long-term trend of mortality decline changed the stakes related to marriage. The other drivers are related to a decline in gender inequality: new methods of family planning, and the increasing participation of women in the labour force.

A dramatic mortality decline at adult ages

For two centuries, economic and medical progress has led to a dramatic decline in mortality. The decline in adult mortality led to the idea that the endurance of a couple's history was in the hands of the partners, not of chance. Taking France as an example of these trends that spread throughout all European countries, one can see why the fear of death has left the picture, as far as couple formation and fertility are concerned (Ariès 1977). For two young adults entering a relationship, the likelihood that both would survive after 50 years of union increased from 15 per cent in 1900 to 41 per cent in 1955, and 68 per cent in 2010 (Table 2.1). This decline in adult mortality was related to the near disappearance of maternal mortality (from 10 per 1000 in 1900 to 2 per 1000 in 1950 and 0.1 per 1000 in 2010), which made the threat of death less prominent in the event of a pregnancy. Moreover, the decline in infant mortality (from 120 per 1000 in 1900 to 50 per 1000 in 1950 and 4 per 1000 in 2010) postponed the threat

Table 2.1 Mortality risks during adulthood, France, 1900, 1955 and 2010

For a person alive at age 20, probability to be still alive at Age . . .				For two persons alive at age 20, probability that both are still alive after . . . (%)			
	Period				Period		
	1900	1955	2010		1990	1955	2010
Age 45	79	95	98	25 years	63	90	96
Age 70	38	64	83	50 years	15	41	68

Sources: Period life tables. Years 1900 and 1955: Vallin and Meslé (2001). Year 2010: Beaumel and Pla (2012)

of death until later in couples' trajectories – a threat that in the past was prominent at all ages.

Increasing individualism and female empowerment through labour force participation
Related to this decline in mortality and fertility during the demographic transition, the requirements between partners have increased: a married couple are now expected to experience intimate commitments, a loving feeling between the partners. Marriage has become less and less a matter of alliance between families or lineages, and more and more the commitment of two individuals, the choice of the partner being made by the partners themselves and not by their families.

The increase in female labour force participation has been a trend in all European countries, related to the increase in the services sectors, offering many jobs as clerks and sellers, and to the will of couples to increase their standard of living with two salaries instead of only one. Despite large country specificities related to part-time jobs, wage inequalities and work–life balance (Thévenon 2009), the development of salaried status has changed the relative status of partners: while a woman who is professionally inactive or working within the family depends on her husband, becoming a salaried worker with an employer outside the family makes her less dependent on her family and husband. This allowed women to envision a separate life and to obtain more bargaining power within the relationship.

Efficient and feminine methods of family planning
The fertility decline was first related to a decline in high-order births, during the demographic transition in the nineteenth century. The ongoing control of fertility by couples, at least to avoid having too many children,

became more and more prevalent and births of parity four or more went on declining even during the baby boom period. The non-medical contraceptive methods, withdrawal and periodic abstinence, were efficient in decreasing couples' fertility, but were nevertheless leading to many unwanted births. During the 1960s, the increase in non-marital sexual activity among young adults first led to many unplanned pregnancies and then to an increase in marriages, especially shotgun marriages with a pregnant bride. The development of the contraceptive pill in the 1960s and its diffusion in Europe during the 1970s changed this situation and gave a new power to women: couples (and especially women), as well as women living outside of a union, could efficiently control their fertility and have sexual intercourse without fear of becoming pregnant. This easier fertility control, thanks to efficient contraceptive methods and, some years later, to the possibility of having recourse to an abortion in the event of an unwanted pregnancy, allowed a disconnection between sexuality and fertility, and thus the disconnection of sexual debut and the question of entering into a stable union or getting married, especially for women. The median age at first intercourse – around 18 for men and women born in 1970 (Bozon 2003) – is far from the median ages at marriage: between 25 and 30. The Pill, as well as other efficient contraceptive methods, such as the intra-uterine device and voluntary sterilization, are now widely used in Europe, leading to a large decline in unwanted pregnancies, and the recourse to abortion is available in most European countries. The number of unwanted births has declined and they have become rare, even if a non-negligible proportion of births are still unplanned (between 8 per cent and 15 per cent among European sub-regions in 2012; see Sedgh et al. 2014). The wide use of efficient contraceptive methods allowed unmarried cohabitation to last without any pregnancy. This also led to the possibility to give birth without getting married, and cohabitation could then become a long-lasting alternative to marriage, for childless couples as well as for parents (Perelli-Harris et al. 2010b).

Social differences vary with the institutional context

The trends toward more diverse partnership behaviours have been general, but many country specificities remain and the social contrasts in family behaviour have been and still are very diverse in Europe: from one social context to another, as well as from one period to the other in the same country, social differences may have vanished or even reversed. For instance, the choice between marriage and cohabitation has varied among social groups, but social differences may not be considered a consequence of a diffusion process: in the 1960s, unmarried cohabitation was more common among the least-educated, unskilled workers. In the 1970s, the diffusion of unmarried cohabitation took place among young urban highly educated couples (Villeneuve-Gokalp 1991), a trend that subsequently vanished in the 1990s. New forms of partnerships, like the Pacs in France, are currently preferred by the most educated (Bailly and Rault 2013).

Social differences strongly vary with the institutional context. For instance, female employment increases divorce risks in many countries, but not in France (Cooke and Baxter 2010); unmarried couples were more fertile among most-educated couples in the 1980s, but the difference has reversed recently (Perelli-Harris et al. 2010b). Social differences may also have strong influences on relationship trends: in France, divorce risks are increasing together with women's education levels, but the proportion of children with separated parents is lower among children whose mothers are highly educated; whereas among the least-educated, couples have children and then experience separation, while couple disruptions of (still) childless couples are more prevalent among the most educated.

CONSEQUENCES FOR PARTNERSHIP IN EUROPE

These trends led to a decline in gender inequality which, together with an increasing demand for intimate commitment, led to a progressive disaffection with regard to marriage as an institution. It also changed the ways individuals experience their partnership and family histories.

The Decline in Gender Inequality

The use of feminine and efficient contraceptive methods, as well as the rise in female labour force participation, together with the increasing educational attainment of women compared to men, can be considered as the main drivers of the change in partnership in Europe. The increase in the overall level of education has been more pronounced for women than for men, so that in cohorts born after 1960, women are in average more educated than men in many European countries. This trend should lead to more egalitarian relations within the couples. It should also lead to an increase in marriage probabilities for less-educated women, should previous preferences for female hypergamy remain (Van Bavel 2012). This seems not to be the case: on the contrary, in France as in other countries, the proportion of women who have never cohabited with a partner before the age of 50 is declining among the least-educated, while it is increasing among the most-educated, so that the gradient has reversed. Among

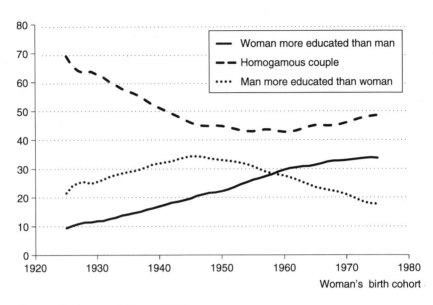

Source: Toulemon and Mazuy (2013).

Figure 2.11   Distribution of French couples by compared level of education of both partners

couples, those where the woman has a higher level of education than the man outnumber those where the man is more educated (Figure 2.11).

This is a very general result, as shown by Esteve et al. (2011) from census samples coming from 38 countries. The change in the structure of female and male population by level of education did not lead to an increasing 'marriage squeeze' for highly educated women, but to a change in male and female preferences: the female hypergamic model is being replaced by an hypogamic model. This shows that family formation norms and preferences are changing rapidly, and that family behaviour can change and become more flexible. Despite the fact that gender inequalities are still prevalent in Europe, at work and in the family (Hamel et al. 2015), the change in men's and women's mating preferences and in sexual behaviour show a decline in gender inequalities and an increasing similarity between men's and women's partnership histories.

Less gender inequality is strongly associated to more unmarried cohabitation. The relation between gender equality and union disruptions is now mixed (Lyngstad and Jalovaara 2010), but the relation used to be positive when unmarried cohabitation and divorce were less common. Furthermore, egalitarian couples used to be less often married and more prone to union disruption or divorce. The relation may have changed in the most egalitarian countries, but the trend towards less gender inequality has been part of the increasing frailty of unions until now.

More Complex Partnership Histories

Because of the increase in divorce, separation and second unions, partnership histories of men and women are becoming more complex. Children may keep some ties with both parents after the separation, sometimes commuting between parental households; adults must in those cases continue being in regular contact with their previous partner. If they enter a new union, a new relationship is established between the new partner and their stepchildren, and this new relationships enriches the family ties. The family network can thus be enlarged at different points in time. The parent of a new step-parent may become a 'step-grand-parent'; similarly other new links can be created (uncles and aunts, cousins, and so on) in the case of a union. Some unions create new networks which are only partially connected: when the previous partner of a parent enters into a new union, the children gain a new step-parent and may then have new half-brothers and half-sisters in another household. But the (first) parent will not gain step-children from this new union of their previous partner. The frontier of the family thus goes beyond the household, each member having their 'own family'.

Statistical Issues on Emerging Forms of Households and Families

Facing these new family behaviours, the United Nations and Eurostat have identified new challenges for the 'measurement of emerging forms of families and households' (Freguja and Valente 2011), with new categories to be identified in censuses and surveys:

- Reconstituted couples: a previous marriage or registered partnership.
- Reconstituted families: a non-common child, a child of only one partner.
- Commuters between households (sharing their time between two homes): children, young adults, partners (both partners or one partner commuting within couples).
- Living apart together: partners having an intimate relationship, living in separate households, with no shared household.
- A synthesis: living apart within a network. Inhabitants having their family beyond the household.
- New family bonds: same-sex couples, cohabiting or legally registered (also LATs).

These new family forms are far from being accurately observed in overall statistics, so that specific family types are ignored, leading to an underestimation of the complexity of partnership relations between adults, when family statistics are based on household composition, with a limited number of identified ties. Questions must remain simple in order to be understood in a similar way in all groups in all countries, but they would need to be enlarged in two directions in order to better identify these family ties: using more accurate categories of family ties within the household, and including some family ties beyond the household.

Other Consequences for Family Behaviour

Changing partnerships have many consequences for other demographic behaviours, such as fertility. In European countries where some family policies have been implemented, it is not clear whether these policies must cope with the consequences of changes in partnership behaviour and provide support to all families, or encourage behaviour with supposed 'positive externalities', most often lower poverty, higher gender equality and higher fertility.

Flexibility of family forms as fuel for fertility

When European countries are compared, those where the family forms are more diverse are those where fertility is the highest: countries experiencing a high mean age at marriage, common unmarried cohabitation and a large proportion of births out of marriage are those where fertility is highest. The individualization of behaviours, with a strong support from the state through family policy, and high female labour force participation, is associated to higher fertility than strict family systems where marriage is still common (Luci-Greulich and Thévenon 2013). Although direct causation is very difficult to establish, these correlations show that it is not the retreat of marriage per se, but the lack of other forms of unions as socially accepted alternatives, which lowers the fertility level.

Consequences of couple disruptions on children

Divorce is by definition related to many changes in children's and adults' daily living conditions, and most studies find negative consequences for adults, some of them being temporary. Specific effects of divorce on children's well-being or school attainment have been found in the United States and Great Britain (Sigle-Rushton et al. 2005), but no general result could be ascertained, the causal relationship being difficult to identify (Ní Bhrolcháin et al. 2000); moreover, Amato (2010) emphasizes the role of pre-divorce marital discord on the impact of divorce. The 'conviction

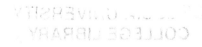

that growing up in stable nuclear families forms the sole guarantee for the cognitive, social and emotional well-being of the next generation', as written in the Introduction, is not evidence-based: family forms have often been diverse and the emotional well-being of children is surely not mainly dependent on growing up in stable nuclear families. The increase in the proportion of children with separated parents thus cannot be considered as a threat on the well-being of the next generation.

Family policies
Family policies towards helping work–family balance were established in some European countries, for reasons based on different ideological motives: in Northern Europe the point was about gender equality, and the state wanted to encourage women to work, even if they had young children; in France the issue was about the fertility level and the aim of the family policy was to encourage women to have children, even if they were working. Pro-natalist policies are becoming more prevalent, due to the low level of fertility. Many other policies such as housing policy and education policies may be related to family policies, even if their aims are more related to other social goals, such as fighting against poverty, or providing equal opportunities. Countries with the greatest acceptance of diverse family forms and partnership behaviours, and more proactive measures for improving work–life balance, are the ones where fertility has remained high despite large changes which occurred in partnership behaviour. The impact on social inequalities and poverty is less easy to evaluate, as some paradoxical side-effects are present. For instance, giving a specific allowance to lone parents may improve their living conditions, but may also make union disruptions easier. Then a voluntarist policy to support lone parents (lone mothers most of the time) may lead to an increase in lone families (and then to an increase in poverty among families). Although there is no doubt that in many cases some parents (mostly women) rightly prefer a union disruption in cases of marital dispute, this may lead to an increase in child poverty, implying a 'coping' policy. The increasing focus on gender equality within family policies currently offers a consistent umbrella to these diverse policies in Europe.

CONCLUSION

The retreat of marriage has led to many changes in family behaviour. This trend is now common to all countries in Europe, but the family forms are still highly differentiated from one country to the next. New family forms have emerged, many of them being difficult to identify in censuses and surveys. The decline of marriage as an institution is part of a major change in European societies, related to decreasing gender inequality and the desire for more flexible family arrangements: alternative forms of union have emerged as long-term alternatives to marriage, when they possess strong legal bases, without referring to the traditional family roles within marriage. These changes lead to more complex family histories, due to an increase in the proportion of union disruptions. New forms of union relationships, as well as new relations between children and adults, and between previous partners (especially if they share common children) are being built in many countries. In order to encourage more inclusive family networks, new forms of family relations must be recognized, taking into account the possibility of successive unions for different members of the family. A decline in gender inequality within the family appears to be the more consistent driver of changes in partnership behaviour, as well as in other social behaviour. This is an ongoing process which, in order to reach its potential of complete equality, must be accompanied by other changes in the society: changes in family behaviour imply less gender inequality in other spheres of society.

NOTE

*   Institut national d'études démographiques, Paris, France, toulemon@ined.fr. Paper presented at the UCSIA International Workshop on The Family Kaleidoscope, Evolving Partnerships and Parenting, University of Antwerp, 19–21 March 2014.

REFERENCES

Amato, P. (2010), 'Research on divorce: continuing developments and new trends', *Journal of Marriage and Family*, 72 (3), 650–666.
Ariès, P. (1977), *L'homme devant la mort*, Paris: Le Seuil.
Avdeev, A., T. Eremenko, P. Festy, J. Gaymu, N. Le Bouteillec and S. Springer (2011), 'Populations and demographic trends of European countries, 1980–2010', *Population*, 66 (1), 9–130, accessed 22 October 2015 at https://www.ined.fr/fichier/s_rubrique/209/pop_e_66.2011.1_avdeev.en.pdf.
Bailly, E. and W. Rault (2013), 'Are heterosexual couples in civil partnerships different from married couples?', *Population and Societies*, 497, 1–4, accessed 22 October 2015 at http://www.ined.fr/en/resources_documentation/publications/pop_soc/bdd/publication/1630/.
Baiocco, R., M. Argalia and F. Laghi (2014), 'The desire to marry and attitudes toward same-sex family legalization in a sample of Italian lesbians and gay men', *Journal of Family Issues*, 35 (2), 181–200.
Beaumel, C. and A. Pla (2012), 'La situation démographique en 2010', Insee Résultats, 131 Société, accessed 22 October 2015 at http://www.insee.fr/fr/publications-et-services/irweb.asp?id=sd2010.

Blondel, B. and M. Kermarrec (2011), *Enquête nationale périnatale 2010. Les naissances en 2010 et leur évolution depuis 2003*, Paris: INSERM, accessed 22 October 2015 at http://www.sante.gouv.fr/IMG/pdf/Les_naissances_en_2010_et_leur_evolution_depuis_2003.pdf.

Bozon, M. (2003), 'At what age do women and men have their first sexual intercourse?', *Population and Societies*, 391, 1–4.

Cooke, L. and J. Baxter (2010), 'Families in international context: comparing institutional effects across Western societies', *Journal of Marriage and Family*, 72 (3), 516–536.

Council of Europe (2006), *Recent Demographic Developments in Europe 2005*, Strasbourg: Council of Europe Publishing.

de Jong Gierveld, J. (2004), 'Remarriage, unmarried cohabitation, living apart together: partner relationships following bereavement or divorce', *Journal of Marriage and Family*, 66 (1), 236–243.

Esteve, A., J. Garcia and I. Permanyer (2011), 'The reversal of the gender gap in education and its impact on union formation: the end of hypergamy', paper presented at the Annual Meeting of the PAA, accessed 22 October 2015 at http://paa2011.princeton.edu/papers/110915.

Freguja, C. and P. Valente (eds) (2011), 'Measurement of different emerging forms of households and families', report by the Task Force on Families and Households, UN-ECE – Eurostat, Conference of European Statisticians, accessed 22 October 2015 at http://www.unece.org/fileadmin/DAM/stats/publications/Families_and_Households_FINAL.pdf.

Frémeaux, N. and M. Leturcq (2013), 'Plus ou moins mariés: l'évolution du mariage et des régimes matrimoniaux en France', *Economie et Statistique*, 462–463, 125–151, accessed 22 October 2015 at http://www.insee.fr/fr/ffc/docs_ffc/ES462E.pdf.

Hamel, C., W. Rault and INED's Demography, Gender and Societies research unit (2015), 'A demographic perspective on gender inequality', *Population and Societies*, 517, 1–4.

Heuveline, P. and J. Timberlake (2004), 'The role of cohabitation in family formation: the United States in comparative perspective', *Journal of Marriage and Family*, 66 (6), 1214–1230.

Levin, I. (2004), 'Living apart together: a new family form', *Current Sociology*, 52 (2), 223–240.

Luci-Greulich, A. and O. Thévenon (2013), 'The impact of family policies on fertility trends in developed countries', *European Journal of Population*, 29 (4), 387–416.

Lyngstad, T. and M. Jalovaara (2010), 'A review of the antecedents of union dissolution', *Demographic Research*, 23 (10), 257–292.

Macura, M. and G. Beets (eds) (2002), *Dynamics of Fertility and Partnership in Europe. Insights and Lessons from Comparative Research*, Vol. 1, UNECE, Geneva: United Nations.

Mazuy, M., M. Barbieri and H. d'Albis (2013), 'Recent demographic trends in France: fertility remains stable', *Population-E*, 68 (3), 329–374, accessed 22 October 2015 at http://www.ined.fr/fichier/s_rubrique/311/population_en_2013_3_france_demographic_situation.en.pdf.

Ní Bhrolcháin, M., R. Chappell, I. Diamond and C. Jameson (2000), 'Parental divorce and outcomes for children: evidence and interpretation', *European Sociological Review*, 16 (1), 67–91.

Pailhé, A., D. Mortelmans, T. Castro, C. Cortina Trilla, M. Digoix, P. Festy, S. Krapf, M. Kreyenfeld, V. Lyssens-Danneboom, T. Martín-García, W. Rault, O. Thévenon and L. Toulemon (2013), 'FamiliesAndSocieties deliverable D2.1. State-of-the-art-report: Changes in the Life Course', accessed 22 October 2015 at http://www.familiesandsocieties.eu/.

Perelli-Harris, B., M. Kreyenfeld, W. Sigle-Rushton, R. Keizer, T. Lappegård, A. Jasilioniene, C. Berghammer, P. Di Giulio and K. Köppen (2010a), 'The increase in fertility in cohabitation across Europe: examining the intersection between union status and childbearing', MPIDR Working Paper, 2009-021, accessed 22 October 2015 at http://www.demogr.mpg.de/papers/working/wp-2009-021.pdf.

Perelli-Harris, B., W. Sigle-Rushton, M. Kreyenfeld, T. Lappegard, R. Keizer and C. Berghammer (2010b), 'The educational gradient of childbearing within cohabitation in Europe', *Population and Development Review*, 36 (4), 775–801.

Prioux, F. (2006), 'Cohabitation, marriage and separation: contrasts in Europe', *Population and Societies*, 422, 1–4, accessed 22 October 2015 at http://www.ined.fr/en/resources_documentation/publications/pop_soc/bdd/publication/1162/.

Sedgh, G., S. Singh and R. Hussain (2014), 'Intended and unintended pregnancies worldwide in 2012 and recent trends', *Studies in Family Planning*, 45 (3), 301–314.

Sigle-Rushton, W., J. Hobcraft and K. Kiernan (2005), 'Parental divorce and subsequent disadvantage: a cross-cohort comparison', *Demography*, 42 (3), 427–446.

Sobotka, T. and L. Toulemon (2008), 'Overview chapter 4: changing family and partnership behaviour. Common trends and persistent diversity across Europe', *Demographic Research*, 19 (6), 85–138, Special Collection 7: Childbearing Trends and Policies in Europe, accessed 22 October 2015 at http://www.demographic-research.org/volumes/vol19/6/.

Thévenon, O. (2009), 'Increased women's labour force participation in Europe: progress in the work life balance or polarization of behaviours?', *Population-E*, 64 (2), 235–272.

Toulemon, L. (2013), 'Les pères dans les statistiques', *Informations sociales*, 176, 8–13.

Toulemon, L. and M. Mazuy (2013), 'Fertility in France remains high among all social groups', poster presented at the seminar on Changing Families and Fertility Choices, Oslo, 6–7 June.

Vallin, J. and F. Meslé (2001), 'Tables de mortalité françaises pour les XIXe et XXe siècles et projections pour le XXIe siècle', Données statistiques, Paris: INED, accessed 22 October 2015 at http://www.ined.fr/fr/ressources_documentation/publications/donnees_statistiques/bdd/publication/110/.

Van Bavel, J. (2012), 'The reversal of gender inequality in education, union formation and fertility in Europe', *Vienna Yearbook of Population Research*, 10, 127–154.

Villeneuve-Gokalp, C. (1991), 'From marriage to informal union: recent changes in the behaviour of French couples', *Population, an English selection*, 3, 81–111.

Waaldijk, K. (ed.) (2005), 'More or less together: levels of legal consequences of marriage, cohabitation and registered partnership for different-sex and same-sex partners', Documents de travail de l'Ined, 125, Paris: INED, accessed 22 October 2015 at https://www.ined.fr/fichier/s_rubrique/19409/document_de_travail_125.fr.pdf.

PART II

Looking at gender

3. Gender inequality in the division of housework over the life course: a European comparative perspective

Tine Kil, Karel Neels and Jorik Vergauwen

INTRODUCTION

Historically, the 'male breadwinner, female carer' model, characterized by a gendered division of paid and domestic work, has been a key assumption underlying the development of welfare states in post-war Western Europe (Pascall and Lewis 2004). In recent decades, however, various institutions in society have shifted from the male breadwinner model towards a gender equity model, where gender is no longer a determinant of who is responsible for carrying out paid work, housework or childcare in a household (McDonald 2000b). This shift has occurred at different speeds in different domains of society. Gender inequity has largely disappeared from institutions such as education and employment. Over the last 50 years, female participation in higher education and the labour market has increased significantly, and the distribution of paid work between partners has become more equal on average (Crompton 1999). In contrast, gender roles in the family and parenting have adjusted slowly (McDonald 2000a). The more equal distribution of paid work is only partly compensated by a more equal distribution of housework and childcare (Altintas 2009; Lachance-Grzela and Bouchard 2010). According to Goldscheider, the revolution towards gender equality therefore runs in two stages (Goldscheider 2000; Goldscheider et al. 2010). The first part of the gender revolution, in which women enter the public sphere of education, employment and politics, has largely been accomplished (Bernhardt et al. 2008). The second part of the revolution, however, in which men join the private sphere and take up their part of the responsibility for housework and childcare, has lagged behind.

The gendered division of housework implies that working women face a 'double shift', with paid work on the one hand, and housework and childcare on the other (Hochschild and Machung 1989). Empirical work on the gender division of housework suggests that there is not so much a double workload but rather a dual responsibility (Elchardus and Glorieux 1994; Glorieux et al. 2006). Women are forced to combine various roles to a greater extent, which can lead to role nuisance, role conflicts, increased planning burden and time pressure. An unequal household division of labour further limits the ability of women to participate in public life and fully realize their role in the professional, social and political spheres (Poeschl, in Lachance-Grzela and Bouchard 2010). An unequal distribution of domestic work also increases the risk of dissatisfaction about it, which in turn is related to low psychological well-being, less perceived social support and reduced family stability (Claffey and Manning 2010). Similarly, the incompatibility between women's roles in the public and private spheres has been suggested as a major cause of low fertility in developed countries (McDonald 2006, p. 162).

The micro factors affecting the distribution of domestic work have been studied extensively in recent decades. Research into the effect of (national) context emerged more recently. Studies that focus specifically on the influence of national context on the gendered division of domestic work from a life course perspective are, nevertheless, rather limited. An exception is the work by Anxo et al. (2011), but they did not distinguish between housework and childcare, whereas previous research has shown that these are conceptually different (Ishiikuntz and Coltrane 1992). Furthermore, the results of their study are limited to separate country analyses. Our chapter focuses specifically on housework and contributes to the literature by documenting how gender inequality in the division of housework changes over the life course and different stages of family formation, and by showing how the gender division of domestic work depends on the institutional and social context in which couples live. Drawing on data from Round 5 of the European Social Survey (ESS) and using multilevel models we first document how the gender distribution of domestic work over the life course is affected by individual and household characteristics (time availability, relative resources and gender ideology), as well as the cultural and policy context (gender culture, full-time childcare, availability of parental leave for men, and neutrality of the tax system). Subsequently, we show how the effect of individual characteristics on the gender distribution of domestic work depends on the cultural and policy context in which couples live.

THEORETICAL BACKGROUND AND RESEARCH QUESTIONS

Determinants of the Division of Housework at the Individual and Household Level

In recent decades several studies have looked into factors at the individual and household level that affect the distribution of domestic work. The available literature has identified three major factors: time availability, relative resources and gender ideology.

Becker (1991) explains the division of housework from a rational, economic perspective. He argues that families seek to maximize utility by distributing tasks as efficiently as possible. Each member must therefore specialize in what they do best, paid or domestic work. Productivity depends on biological factors, different experiences and investment in human capital over the life course. This makes that men better engage in paid work and women in domestic work. A recent application of this theoretical framework is the perspective of time availability, in which the distribution of housework depends on the time available to partners. The partner who spends less time on other activities such as labour force participation will have more time available to take up a larger share of the housework.

The second approach emphasizes the importance of relative resources that partners contribute to the household. Housework is considered an annoying task, distribution of which is achieved as a result of negotiation. Negotiation takes the form of a power struggle: the partner who has the best negotiating position – based on material resources – may limit their share of the housework (Brines 1993).

The last perspective looks into the distribution of domestic work as the result of gender ideology. In this respect, women with attitudes conforming to the 'male breadwinner, female carer' ideal will perform a larger share of the household chores. Gender ideology is viewed as the result of socialization in the role that is associated with the gender category to which one belongs. An alternative theory is the 'gender construction or doing gender' perspective. From this perspective, domestic work is a process through which individuals define their gender identity. West and Zimmerman (1987) view gender as a set of routines that are embedded in everyday interaction which must be constantly exercised and confirmed in interaction with others.

A review of the literature by Lachance-Grzela and Bouchard (2010) suggests that the gender division of housework is a complex process that is best explained by a combination of the aforementioned factors. The first part of the first research question (1a) therefore looks into the effects of individual-level and household-level factors such as time availability, relative resources and gender ideology on the gender distribution of housework.

A Life Course Approach of the Gendered Division of Housework

The life course is approached using Glick's classic idea of the 'family cycle' (in Buhlmann et al. 2010). He argues that families go through a sequence of typical life stages at normatively defined ages. Glick therefore distinguishes between marriage, childbearing, children leaving home and dissolution of the family. Later on, categories were added that vary depending on age and institutional role of the children, ranging from families with pre-school children to empty-nest families.

The form and extent of gender inequality vary throughout the life span (Anxo et al. 2010). Research by Anxo et al. (2011) on the household division of labour by age in France, Italy, Sweden and the United States based on cross-sectional data shows that gender differences in paid work, housework, childcare and leisure are smaller at younger and older ages. At working age they are largest, especially when children are present in the family (Buhlmann et al. 2010). Grunow et al. (2012) show (based on longitudinal data for West Germany) that many couples try to distribute housework evenly in the beginning of their relationship. But after this initial stage the distribution gets more traditional and a routine is created.

Research by Lundberg and Rose (1999) based on longitudinal data from the American Panel Study of Income Dynamics shows that especially parenthood is often accompanied by a specialization of gender roles in paid and unpaid work. Specialization patterns, however, apply more to the older birth cohorts, suggesting that gender roles have changed over time. Also Martinengo et al. (2010) found (based on cross-sectional data) that parenting entails a more gendered division of work and family life. In their interpretation, the current generation is mainly egalitarian, but the general image about parenting that manifests itself when becoming a parent has a greater impact than other cultural norms such as gender egalitarianism. Studies based on longitudinal data from Australia (Baxter et al. 2008) and the United States (Nomaguchi and Milkie 2003) show that every birth significantly increases the time spent on housework for women. For fathers, the birth of a first child triggers no change in the time spent on housework, and the second birth even reduces the time spent on housework (Baxter et al. 2008). Similarly an American study with longitudinal data (Sanchez and Thomson 1997) shows that the transition to a second or subsequent child is accompanied by a slight increase in the working hours of the father. These findings show that children imply more housework, and that mainly mothers take up these extra tasks.

The second part of the first research question (1b) therefore is whether the effects of time availability, relative resources and gender ideology differ over the life course.

The Influence of National Context

Decision making regarding the distribution of domestic work in the family is embedded in a social context and is influenced by norms, values and the prevailing culture in a particular society (Lappegård et al. 2012). Numerous studies have recently looked into the relationship between the household division of labour and macro-indicators (Batalova and Cohen 2002; Fuwa 2004; Fuwa and Cohen 2007; Geist 2005; Hook 2010; Knudsen and Waerness 2008; Lappegård et al. 2012; van der Lippe et al. 2011).

Several researchers have investigated the influence of gender equality in the public sphere. This research is often based on the Gender Empowerment Measure (GEM) of the United Nations (Batalova and Cohen 2002; Fuwa 2004) and female labour market participation (Fuwa 2004; Hook 2006, 2010). The findings largely confirm that the visibility of women in positions of public authority and prestige affects the standards with respect to the gender distribution of work (Batalova and Cohen 2002). The presence of women in the public sphere has a positive impact on gender equality in the private sphere of the family.

The impact of social policies on gender equality has also been considered. Geist (2005) notes that couples in conservative countries divide housework less equally than couples in social democratic countries. The regimes of conservative welfare states actively encourage traditional gender roles, while social democratic regimes encourage gender equality. Liberal regimes are more heterogeneous and take an intermediate position. Also family policies are taken into account. Public childcare can limit the female caregiver and homemaker role through its influence on female employment and financial independence (Hook 2006). On the other hand, it hardly affects the role of the father in the household. The state takes over some parts of the traditional 'female' tasks, but does not encourage men to become more involved in childcare and domestic work. Hence cross-national analyses find no significant effects of public childcare on the division of housework (Hook 2006, 2010). In contrast, research by van der Lippe et al. (2011) shows that public spending on childcare is negatively related with the time spent by women on housework if children are present in the household.

Parental leave is suggested to have the opposite effect. Since it is used predominantly by mothers, it can discourage a more egalitarian division of household labour participation because it reinforces the 'male bread-winner, female homemaker' model, affecting financial resources and long-term employment opportunities for women. In contrast to this hypothesis Fuwa and Cohen (2007) found a positive relationship between the length of parental leave and equality of the household division of labour. Hook (2006) nuanced this finding, suggesting that the argument would only apply to countries where fathers can take up parental leave, as availability of parental leave to both partners discourages gender specialization and the persistence of traditional gender roles. In countries where fathers are not entitled to parental leave, there exists a negative relationship between the length of parental leave and gender equality in the household division of labour.

In sum, there is some evidence that gender and policy contexts have an effect on the division of housework in the households, but results are incon-sistent and the effects are usually small (Lachance-Grzela and Bouchard 2010). Given that household tasks take place in the private sphere of family life, it is suggested that policies struggle to affect them. Welfare state policy is primarily focused on the organization of care and less on the organiza-tion of housework. Therefore the effect on housework is rather indirect and caused by the relatively strong relationship between care and house-work among parents of young children. But family policies also contribute to the division of housework via the normative and symbolic construction of families. Policy measures induce the institutionalization of a dominant and normative family structure (Bourdieu 1996). Private gender equality is therefore more common in a society where gender equity is accepted as the dominant cultural value and where institutions support it.

Buhlmann et al. (2010) suggest that the extent to which parenthood induces a traditional division of housework depends on the social context in which a couple resides. Although the birth of a child entails a more unequal division of labour, care and housework in all countries, the ability to return to a more equal distribution of work and care would depend on the institutional context. In countries where policy supports a dual earner model, it is easier to re-establish a more equal division of labour and care. In countries where institutions support a male breadwinner model or where family policy remains limited, the pattern of an egalitarian distribu-tion of housework often does not recover.

The second research question looks into the influence of contextual ele-ments on gender inequality in the private sphere: what is the importance of policy and culture for the gendered division of housework (2a) and do the effects of such contextual factors vary over the life course (2b)?

To assess the interplay between social contexts and individual character-istics on the division of housework, the third research question concerns the cross-level interaction effects between micro-level and macro-level variables: are the effects of the individual-level variables influenced by the country-level variables in the different life course stages?

DATA AND METHODS

Data

The analyses use data from ESS Round 5, a standardized, cross-sectional, repeated survey on the living conditions and political attitudes of European residents. The interviews were conducted in 2010, 2011 and 2012. Round 5 includes a module on 'Work, family and well-being' that provides data about housework. The sample includes 24 countries: Belgium, Bulgaria, Cyprus, Czech Republic, Denmark, Estonia, Finland, France, Germany, Greece, Hungary, Ireland, Lithuania, the Netherlands, Norway, Poland, Portugal, Russia, Slovakia, Slovenia, Spain, Sweden, Switzerland and the United Kingdom. Because this research investigates gender equality within households, the sample was restricted to respondents in heterosexual couples. The total number of sampled respondents was 24045, ranging from 655 in Lithuania to 1722 in Germany.

Because this study uses a life course perspective, different life stages are examined separately. For the classification we used a variant of the family cycle approach developed by Glick (Buhlmann et al. 2010). This typology reflects the life events and life stages of a large part of the population, such as the birth of a child, the transition to retirement, and so on (Anxo et al. 2011). We distinguished between couples who are in different life stages, based on the age of women, the presence of children in the household and the age of the youngest resident child. We distinguished six different groups: (1) young couples (<45 years old) without children; (2) couples (<60 years old) with young children (<6 years old); (3) couples (<60 years old) with children aged 6–15; (4) couples (<60 years old) with teenage children aged 16–25; (5) midlife 'empty-nest' couples (45–59 years old) without resident children; and (6) older couples (>59 years old).

The age of the respondents ranges from 16 to 94 with the average age being 50. Looking at the sample distribution over the life stages, 28.6 per cent of women in the sample are older than 60. But there are also substantial differences between countries. Almost half (45.1 per cent) of Portuguese couples are in the oldest life stage (>60 years old), while this group is limited to 19.6 per cent in the Polish sample (see Table 3.1).

Table 3.1 Sample distribution by country and life course stage, respondents in a heterosexual couple aged 16–94

	Aged <45, no child (%)	Aged <60, child aged <6 (%)	Aged <60, child 6–15 (%)	Aged <60, child aged 16–25 (%)	Aged 45–59, no child (%)	Aged >59 (%)	Total %	Total N
Belgium	9.1	20.7	15.1	13.1	14.0	28.0	100.0	992
Bulgaria	5.0	13.9	16.0	12.2	16.9	36.0	100.0	1076
Czech Republic	11.6	18.5	14.8	14.2	13.0	27.8	100.0	859
Cyprus	9.4	18.1	13.5	16.1	9.9	33.0	100.0	554
Switzerland	10.4	18.2	15.2	14.8	17.2	24.3	100.0	1023
Germany	11.2	15.8	14.3	9.4	19.4	29.9	100.0	1662
Denmark	8.5	16.0	19.7	8.6	17.3	30.0	100.0	978
Estonia	6.4	21.7	14.7	13.6	14.4	29.2	100.0	890
Spain	13.0	21.6	17.4	15.4	9.0	23.6	100.0	1026
Finland	12.2	20.6	11.6	7.6	17.0	30.9	100.0	1087
France	10.4	22.4	14.6	8.0	14.6	29.9	100.0	915
United Kingdom	12.0	22.9	12.7	7.3	16.0	29.2	100.0	1168
Greece	12.0	20.0	17.2	11.3	10.7	28.8	100.0	1359
Hungary	8.0	20.2	16.8	15.2	14.6	25.2	100.0	822

Ireland	14.7	26.9	14.5	7.4	12.0	24.4	100.0	1089
Lithuania	17.8	18.1	10.8	12.4	20.0	30.9	100.0	619
Netherlands	12.8	19.4	15.4	8.8	16.2	27.4	100.0	1072
Norway	11.2	24.0	15.8	7.6	16.3	25.2	100.0	976
Poland	10.1	27.8	16.1	15.5	11.0	19.6	100.0	864
Portugal	6.4	11.7	15.2	8.4	13.2	45.1	100.0	891
Russia	14.6	20.0	15.9	14.3	16.1	19.0	100.0	861
Sweden	12.2	19.8	13.0	8.2	15.8	31.0	100.0	882
Slovenia	6.1	19.2	16.0	18.9	9.8	29.9	100.0	692
Slovakia	5.9	14.4	16.6	19.1	14.6	29.4	100.0	881
Total	10.3	19.6	15.2	11.6	14.7	28.6	100.0	23 238

Source: ESS Round 5 (2010).

Dependent Variable

The dependent variable is the relative division of housework. We look at the proportion of household tasks for which the female partner is responsible. The possible values of the indicator range from 0 to 100, where 0 refers to a distribution where the male partner performs all tasks and 100 to a distribution where the female partner performs all tasks. As housework and childcare are conceptually different (Ishiikuntz and Coltrane 1992) and the meaning and delineation of childcare is more complex (Altintas 2009; Pfau-Effinger 2010), we focus on housework. ESS Round 5 (ESS5) includes two questions that measure how many hours per week the respondent and his partner spend in total on housework, which is restricted to cooking, washing, cleaning, shopping and maintenance tasks. The first four tasks are typically female and more routine, non-discrete and time-consuming while maintenance tasks are rather 'male', interrupted, occasionally, flexible and less time-consuming. Recent studies (Batalova and Cohen 2002; Fuwa 2004) have focused on the distribution of typically female tasks. However, this may underestimate the actual contribution of the male partner. As a result, it seems more useful to consider both.

The measure for time spent on housework is based on answers to survey questions. Comparisons of estimates of time spent on housework by questionnaires and time diaries show that the reported hours people spend on domestic labour are much higher in questionnaires (Bianchi et al. 2000). This problem is especially present when household tasks are questioned separately and the time is then added up, as simultaneous activities are counted twice (Coltrane 2000). This bias can be partially avoided by the more general question ('how many hours do you spend weekly on housework in total?') that ESS5 uses. In addition, the dependent variable is relative thus the estimation of the absolute contribution is less important.

Independent Variables

Micro-level variables
Time availability is operationalized as the total number of hours that the female partner on average spends on paid work per week. Relative resources is operationalized as the proportion of household income for which the female partner is responsible. There are seven categories: (0) none; (1) very small; (2) under a half; (3) about half; (4) more than half; (5) very large; and (6) all.

For the operationalization of gender ideology two items were used that estimate the extent to which one agrees with the assumptions of the male breadwinner model. The statements are: 'When jobs are scarce, men should have more right to work than women', and 'A woman should be prepared to cut down on her paid work for the sake of her family'. The responses to these items were measured using a five-point scale ranging from 'agree strongly' to 'disagree strongly'. The correlation (Pearson) between the two items was 0.49 ($p < 0.001$). The scores on the two scales were added together and divided by two to form an indicator of gender ideology. This variable is coded so that 0 is equivalent to a gender ideology that corresponds to the male breadwinner model and 4 is equivalent to a gender ideology that rejects these ideas.

We also include some control variables to the models. The average number of working hours per week of the male partner and the household size fit within the time availability perspective. We additionally add information on the education of both partners (coded in seven ordinal International Standard Classification of Education – ISCED – categories) and whether the couple is married. A higher level of education and unmarried cohabitation are usually associated with more progressive values such as gender egalitarianism. Furthermore also age and sex of the respondent were entered as control variables. We take into account gender as earlier research (Kamo 2000; Lee and Waite 2005) shows that men and women estimate their own and their partners time spent on housework differently.

Macro-level variables
The contextual variables reflect policies that address gender equity in family-oriented institutions (Saraceno and Keck 2011) and gender culture. All contextual variables were standardized.

The first policy variable considers the use of full-time formal childcare, which is measured as the percentage of children between 0 and 2 years old that spend more than 30 hours per week in formal childcare. Formal childcare includes all types of organized care by a public or private structure. It draws on data from Eurostat (2010).

The second indicator considers availability of parental leave for men, where we used the number of months of parental leave that is exclusively reserved for the parents together or that is explicitly reserved for fathers in 2009 (Multilinks Database 2011). In most countries, parents can decide who receives the leave and how the effective parental care period is divided between father and mother. This indicator only considers the regulation that creates additional rights when both parents share the time (Keck and Saraceno 2011).

The third variable concerns the fiscal support for dual earner couples or the neutrality of the tax system. Tax systems are neutral when they do not influence the distribution of paid work between couples and create equal work incentives for both partners (OECD 2012a). It is operationalized as the extent to which a single earner couple has to pay more or less taxes than a dual earner couple with the same income (200 per cent of the median income) and the same household composition. A negative value indicates that a single earner family pays less taxes than a similar dual earner household whereas a positive value indicates the reverse. We used data for 2010 from OECD (2012b).

Besides the policy variables, we used an indicator of progressive gender culture and support for the dual worker/dual carer model. To construct the cultural variable we used data from the 2008 European Value Study (EVS 2011). The survey consists of approximately 1500 respondents per country and contains mostly countries that also participated in ESS Round 5. The survey examines the specific support of sharing roles within the household, while ESS Round 5 does not explore these issues. A factor analysis was performed on eight items that measure the extent to which respondents agree with the male breadwinner model and a gendered division of housework and childcare. The factor we use examines the egalitarian ideas of gender roles within the family. Principal axis factoring with varimax rotation showed that following statements load the strongest on the factor: 'In general, fathers are as well suited to look after their children as mothers' (0.55), 'Men should take as much responsibility as women for the home and children' (0.54), 'A working mother can establish just as warm and secure a relationship with her children as a mother who does not work' (0.49) and 'A pre-school child is like to suffer if his or her mother works' (−0.42). The possible answers consisted of a Likert scale with four points ranging from total agreement (1) to total disagreement (4). The standardized factor scores are constructed from the weighted person data and aggregated by country. The scale is coded in such a way that a higher value means a more progressive gender culture.

Analysis

We used multilevel models where individuals (level 1) are nested in countries (level 2). Multilevel regression creates the possibility to test the combined effects of individual-level variables and country-level variables. For each life course stage ten models were estimated using the relative division of housework as the dependent variable.

$$Y_{ij} = \gamma_{00} + \mu_{0j} + r_{ij} \tag{3.1}$$

Model (3.1) only includes constants at both the individual level and the country level, where Y_{ij} reflects the proportion of the housework that the female partner is responsible for in couple i in country j; γ_{00} represents the grand mean (intercept); μ_{0j} is the country-specific deviation from the grand mean (random intercept) and r_{ij} represents the individual-level deviation from the country-specific mean (individual-level residual).

$$Y_{ij} = \gamma_{00} + \gamma_{10}TA_{ij} + \gamma_{20}RR_{ij} + \gamma_{30}GI_{ij} + \Sigma\gamma_{k0}X_{ikj} + \mu_{0j} + r_{ij} \quad (3.2)$$

Model (3.2) includes the three individual-level variables of interest as well as a number of control variables, where TA_{ij} stands for time availability; RR_{ij} for relative resources and GI_{ij} for gender ideology. The X_{ikj} denote the control variables (working hours of male partner, household size, marital status, education, age and gender). The terms γ_{10}, γ_{20}, γ_{30} and γ_{k0} reflect the slopes for time availability, relative resources, gender ideology and the different control variables respectively. The remaining terms have the same meaning as in the first model.

$$Y_{ij} = \gamma_{00} + \gamma_{10}TA_{ij} + \gamma_{20}RA_{ij} + \gamma_{30}GI_{ij} + \Sigma\gamma_{kj}X_{ikj} + \gamma_{01}Z_j + \mu_{0j} + r_{ij}$$

$$(3.3\text{–}3.6)$$

Models (3.3)–(3.6) each include a macro-level variable Z_j as an independent variable, where γ_{01} reflects the slope of the macro-variable in each model.

$$Y_{ij} = \gamma_{00} + \gamma_{10}TA_{ij} + \gamma_{20}RA_{ij} + \gamma_{30}GI_{ij} + \Sigma\gamma_{kj}X_{ikj} + \gamma_{0j}Z_j + \gamma_{1j}TA_{ij}Z_j$$

$$+ \gamma_{2j}RA_{ij}Z_j + \gamma_{3j}GI_{ij}Z_j + \mu_{0j} + r_{ij} \quad (3.7\text{–}3.10)$$

In models (3.7)–(3.10) the cross-level interaction effects between the three key individual-level variables and each of the macro-variables were included, with $\gamma_{1j}TA_{ij}Z_j$, $\gamma_{2j}RA_{ij}Z_j$ and $\gamma_{3j}GI_{ij}Z_j$ refer to the slopes of the cross-level interaction effects. The random slopes of the models have also been tested but were not included in the model specifications, as they were rarely significant.

RESULTS

The Null Model

In the first model (Table 3.2), the values of the intercepts reflects the average division of housework in the various life stages. In the average European couple the woman is responsible for more than half of the housework, but gender inequality varies over life stages. As expected, the

Table 3.2   The multilevel null models for the distribution of housework in different life course stages, respondents in a heterosexual couple aged 16–94

	Life course stage					
	1	2	3	4	5	6
Intercept	64.26***	71.40***	71.75***	72.13***	68.50***	70.17***
Variance						
Intercept (level 2)	31.91***	26.31***	34.27***	31.47***	34.35***	34.71***
Residual level 1	347.09***	321.82***	33.56***	349.23***	374.53***	429.57***
ICC	8.42%	7.56%	9.32%	8.26%	8.40%	7.48%
AIC	21 392.90	39 794.20	30 982.60	23 487.10	30 341.20	55 944.40
N	2455	4613	3575	2695	3455	6614

Notes:
Life course stages: 1 = woman aged <45, no resident child; 2 = woman aged <60, resident child aged <6; 3 = woman aged <60, resident child aged 6–15; 4 = woman aged <60, resident child aged 16–24; 5 = woman aged 45–59, no resident child; 6 = woman aged >59.
ICC = intra-class correlation coefficient.
Significance levels: * p <0.1, ** p <0.05, *** p <0.01.

Source: ESS Round 5 (2010).

inequality in terms of housework is largest when children are present. For couples with resident children, women perform 71 to 72 per cent of the housework. The gender inequality is lowest (64 per cent) among young couples without children. Further, the variance components show that there is significant variation between countries, with the country-level accounting for 7.5 per cent (stage 6) to 9.3 per cent (stage 3) of the variance in the relative share of housework performed by women.

Individual-level Covariates

In Table 3.3 the individual-level variables are added. Time availability (the average number of working hours per week of the female partner), relative resources (the proportion of household income that the woman is responsible for) and gender ideology (the extent to which progressive values regarding gendered roles are supported) are negatively related to the proportion of the housework that the woman is responsible for. The effects are significant at every life stage. Only for couples with children between 16 and 24 years old a progressive gender ideology has an insignificant effect.

Standardization of the effects (Table 3.4) indicates that the average number of working hours of women and men is most strongly related to the division of housework in each life stage. If the average number of hours a woman spends on paid work increases with one standard deviation, the average proportion of the housework that the woman is responsible for decreases with approximately 0.20 standard deviations. Only for retired couples is the effect of time availability less strong (−0.11), but this may be due to the fact that these people simply spend less time on paid work.

The effects of relative resources and gender ideology are smaller than those of time availability and differ strongly across life stages. The effect of relative resources is relatively small for young couples without children, but roughly three times larger among couples with young children. The older the youngest child, the smaller this effect. This observation can be linked to the fact that economic dependence implies a relatively larger risk in combination with young children. The financially dependent spouse has more to lose in this case in the event of separation. As a result, relative income power may play a larger role in the negotiation of the division of housework.

Gender ideology appears to have a more articulated impact for young couples and older couples without children. Especially when children are present in the household the effect of gender ideology is relatively weak. The practical need for domestic work associated with children and the cultural meaning of parenthood may partially outweigh the effect of gender ideology.

Table 3.3 Multilevel models including individual determinants of the distribution of housework in different life course stages, respondents in a heterosexual couple aged 16–94

	Life course stage					
	1	2	3	4	5	6
Intercept	68.39***	73.67***	73.65***	64.14***	55.18***	72.64***
Time availability (work hours woman)	−0.20***	−0.21***	−0.20***	−0.22***	−0.21***	−0.21***
Relative resources (income w/m, 0–6)	−0.73**	−1.93***	−1.82***	−1.18***	−1.55***	−1.31***
Gender ideology (0–4)	−2.91***	−2.38***	−2.19***	−0.74	−2.06***	−1.88***
Work hours man	0.22***	0.230***	0.23***	0.18***	0.24***	0.14***
Educational level m	−0.06	−0.31***	−0.37***	−0.29**	−0.28**	−0.06
Educational level w	−0.77***	−0.54***	−0.49***	−0.53***	−0.37***	−0.03
Married	1.51	−0.56	0.28	2.05	1.75*	4.76***
Household members	0.72**	1.56***	0.45	0.60	2.31*	0.96***

	1	2	3	4	5	6
Age woman	0.05	−0.06	0.07	0.18**	0.27***	−0.06
Woman	3.04	1.44	2.51*	3.23*	3.92**	2.05*
*Woman*GI*	0.66	1.47***	0.82	0.14	−0.32	0.60
Variance						
Intercept (level 2)	21.36***	13.62***	273.08***	15.55***	20.54***	30.92***
Residual level 1	294.38***	250.56***	17.38***	306.72***	307.69***	410.90***
ICC	6.76%	5.15%	5.98%	4.83%	6.26%	6.99%
R^2 Level 2	31.48%	46.79%	47.51%	47.43%	38.78%	10.67%
AIC	187973.20	35130.00	27002.80	20138.20	27148.80	55833.50
N	2220	4193	3189	2346	3162	6295

Notes: Life course stages: 1 = woman aged <45, no resident child; 2 = woman aged <60, resident child aged <6; 3 = woman aged <60, resident child aged 6–15; 4 = woman aged <60, resident child aged 16–24; 5 = woman aged 45–59, no resident child; 6 = woman aged >59. ICC = intra-class correlation coefficient. Significance levels: * p <0.1, ** p <0.05, *** p <0.01.

Source: ESS Round 5 (2010).

Changing family dynamics and demographic evolution

Table 3.4   Standardized effects (and their standard errors) for the effects of the individual variables on the distribution of housework (Table 3.3) for different life course stages for cohabiting couples of the opposite sex (16–94 years old)

	Life course stage					
	1	2	3	4	5	6
Distribution of housework	(19.50)	(18.64)	(19.11)	(19.58)	(20.19)	(21.66)
Time availability	−0.20	−0.21	−0.20	−0.22	−0.21	−0.11
(work hours woman)	(19.22)	(19.28)	(19.03)	(19.74)	(19.74)	(11.93)
Relative resources	−0.05	−0.15	−0.13	−0.09	−0.11	−0.08
(income w/m, 0–6)	(1.39)	(1.40)	(1.41)	(1.42)	(1.39)	(1.27)
Gender ideology	−0.13	−0.09	−0.10	−0.03	−0.11	−0.07
(0–4)	(1.01)	(1.02)	(1.05)	(1.03)	(1.02)	(1.01)
Work hours man	0.20	0.22	0.22	0.19	0.27	0.10
	(18.11)	(17.57)	(18.26)	(20.42)	(22.48)	(15.51)
Educational level man	−0.01	−0.04	−0.05	−0.04	−0.04	−0.01
	(3.26)	(2.40)	(2.52)	(3.03)	(2.72)	(3.55)
Educational level woman	−0.10	−0.07	−0.07	−0.06	−0.05	0.00
	(2.40)	(2.60)	(2.79)	(2.17)	(2.81)	(3.38)
Married	0.04	−0.01	0.01	0.03	0.03	0.05
	(0.49)	(0.43)	(0.35)	(0.27)	(0.34)	(0.22)
Household members	0.03	0.09	0.02	0.02	0.03	0.03
	(0.71)	(1.08)	(0.90)	(0.80)	(0.29)	(0.73)
Age woman	0.02	−0.02	0.02	0.05	0.05	−0.02
	(6.93)	(6.71)	(5.97)	(5.44)	(3.99)	(6.49)
Woman	0.12	0.13	0.11	0.09	0.08	0.07
	(0.50)	(0.50)	(0.50)	(0.50)	(0.50)	(0.50)
*Woman * GI*	0.02	0.04	0.02	0.00	−0.01	0.01
	(0.50)	(0.51)	(0.52)	(0.51)	(0.51)	(0.51)

Notes:
The standard errors are presented in parentheses.
Life course stages: 1 = woman aged <45, no resident child; 2 = woman aged <60, resident child aged <6; 3 = woman aged <60, resident child aged 6–15; 4 = woman aged <60, resident child aged 16–24; 5 = woman aged 45–59, no resident child; 6 = woman aged >59. ICC = intra-class correlation coefficient.

Source: ESS Round 5 (2010).

Furthermore it is striking that for the elderly couples less variance is explained than in the other groups. This is may be due to the physical capabilities which account for a large fraction of the distribution of domestic work and/or the fact that housework habits are formed in previous life stages and persist in later life stages.

Contextual Factors

In Table 3.5 the four macro-level variables are included. The effects of the individual variables are not shown, since they hardly change when adding the macro-level variables.

For almost all couples – except among couples with a child aged 6–15 (life stage 3) and older couples (life stage 6) – the progressivity of the overall gender culture has a significant positive effect on gender equality in the division of housework. For young couples without children, a standard deviation increase in the progressivity of the national gender culture decreases the share of housework for which women are responsible by 8.46 per cent. The variance components show that the gender culture explains 18.35 per cent of the variance at country level (R^2 level 2 in Table 3.5 minus R^2 level 2 in Table 3.3). In the other life stages gender culture still explains about 10 per cent of the variance at the country level. This is quite small, since the variance at the country level was not higher than 10 per cent in the null model (ICC, Table 3.2).

The three policy variables show no significant effects and only explain a small proportion of the variance. Only for older couples (life stage 6) the availability of parental leave for men has a significant negative effect on gender equality.

Cross-Level Interactions

Table 3.6 examines the interaction effects between the three main micro-level variables of interest and the four macro-level variables which show a number of interesting results, particularly for couples with young children.

For young couples without children (life stage 1) there are no significant interaction effects between gender culture and the micro-level variables. But it is notable that the main effect of gender culture has increased (b = −13.933) compared to the latter model. The other interaction terms do not contribute to the model fit.

For couples with young children (life stage 2) there is a significant interaction between gender culture and full-time childcare at the aggregate level and gender ideology at the individual level. Figure 3.1 gives a visual

Table 3.5   Multilevel models of the macro determinants for the distribution of housework for different life course stages, controlling for the individual determinants, respondents in a heterosexual couple aged 16–94

	Life course stage					
	1	2	3	4	5	6
Intercept	68.66***	73.63***	73.45***	63.66***	55.10***	72.66***
Gender culture	−8.46**	−7.17***	−4.75	−6.16**	−7.45**	−2.88
Variance						
Intercept (level 2)	14.93***	9.49***	16.10***	13.04***	16.50***	31.58***
Residual level 1	294.49***	250.56***	273.09***	306.73***	307.68***	410.91***
ICC	4.82%	3.65%	5.57%	4.08%	5.09%	7.14%
R² Level 2	49.83%	61.61%	51.03%	54.77%	49.76%	8.83%
AIC	18962.40	35118.20	26996.30	20130.00	27139.20	55828.40
N	2220	4193	3189	2346	3162	6295
Intercept	68.80***	73.63***	74.02***	63.57***	52.97***	71.24***
Full-time childcare	−0.91	−1.23	−0.32	−0.85	−0.63	1.01
Variance						
Intercept (level 2)	22.43***	12.40***	18.21***	15.70***	21.92***	30.19***
Residual level 1	291.63***	246.12***	269.76***	301.83***	306.18***	408.86***
ICC	7.14%	4.79%	6.32%	4.94%	6.68%	6.80%
R² Level 2	28.49%	51.24%	45.29%	47.11%	35.05%	13.82%
AIC	17550.70	332521.60	25702.60	19027.30	25724.50	53848.10
N	2056	4010	3040	2221	2998	6075

Intercept	68.69***	73.71***	74.08***	65.13***	52.74***	72.29***
Parental leave men	0.99	0.23	1.18	0.05	1.02	2.41**
Variance						
Intercept (level 2)	23.38***	15.11***	17.06***	17.66***	21.624***	27.59***
Residual level 1	291.50***	250.88***	270.02***	299.22***	302.43***	406.99***
ICC	7.42%	5.68%	5.94%	5.57%	6.67%	6.35%
R^2 Level 2	25.77%	41.44%	48.44%	41.46%	35.91%	19.94%
AIC	17610.40	33543.00	25619.70	18873.60	25816.20	53181.10
N	2063	4003	3030	2205	3013	6003
Intercept	68.35***	73.15***	73.98***	63.76***	53.20***	72.08***
Neutrality tax system	−0.37	−0.69	0.15	0.61	0.28	1.79
Variance						
Intercept (level 2)	14.33***	11.92***	18.00***	16.47***	20.02***	26.98***
Residual level 1	294.65***	254.42***	267.22***	298.61***	306.18***	401.56***
ICC	7.30%	4.63%	6.31%	5.23%	6.14%	6.30%
R^2 Level 2	28.46%	52.96%	45.90%	44.94%	40.20%	21.65%
AIC	17151.10	32923.70	25183.10	18379.30	25292.90	52205.80
N	2014	3940	2982	2148	2948	5902

Notes:

The coefficients for the micro-variables are not shown.

The macro-data for some countries are missing, so these countries are not included in the analysis. Full time childcare: Russia, Parental leave men: Czech Republic, Neutrality tax system: Switzerland and Russia.

Life course stages: 1 = woman aged <45, no resident child; 2 = woman aged <60, resident child aged <6; 3 = woman aged <60, resident child aged 6–15; 4 = woman aged <60, resident child aged 16–24; 5 = woman aged 45–59, no resident child; 6 = woman aged >59.

ICC = intra-class correlation coefficient.

Significance levels: * p <0.1, ** p <0.05, *** p <0.01.

Sources: ESS Round 5 (2010); EVS (2011); Multilinks Database (2011, data for 2009); Eurostat (2008); OECD (2012b, data for 2010).

Table 3.6   Multilevel models of the most important individual determinants, macro determinants and cross-level interactions for the distribution of housework in different life course stages, controlling for other individual determinants, respondents in a heterosexual couple aged 16–94

	Life course stage					
	1	2	3	4	5	6
Intercept	68.718***	73.474***	73.584***	64.313***	55.455***	72.640***
Time availability	-0.204***	-0.203***	-0.199***	-0.219***	-0.211***	-0.187***
* GC	0.076	0.004	-0.60	-0.086	0.006	-0.312***
Relative resources	-0.701**	-1.932***	-1.850***	-1.175***	-1.591***	-1.304***
* GC	0.427	0.544	-0.312	0.320	-2.299**	-0.184
Gender ideology	-2.739***	-3.657***	-2.171***	-0.690	-2.001***	-1.850**
* GC	0.914	-2.459**	-1.592	-2.459	0.259	1.335
GC	-13.933**	-2.140	1.923	2.085	-2.892	-3.224
AIC	18959.00+	35112.70+	26992.10+	20124.20–	27132.20+	55805.10+
Intercept	68.867***	73.374***	74.233***	64.472***	53.143***	71.128***
Time availability	-0.208***	-0.206***	-0.197***	-0.215***	-0.213***	-0.188***
* FTCC	0.042*	-0.020	-0.010	-0.020	-0.006	-0.075***
Relative resources	-0.713**	-1.706***	-1.684***	-1.210***	-1.505***	-1.222***
* FTCC	-0.015	0.976***	0.226	-0.106	0.044	0.153
Gender ideology	-2.916***	-2.416***	-2.442***	-0.772	-2.115***	-1.834***
* FTCC	0.146	-0.786**	-0.739**	-0.797*	-0.365	0.176
FTCC	-2.376	-0.761	1.484	1.909	-0.423	0.650
AIC	17552.40–	33508.40+	25704.60–	19028.00–	25730.50–	53841.00+

Intercept	68.585***	73.744***	74.233***	65.574***	52.384***	72.695***
Time availability	−0.201***	−0.202***	−0.197***	−0.211***	−0.212***	−0.196***
* APLM	0.021	−0.011	−0.010	−0.025	−0.043	−0.051**
Relative resources	−0.796**	−1.757***	−1.684***	−1.116***	−1.518***	−1.242***
* APLM	0.012	0.081	0.226	1.073***	−0.235	0.036
Gender ideology	−2.934***	−2.432***	−2.442***	−1.085*	−2.062***	−1.845***
* APLM	−0.348	−0.404	−0.739*	−0.972**	−0.518	−0.453
APLM	1.367	1.361	1.484	0.981	4.037**	3.745**
AIC	17615.00−	33548.60−	25623.50−	18866.20+	25810.60+	53178.10+
Intercept	68.567***	73.129***	74.038***	63.754***	53.532***	72.378***
Time availability	−0.216***	−0.204***	−0.196***	−0.205***	−0.213***	−0.209***
* NTS	0.043**	−0.013	0.014	−0.004	0.006	−0.056***
Relative resources	−0.564*	−1.942***	−1.805***	−1.334***	−1.611***	−1.404***
* NTS	−0.462	0.022	−0.036	0.351	−0.288	0.077
Gender ideology	−2.985***	−2.402***	−2.315***	−0.962*	−2.229***	−1.914***
* NTS	0.070	−0.652**	−0.525	0.094	−0.853**	−0.454
NTS	−0.592	1.116	1.111	−0.264	2.801*	2.812*
AIC	17152.60−	32925.50−	25187.90−	18383.90−	25292.30+	52203.70+

Notes:

The coefficients for the micro-variables are not shown.

The macro-data for some countries are missing, so these countries are not included in the analysis. Full-time childcare, Russia; Parental leave men, Czech Republic; Neutrality tax system, Switzerland and Russia.

Life course stages: 1 = woman aged <45, no resident child; 2 = woman aged <60, resident child aged <6; 3 = woman aged <60, resident child aged 6–15; 4 = woman aged <60, resident child aged 16–24; 5 = woman aged 45–59, no resident child; 6 = woman aged >59.

Contextual variables: GC = gender culture; $FTCC$ = % of 0–2-year-olds in childcare (>30 hours/week); $APLM$ = quotes parental leave for men; NTS = neutrality tax system.

AIC: + AIC is smaller than in former model (improvement); − AIC is bigger than in the former model (deterioration).

Significance levels: * p <0.1, ** p <0.05, *** p <0.01.

Sources: ESS Round 5 (2010); EVS (2011); Multilinks Database (2011, data for 2009); Eurostat (2010, data for 2008); OECD (2012b, data for 2010).

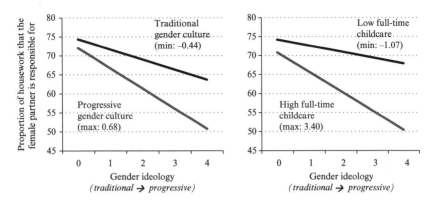

Notes:
Conditional on high versus low standardized values for gender culture (left) and high
versus low standardized values for usage of full-time childcare (right) among young couples
(aged <60) with young children (aged <6).
The values for the division of housework are calculated based on the highest (max) and
lowest value (min) for the macro-variables. The effects of the other micro-variables are held
constant on the value of zero.

Sources: ESS Round 5 (2010), EVS (2011), Eurostat (2010, data for 2008).

Figure 3.1   The effect of gender ideology on the division of housework

representation of these effects. The negative effect of gender ideology on
the proportion of housework that women perform is more articulated in
settings characterized by a progressive national gender culture (left panel)
and a higher full-time use of childcare (right panel). For couples with a
strong traditional gender ideology (0) the national gender context hardly
plays a role in the division of housework, while it does for couples with
progressive gender values (4).

Although Table 3.3 showed that gender values at the individual level play
a less important role for couples with children, the cross-level interaction
shows that the effect of progressive gender values is larger in countries
with a gender egalitarian culture and policy context. The national gender
context therefore seems of great importance to avoid that traditional
gender roles to come into place after the transition to parenthood. In an
environment that confirms gender egalitarian ideas it is easier to convert
these ideas effectively into behaviour.

For couples with children aged between 6 and 15 (life stage 3) and
couples with children aged between 16 and 24 (life stage 4), most models
including cross-level interactions do not improve the model fit.

For couples between 45 and 59 years old without children (life stage 5)
gender culture has a significant effect in its interaction with relative

resources, with the negative effect of relative ressources being reinforced in settings characterized by a progressive gender culture.

For older couples (life stage 6) the macro-level variables have a strong effect in their interaction with time availability. In countries with a progressive gender culture, with a high full-time use of childcare, where parental leave is available for fathers and tax systems are rather neutral, the negative effect of time availability is more articulated. A closer look into the distribution of the respondents shows that about 85 per cent of the women aged 60 and older in the sample do not work whereas couples who do work are rather exceptional. It is not useful to draw conclusions on these cases. The gendered division of domestic work is probably more difficult to grasp in these older households as they have less contact with childcare and parental leave and their habits on the division of housework are formed much earlier in the life course or may depend on physical capabilities of both partners.

DISCUSSION AND CONCLUSION

The aim of this study was to examine how individual and contextual characteristics affect the gendered division of domestic work through different stages over the life course. This approach is innovative as it looks into the influence of contextual variables on private gender equality from a life course perspective. The results showed that on average women are responsible for the bulk of the housework in all countries at all life stages. However, the gender disparity is lowest among young couples without children and greatest among couples with children, confirming results of longitudinal studies (Baxter et al. 2008; Lundberg and Rose 1999; Nomaguchi and Milkie 2003; Sanchez and Thomson 1997).

At all phases of the life course, gender equality is higher as working hours of women increase, as the proportion of household income for which a woman is responsible is larger and as the progressivity of the gender values is stronger. Across the phases of the life course the impact of time availability seems to be rather similar. The relative proportion of time spent on unpaid work is most strongly related to the proportion of time spent on paid work compared to the other variables.[1] The effect of relative resources on gender inequality is smallest among young couples without children and largest among couples with young children.

The effect of gender ideology is again strongest among young couples without children and smaller among couples with children living at home. Ideas about gender roles have a relatively large impact on the division of housework in the childless life stages. Gender egalitarian ideas are thus more easily translated into reality when couples are in life stages without children. The results suggest that when couples make the transition to parenthood, the effect of gender values is partly outweighed by the culturally dominant ideas related to parenting. This interpretation supports the argument of Martinengo et al. (2010) that cultural ideas about parenting are stronger than cultural ideas about gender equality.

In general national gender culture plays a significant role in the distribution of domestic work (except for households with children aged 6–15 and older couples). A more progressive national gender culture is significantly related to a larger private gender equality. The decision on the division of housework in the family is thus embedded in a cultural context and gender culture is found to have an influence on the behaviour of individuals, regardless of personal beliefs.

For couples with young children and progressive gender values, the gender culture also matters in a different way. These households are more capable of converting their egalitarian values into reality in a country with a progressive gender culture and where childcare is frequently used full-time. For couples with a progressive gender ideology the national gender context is thus of great importance at this key moment in the life course. Although individual gender values play a relatively minor role in couples with young children, the effects of progressive gender values at the individual level are greater in countries where the childcare policy and cultural context also support gender equality. A progressive gender context in terms of culture and formal childcare seems to be crucial for these couples to convert progressive ideas and values into reality. Possibly, this effect may be underestimated as people adjust their ideas to their behavior to resolve cognitive dissonance (Buhlmann et al. 2010).

A similar conclusion was made by Buhlmann et al. (2010) about value–practice configurations in gender equality in paid work. Context has an effect on the extent to which gender values can be translated into reality in paid and unpaid work. Couples seem to divide work quite equally at the beginning of their relationship but the extent to which they can keep up this equal division after childbirth depends on support of the context. Young families therefore benefit from a progressive value context and policies encouraging spouses to divide work more equally and averting the domination of emerging parenting practices and ideas over gender ideology.

While the effect of gender culture was clear and reasonably strong, the effects of the policy variables and their cross-level interactions were not. The uncertainty about the effects of policy can be the result of different elements. Policy on gender equality often has to be present for some time before it can affect the ideals and actual behaviour of individuals (Bernhardt et al. 2008), and there may be discrepancies between cultural ideas and policy measures that lead to unwanted or unexpected effects

(Pfau-Effinger 2005). Furthermore, the policy context is often complex and it is difficult to isolate the effect of a policy measure since in many countries the policy package is not homogeneous and is inconsistent in certain areas (Anxo et al. 2010).

This study was conducted using data from ESS Round 5 (2010) for 24 European countries. An advantage of the data is that characteristics of both the respondent and their partner were available for certain sections of the questionnaire. However, there are limitations associated with the use of survey data. First, the sample is limited (an average 1002 people per country), especially since the sample was further divided into six life stage categories. Furthermore, the survey was designed to determine only the total time spent on a set of household chores per week. It was therefore not possible to make a distinction between typically male and typically female tasks. However, this also has advantages since the overestimation of the time spent by duplication of tasks was reduced and the unequal distribution of domestic work is not overrated (which is likely to occur when one ignores typically male jobs). A third potential problem is that the data are cross-sectional. Given that different life stages therefore relate to different birth cohorts, it is not possible to distinguish between age, period and cohort effects. To determine how the division of labour varies throughout the life span, longitudinal data with a longitudinal measurement of the division of labour are required.

ACKNOWLEDGEMENTS

This research was supported by grants from the Flemish Research Council (G012011N) and the Research Council of the University of Antwerp (BOF-DOCPRO2013). An earlier version of this chapter was awarded the Pierre Francois Verhulst prize 2013 of the Vereniging voor Demografie (VVD) and the Société Démographique Francophone de Belgique (SDFB).

NOTE

1. But this relationship is not exogenous as the relationship between time spent on housework and time spent on paid work is simultaneous.

REFERENCES

Altintas, E. (2009), *State-of-the-art Report: Division of Domestic Labour*, EqualSoc, Oxford: University of Oxford.

Anxo, D., G. Bosch and J. Rubery (2010), 'Shaping the life course: a European perspective', in D. Anxo, G. Bosch and J. Rubery (eds), *The Welfare State and Life Transitions: A European Perspective*, Cheltenham, UK and Northampton, MA, USA: Edward Elgar Publishing, pp. 1–77.

Anxo, D., L. Mencarini, A. Pailhe, A. Solaz, M.L. Tanturri and L. Flood (2011), 'Gender differences in time use over the life course in France, Italy, Sweden, and the US', *Feminist Economics*, 17 (3), 159–195.

Batalova, J.A. and P.N. Cohen (2002), 'Premarital cohabitation and housework: couples in cross-national perspective', *Journal of Marriage and Family*, 64 (3), 743–755.

Baxter, J., B. Hewitt and M. Haynes (2008), 'Life course transitions and housework: marriage, parenthood, and time on housework', *Journal of Marriage and Family*, 70 (2), 259–272.

Becker, G.S. (1991), *A Treatise on the Family*, Cambridge, MA: Harvard University Press.

Bernhardt, E., T. Noack and T.H. Lyngstad (2008), 'Shared housework in Norway and Sweden: advancing the gender revolution', *Journal of European Social Policy*, 18 (3), 275–288.

Bianchi, S.M., M.A. Milkie, L.C. Sayer and J.P. Robinson (2000), 'Is anyone doing the housework? Trends in the gender division of household labor', *Social Forces*, 79 (1), 191–228.

Bourdieu, P. (1996), 'On the family as a realized category', *Theory, Culture and Society*, 13 (3), 19–26.

Brines, J. (1993), 'The exchange value of housework', *Rationality and Society*, 5 (3), 302–340.

Buhlmann, F., G. Elcheroth and M. Tettamanti (2010), 'The division of labour among European couples: the effects of life course and welfare policy on value practice configurations', *European Sociological Review*, 26 (1), 49–66.

Claffey, S.T. and K.R. Manning (2010), 'Equity but not equality: commentary on Lachance-Grzela and Bouchard', *Sex Roles*, 63 (11–12), 781–785.

Coltrane, S. (2000), 'Research on household labor: modeling and measuring the social embeddedness of routine family work', *Journal of Marriage and the Family*, 62 (4), 1208–1233.

Crompton, R. (1999), *Restructuring Gender Relations and Employment: The Decline of the Male Breadwinner*, Oxford: Oxford University Press.

Elchardus, M. and I. Glorieux (1994), 'The search for the invisible 8 hours. The gendered use of time in a society with a high labour force participation of women', *Time and Society*, 3 (1), 5–28.

European Social Survey (ESS) Round 5 (2010), 'Data file edition 3.0', Norway: Norwegian Social Science Data Services – Data Archive and distributor of ESS data.

Eurostat (2010), *Formal Child Care by Duration and Age Group (EU-SILC)*, Luxembourg: Eurostat.

EVS (2011), *European Values Study 2008: Integrated Dataset (EVS 2008)* (ZA4751 Data File Version 2.0.0 ed.), Cologne: GESIS Data Archive.

Fuwa, M. (2004), 'Macro-level gender inequality and the division of household labor in 22 countries', *American Sociological Review*, 69 (6), 751–767.

Fuwa, M. and P.N. Cohen (2007), 'Housework and social policy', *Social Science Research*, 36 (2), 512–530.

Geist, C. (2005), 'The welfare state and the home: regime differences in the domestic division of labour', *European Sociological Review*, 21 (1), 23–41.

Glorieux, I., S. Koelet, I. Mestdag and J. Minnen (2006), *De 24 uur van Vlaanderen. Het dagelijks leven van minuut tot minuut*, Leuven: LannooCampus.

Goldscheider, F.K. (2000), 'Men, children and the future of the family in the third millennium', *Futures*, 32 (6), 525–538.

Goldscheider, F.K., L.S. Olah and A. Puur (2010), 'Reconciling studies of men's gender attitudes and fertility: Response to Westoff and Higgins', *Demographic Research*, 22, 189–197.

Grunow, D., F. Schulz and H.P. Blossfeld (2012), 'What determines change in the division of housework over the course of marriage?', *International Sociology*, 27 (3), 289–307.

Hochschild, A.R. and A. Machung (1989), *The Second Shift: Working Parents and the Revolution at Home*, New York: Viking.

Hook, J.L. (2006), 'Care in context: men's unpaid work in 20 countries, 1965–2003', *American Sociological Review*, 71 (4), 639–660.

Hook, J.L. (2010), 'Gender inequality in the welfare state: sex segregation in housework, 1965–2003', *American Journal of Sociology*, 115 (5), 1480–1523.

Ishiikuntz, M. and S. Coltrane (1992), 'Predicting the sharing of household labor – are parenting and housework distinct?', *Sociological Perspectives*, 35 (4), 629–647.

Kamo, Y. (2000), '"He said, she said": assessing discrepancies in husbands' and wives' reports on the division of household labor', *Social Science Research*, 29 (4), 459–476.

Keck, W. and C. Saraceno (2011), *Database on Intergenerational Policy Indicators: Methodological Report*, Berlin: Social Science Research Center Berlin.

Knudsen, K. and K. Waerness (2008), 'National context and spouses housework in 34 countries', *European Sociological Review*, 24 (1), 97–113.

Lachance-Grzela, M. and G. Bouchard (2010), 'Why do women do the lion's share of housework? A decade of research', *Sex Roles*, 63 (11–12), 767–780.

Lappegård, T., R. Kjeldstad and T. Skarðhamar (2012), *The Division of Housework: Does Regional Context Matter?*, Oslo: Statistics Norway.

Lee, Y.S. and L.J. Waite (2005), 'Husbands' and wives' time spent on housework: a comparison of measures', *Journal of Marriage and Family*, 67 (2), 328–336.

Lundberg, S. and E. Rose (1999), 'The determinants of specialization within marriage', Working Paper UWEC 2005–07, Seattle: University of Washington.

Martinengo, G., J.L. Jacob and E.J. Hill (2010), 'Gender and the work–family interface: exploring differences across the family life course', *Journal of Family Issues*, 31 (10), 1363–1390.

McDonald, P. (2000a), 'Gender equity in theories of fertility transition', *Population and Development Review*, 26 (3), 427–439.

McDonald, P. (2000b), 'Gender equity, social institutions and the future of fertility', *Journal of Population Research*, 17 (1), 1–16.

McDonald, P. (2006), 'Low Fertility and the state: the efficacy of policy', *Population and Development Review*, 32 (3), 485–510.

Multilinks Database (2011), *Leave Dedicated to Fathers*, Berlin: Social Science Research Center Berlin.

Nomaguchi, K.M. and M.A. Milkie (2003), 'Costs and rewards of children: the effects of becoming a parent on adults' lives', *Journal of Marriage and Family*, 65 (2), 356–374.

OECD (2012a), 'Neutrality of tax/benefit systems', accessed 17 September 2015 at www.oecd.org/els/soc/PF1_4_Neutrality_of_tax_benefit_systems.pdf.

OECD (2012b), 'OECD Family Database', accessed 17 September 2015 at www.oecd.org/social/family/database.

Pascall, G. and J. Lewis (2004), 'Emerging gender regimes and policies for gender equality in a wider Europe', *Journal of Social Policy*, 33, 373–394.

Pfau-Effinger, B. (2005), 'Culture and welfare state policies: reflections on a complex interrelation', *Journal of Social Policy*, 34, 3–20.

Pfau-Effinger, B. (2010), 'Cultural and institutional contexts', in J. Treas (ed.), *Dividing the Domestic: Men, Women, and Household Work in Cross-National Perspective*, Stanford, CA: Stanford University Press, pp. 125–146.

Sanchez, L. and E. Thomson (1997), 'Becoming mothers and fathers – parenthood, gender, and the division of labor', *Gender and Society*, 11 (6), 747–772.

Saraceno, C. and W. Keck (2011), 'Towards an integrated approach for the analysis of gender equity in policies supporting paid work and care responsibilities', *Demographic Research*, 25, 371–405.

van der Lippe, T., J. de Ruijter, E. de Ruijter and W. Raub (2011), 'Persistent inequalities in time use between men and women: a detailed look at the influence of economic circumstances, policies, and culture', *European Sociological Review*, 27 (2), 164–179.

West, C. and D.H. Zimmerman (1987), 'Doing gender', *Gender and Society*, 1 (2), 125–151.

4. Intersectionality in young adults' households: a quantitative perspective

Dimitri Mortelmans, Petra Meier and Christine Defever*

INTRODUCTION

The transition from adolescence to adulthood is 'demographically dense' (Rindfuss 1991) in that it tends to involve a number of significant demographic transitions. These comprise steps in life such as leaving (the parental) home, finishing school, starting work and becoming financially autonomous, getting married or otherwise settled, and eventually becoming a parent. These events may accumulate and partially overlap (Shanahan 2000) and studies have shown that entry into adulthood has become late, protracted and complex over time (Billari and Liefbroer 2010). Nowadays, many events occur rather late in young adulthood as compared to earlier times: youngsters live longer with their parents, study longer, and marriage and parenthood are postponed. Moreover, the time-span between the first and the last transition – typically leaving home and entry into marriage and/or parenthood – is expanding. Furthermore, the transition to young adulthood is complex, in that the sequencing of the events is highly variable and some of these events can even be repetitive. For example, youngsters increasingly leave the parental home but return after a broken relationship or during a period of unemployment, to leave the home again later. Significant economic and social changes in the latter half of the twentieth century – such as the expansion of secondary and higher education, a decline in the availability of full-time jobs, an increase in the proportion of individuals concurrently pursuing higher education and work, an increase in the labour force participation of women and an increase in cohabitation (Settersten 2008) – shaped these contemporary patterns of the transition to adulthood in Western Europe.

In the period before the transition to young adulthood, denoted with the term 'emerging adulthood' (Arnett 2000), these emerging adults often explore a variety of possible life directions in love, work and worldviews. This mostly turbulent life course period not only shows a wide variety but we hypothesize it to be quite vulnerable to accumulation processes of inequality as well. Emerging adults not only vary in the degree of exploration they choose to pursue, but also, more importantly, this exploration is not equally available to all young people, nor does it have the same implications. Youth arrive at their late teens with vastly differing capacities and resources to navigate the various transitions (Furstenberg 2008), resulting in youth from less advantaged homes being distinctly less well equipped to accomplish these markers of adulthood than their more privileged peers. Experiences in early adulthood, like those in other periods, differ greatly by gender, race, ethnicity and social class. Moreover, the variability within these groups is also striking. It is here that the concept of intersectionality comes in.

The concept of intersectionality reflects the idea that individuals belong to multiple demographic categories such as gender, ethnicity, social class, disability and other forms of socially distinguishing group membership or identity. While intersectionality easily found its way into theoretical accounts (Phoenix and Pattynama 2006), it is much more difficult to empirically assess it (Hancock 2007; McCall 2005; Warner 2008; Weldon 2008), let alone to translate it into policies meant to tackle issues of inequality (Hankivsky and Cormier 2011; Davis 2008; Nash 2008). In this chapter we aim to investigate intersectionality in a quantitative way, so as to reveal possible accumulations of inequalities related to the transition. We thereby use the case of the transition phase from emergent to young adulthood. The next section discusses the concept of intersectionality and the difficulties in assessing it empirically, especially when applying a quantitative approach. The following section of the chapter presents the method and data used. We look at intersectionality in an inter-categorical manner and employ data from the Generations and Gender Programme (GGP) panel survey from six Western European countries (Germany, France, Belgium, the Netherlands, Italy and Norway) that were collected from 2002 until 2010. In the section thereafter we present the results of our analysis for these six European countries. The final section of this chapter comprises the conclusion.

INTERSECTIONALITY AND THE CHALLENGES WHEN ASSESSING IT QUANTITATIVELY

The concept of intersectionality reflects the idea that individuals belong to multiple demographic categories such as gender, ethnicity, social class, disability and other forms of socially distinguishing group membership or identity. It especially stands for the idea that these social categories are intersecting and create instances of opportunity and constraints, where a person can, depending on their particular identity configuration in a particular social context, experience advantage, disadvantage or both at the same time (Collins 1990). Therefore, intersectionality is 'an aspect of social organization' that rejects 'the idea that the effects of interacting social structures can be adequately understood as a function of the autonomous effects of . . . social categories' (Weldon 2008, p. 97). While all these social categories might have effects on themselves, they also have some intersectional effects, whereby these can reinforce or counterbalance discrimination and inequality. As a consequence, social groups are not homogeneous.

The field of intersectionality is burgeoning and the term has even became a buzzword, according to Davis (2008); not only because it has emerged in a number of discursive spaces such as women's studies, sociology, politics, psychology, health science, geography and higher education, but also because the theoretical underpinnings are heavily debated in current writings and in equality policy circles.

In the very beginning, the intersectionality paradigm was used to raise more awareness for (until then) invisible groups. Crenshaw (1991) coined the term to claim that black women are often forgotten in justice and other social systems, as their lived experiences are not comparable to white women, nor can they be reduced to a simple union of the experiences of women and of blacks. By looking at the intersection of, for example, black women, we can give voice to a group that otherwise would have remained unheard. In this respect, Purdie-Vaughns and Eibach (2008) use the term 'intersectional invisibility' to describe the phenomenon where individuals with intersecting subordinate identities are made invisible. Indeed, because we tend to define the standard person as male (androcentrism), white (ethnocentrism) and heterosexual (heterocentrism) in most Western societies, this tendency may cause people with multiple subordinate-group identities to become invisible, as they will be defined as non-prototypical members of their respective identity groups. Intersectionality points to the fact that not only women might face a different situation than men, but also heterosexual women might face a different situation from lesbian women. And the sexual orientation might have different consequences in two differing ethnic groups.

The conceptualization of intersectionality as a way to better represent those who have been left out or ignored, thereby offering a 'content specialization' (Choo and Ferree 2010), is also called the intracategorical approach (McCall 2005). The intracategorical approach starts from the idea that master categories are not enough to understand social reality and tend to focus on particular social groups at neglected points of intersections – for example, black lesbian women – in order to reveal the complexity of lived experiences within such groups. This approach heavily relies on narrative essays whereby the individual's experience is taken as the subject and is extrapolated to the broader social location embodied by the individual.

However, there is tension between the voice approach to intersectionality and the claim that no one is ever 'just' privileged or oppressed (Jordan-Zachary 2007). In studying the conflicting dimensions of inequality, we also need to study the normative cases where power and privilege cluster. As Yuval-Davis points out, researchers tend to study 'others' when taking an intersectional approach, thereby portraying low-status groups as the 'effect to be explained' (cited in Warner 2008). When intersectionality is defined as focusing on those who are marginalized, dominant social groups remain unacknowledged. Therefore, intersectionality quickly evolved to a more inter-categorical approach. This approach not only focuses on the complexity within one specific social group, but also expands its scope across analytical categories by using a multigroup and comparative method. Studies done in this multigroup vein analyse the intersection of the full set of dimensions of multiple categories – for example, black, white, women, men, black women, black men, white women and white men – and thus examine both advantage and disadvantage explicitly and simultaneously (McCall 2005). This approach contrasts with the anticategorical approach (McCall 2005) that rejects the use of fixed categories because a wide range of different experiences, identities and social locations fail to fit neatly into any single 'master' category. This is a more constructionist version of intersectionality (Choo and Ferree 2010) which appeals to those who doubt the stability of social categories at the micro level.

Intersectionality is difficult to assess empirically (Hancock 2007; McCall 2005; Warner 2008; Weldon 2008) or to translate into public policies (Davis 2008; Hankivsky and Cormier 2011; Nash 2008). A dilemma in both research and policy making is that considering all components of a social identity can 'generate an infinite regress that dissolves groups into individuals' (Young 2004, p. 721). In other words, people vary by so many different group memberships that once researchers split groups up, placing people into all the categories in which they may belong, groups are reduced to an assortment of unique individuals (Warner 2008). This problem is reflected in the abundant number of qualitative studies, such as case studies, in the field of intersectionality. In these specific research instances it may be feasible and worthwhile to acknowledge all identities that the individual and/or researcher views as relevant to the research question. But when a researcher's charge is to make generalizations or take on a larger-scale project, they will need to make choices as to which social categories to include. The same dilemma holds true for policy making: incorporating the notion of intersectionality in policies can lead to good governance in that it 'gives voice' to a group and its specific and unique advantages or disadvantages that would otherwise have remained invisible. At the same time, incorporating many social categories in policies may result in governance that targets only a very small group.

In addition, one of the major concerns is that the inter-categorical space can become very complicated with the addition of any one analytical category to the analysis, because it requires an investigation of the multiple groups that constitute the category (McCall 2005). Researchers, therefore, have highlighted the difficulties in applying intersectionality to empirical research, especially in areas that conventionally have relied on quantitative research strategies. Indeed, one of the criticisms of intersectionality theory is that it provides no usable methods for research, particularly quantitative research as conventionally conducted in social and behavioural sciences.

In this chapter we want to take such a quantitative approach to empirically studying intersectionality by looking at it in an inter-categorical manner. We do so with the aim to investigate how and when policies have to incorporate the notion of intersectionality in order to block the accumulation of inequalities related to the transition.

METHOD

Survey

We use the Generations and Gender Programme (GGP) survey to investigate intersectionality in the transition to young adulthood. The GGP is a panel survey of nationally representative samples of the 18–79-year-old population throughout 19 European countries, and its questions probe how public policy and programme interventions affect the relationships between parents and children (generations) and between partners (gender). The survey covers questions on fertility, partnership, the transition to adulthood, economic activity, care duties and attitudes. More specifically, we use the data from the following six Western European countries: Germany, France, Belgium, the Netherlands, Italy and Norway. These data were collected from 2002 until 2010 and are suitable for the analysis we aim to conduct. Because we are interested in the transition from emergent adulthood to young adulthood, we select all respondents aged 18–35 at the time of the interview, resulting in a sample of 15 837 respondents.

Gender, Migrant Background and Social Class

We will investigate intersectionality by taking gender, migrant background and educational attainment of the father into account. The migrant background of the respondent was defined according to their country of birth and that of their parents. Respondents born abroad or born in the country of interview but with at least one parent born abroad were defined as migrants and assigned to one of two migrant groups: coming from EU-25 countries (plus Norway) or coming from non-European Union (EU) countries (in Italy, this difference could not be made due to data limitations). Social class was not asked about directly in the GGP, but we used the educational attainment of the father as proxy. Three groups were made: low social class (ISCED 0 and ISCED 1), middle social class (ISCED 2, ISCED 3 and ISCED 4) and high social class (ISCED 5 and ISCED 6).

As shown in Table 4.1, our sample of 18–35-year-olds contains considerably more women in France and the Netherlands. One-quarter of the respondents has some migrant background, except for Italy and (to a lesser degree) Norway. According to class, most respondents have a father with an International Standard Classification of Education (ISCED) education level of 3 or 4. France has a somewhat different coding scheme, which results in a higher proportion of respondents coming from a lower-educated father.

Indicators of the Transition to Young Adulthood

We use two additional indicators to control whether participants had already experienced the transition of moving outside the parental home. The household status is the dependent variable (see the 'Analytical Strategy' section, below) and is defined as the situation in which the respondent lives. Four categories are discerned: (1) living at home with parent(s); (2) living alone; (3) living with a partner with children; or (4) being a single parent.

As shown in Table 4.2, the German and French samples show the most resemblance; the Italian and, to a lower extent, the Belgian sample differ most from the others. As we know from the demographic literature, Italian youngsters, due to the difficult labour market and housing situation amongst other factors, to a larger extent still live with their parents and postpone moving in with a partner and founding a family. While Belgian 18–35-year-olds tend to live alone to a lesser extent than their European peers from the other countries examined, they do not tend to postpone moving in with a partner and founding a family.

In addition to the characteristics of intersectionality (gender, migrant

Table 4.1 Distribution of gender, migrant status and social class categories, in absolute numbers and percentages, for 18–35-year-olds

	GER		FRA		BEL		NED		ITA		NOR	
	N	%	N	%	N	%	N	%	N	%	N	%
Gender												
Men	1056	43.6	1104	40.7	858	45.6	802	39.0	1320	48.3	2005	49.9
Women	1369	56.5	1611	59.3	1025	54.4	1254	61.0	1416	51.8	2017	50.2
Migrant status												
EU-25 + NOR	255	10.6	236	8.8	245	13.0	97	4.8	0	0.0	93	13.0
Non-EU	356	14.8	363	13.5	258	13.7	181	9.0	79	3.0	262	13.7
Non-migrants	1799	74.7	2084	77.7	1378	73.3	1745	86.3	2579	97.0	3666	73.3
Social class												
Low	70	45.7	962	45.7	278	17.8	309	17.8	1110	41.1	610	18.1
Middle	1524	35.7	752	35.7	774	49.7	951	54.6	1426	52.8	1731	51.3
High	551	18.5	390	18.5	506	32.5	481	27.6	164	6.1	1033	30.6

Source: GGP, Wave 1, own calculations.

Table 4.2   Distribution of household type, in absolute numbers and percentages, for 18–35-year-olds

	GER		FRA		BEL		NED		ITA		NOR	
	N	%	N	%	N	%	N	%	N	%	N	%
Household type												
(1) Living with parents	335	13.8	484	17.8	695	36.9	251	12.2	1648	60.2	694	17.3
(2) Living alone	750	30.9	742	27.3	171	9.1	565	27.5	130	4.8	1193	29.7
(3) Partner with children	1189	49.0	1347	49.6	959	50.9	1174	57.1	926	33.9	1982	49.3
(4) Lone parent	151	6.2	142	5.2	58	3.1	66	3.2	32	1.2	153	3.8

Source: GGP, Wave 1, own calculations.

status and class) we add two control variables: activity status and educational attainment:

- Activity status: respondents were classified as being a student, being employed (employed, self-employed, a family member helping in a family business or military service), being unemployed, or being economically inactive (maternity leave, parental or childcare leave, ill or disabled for a long time, or housekeeping).
- Educational attainment: respondents who were no longer studying were assigned to three groups: having a low educational attainment (ISCED level 0 or 1, corresponding to pre-primary or primary level), a middle educational attainment (ISCED level 2, 3 or 4, corresponding to lower or upper secondary level, or post-secondary non-tertiary level such as preparatory courses) and high educational attainment (ISCED level 5 or 6, corresponding to first or second stage of tertiary education).

Analytical Strategy

Since we are interested in intersectionality, tabular methods of analysis are often used when non-qualitative techniques are implemented (Meier et al. forthcoming). In this chapter, we want to push the analysis one step further by applying a classification and regression tree (CART) to our data. The technique was developed by Breiman and colleagues (Breiman 2001; Breiman et al. 1984) and Zhang and Singer (2013). It was introduced in life course sociology (Singer et al. 1998) and demography (Hobcraft and Sigle-Rushton 2008; Sigle-Rushton 2014) as an alternative way to gain insight into social processes without using strong (linear or non-linear) assumptions on regression models. Classification trees (as used in this chapter) are used with categorical dependent variables, allowing the researcher to gain insight into the most significant variables explaining this outcome. The technique uses a stepwise algorithm that splits the data into more and more homogenous groups. The classic way to do so (implemented in the R-package rpart) is by splitting the data and then pruning the tree from the bottom until an optimal model is achieved (Therneau and Atkinson 1997; Zhang and Singer 2013). An alternative method of CART is a technique called conditional inference trees. This method overcomes issues of overfitting traditional estimating techniques by using permutation tests theory (Hothorn et al. 2006). This method allows significance testing on each successive step, reaching a more optimized model than the traditional CART algorithms. In this chapter, we used the R-package PARTY to estimate the classification trees (Hothorn et al. 2015) on the nominal outcome 'household type'.

RESULTS

In what follows, we will take an intersectional perspective, by concentrating on the trajectories into household type using three social categories: gender, migrant status and social class. The classification tree for each country reveals groups of respondents that may experience a particular path in leaving the parental home, which would have been 'invisible' when only looking at the main social categories separately. In a next stage, we will take a look at the size and proportion of the groups. Reflecting on group size is useful in order to decide whether full intersectionality (according to these three social categories) is efficient for policy making, or whether targeting larger, less homogeneous groups would be a more successful strategy.

In Table 4.3, we present an overview of explanatory variables involved in each country-specific model. For two countries (Belgium and the Netherlands) all variables played a significant role somewhere in the classification. For Germany and Italy, social class seems not to matter in the model, while for Norway and France there is no effect for migrants.

When analysing the classification trees, it is clear that the pathways in all countries are different, despite using the same independent variables. This is a first indication of how intersectionality through CART analysis reveals different interactions that would have remained hidden with regular regressions. One stable characteristic, however, is that all trees start with a split in activity status. When analysing the household status of youngsters aged 18–35, the main determining factor is being a student or not. In Italy and Norway, unemployed youngsters appear to be more similar to students than in other countries, since selecting out the students takes two splits for these countries. When looking at the trajectories of students, the diversity in living arrangements is clearly smaller than for those who are in the labour market. Gender differentiates students in Germany, Italy and Norway, while in Belgium it is migration status, and in the Netherlands it is social class.

Determining the household position of non-students across all six countries is not only more complex in terms of intervening factors, but it is also much more diverse across countries. We will not give an overview of all trajectories, but summarize the most important characteristics. First, being employed plays a major role in arriving at a final state in which children are present in the household. In all countries, there is a strong connection between having children and being employed as an 18–35-year-old. Second, education plays a role in determining the final stages of household type. In all countries, higher educational levels show different living arrangements than lower levels of education. These differences cannot be traced back

Table 4.3 Usage of explanatory variables in CART, models according to country, for 18–35-year-olds

	GER	FRA	BEL	NED	ITA	NOR
Gender	X	X	X	X	X	X
Migrant status	X		X	X	X	
Social class		X	X	X		X
Activity status	X	X	X	X	X	X
Educational attainment	X	X	X	X	X	X

Source: GGP, Wave 1, own calculations.

to a prolonged study career, since students in these age categories have already been split at a higher level in the trees. Next to the activity status and educational status, it is migration status that determines the final living state in the Netherlands and Italy, while social background (class) is more important in Belgium, the Netherlands, France and Norway. Figure 4.1 gives the classification tree for each of the countries.

Although the intersectional perspective seems to reveal interesting findings, it is necessary to take the size of the different groups into account. By combining different social categories so as to generate a social group comprising an intersection of social identities, one is bound to end up with smaller groups of individuals being concerned. This is bound to the complexity of the optimal model. For example, in France the optimal model consists of four groups, while the Netherlands shows ten different groups in the final model. The composition of the groups is unequal and the model produces some small groups, especially those representing more complex trajectories. For example, unemployed women (Norway) or lower-educated women at home are small homogeneous groups. Moreover, migrant men at work are a particular household type in Italy.

CONCLUSION

In this chapter, we wanted to investigate quantitatively how intersectionality is at play in the accumulation of inequalities related to the household position in young adulthood in a number of European countries. We focused on three social categories: gender, social class and migrant status. We used a quantitative approach but kept the analysis and interpretation intuitive by only using classification trees.

By taking an intersectional perspective, we found that gender and social class are important factors to take into account. What a general linear regression could not have revealed is that the circumstances and problems for women from a low social class and a non-EU background are different from country to country. Moreover, men from non-EU countries of middle social class, and women at home of low social class from EU countries, turn up as groups with a specific household position. Intersectionality thus gives visibility to groups that would otherwise have remained invisible.

This is important from an empirical and a social point of view, and this chapter contributes to the ongoing research on intersectionality in two ways. First, we took a new step by studying intersectionality quantitatively. As already stated at the beginning of the chapter, intersectionality has a long history of qualitative research. Although we agree that qualitative studies, such as case studies and interviews, bring added value when

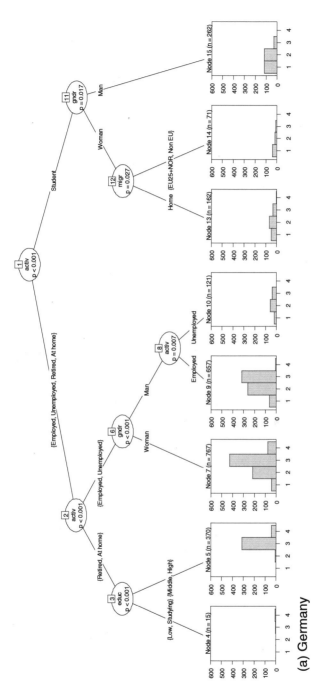

Figure 4.1   Classification tree for Germany, Belgium, the Netherlands, France, Italy and Norway

(a) Germany

93

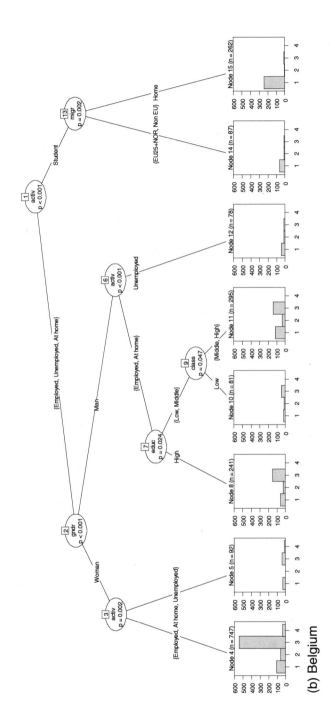

(b) Belgium

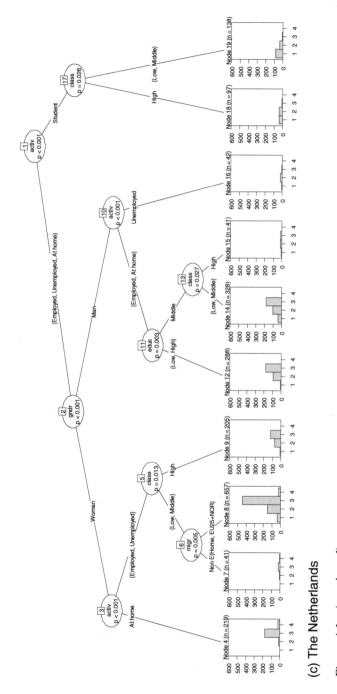

(c) The Netherlands

Figure 4.1 (continued)

95

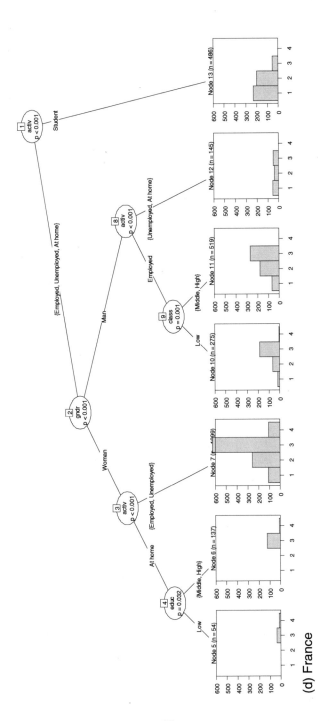

(d) France

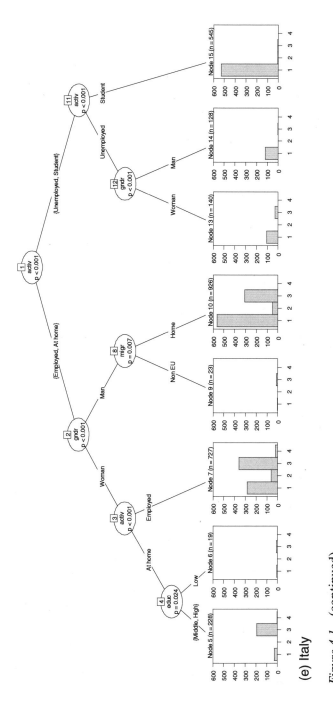

(e) Italy

Figure 4.1 (continued)

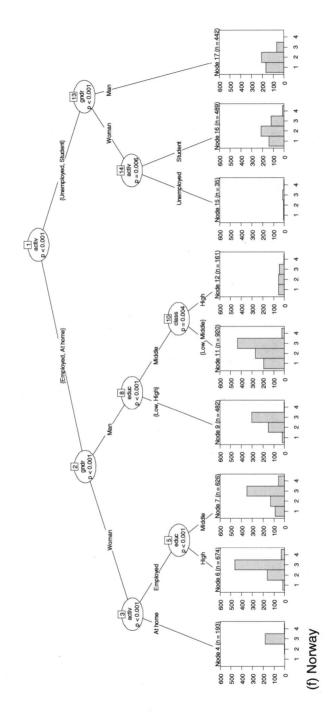

(f) Norway

Figure 4.1 (continued)

looking for more in-depth interpretation and meaning given the reality of facing multiple subordination, we think that quantitative data can overcome some challenges faced in qualitative research. Large datasets give a better overview of the problems faced by a broad representative group. Personal stories are not very informative for policy makers, as it may very well be that the reality of these respondents is only lived by a very small, specific group. We refer to this problem as 'noise': by applying intersectionality in its most extreme form and reducing groups to unique individuals (N = 1), conclusions may not be representative. This is illustrated by our classification trees showing interactions between migration status and gender in several countries. No policy maker should take action based on this finding only. However, if small groups accumulate different problems, action may need to be taken, no matter how small the group is. We therefore think that the multidimensionality of the problem is an important factor to consider when applying intersectionality in policy making. Good governance must take into account not only the accumulation of different disadvantages based on different group memberships, but also the accumulation of different problems faced by these groups. This would make the application of the notion of intersectionality in policy making very effective.

Second, we think that the use of CART analysis is a particularly useful way of quantitatively investigating issues of intersectionality. The technique may open up new perspectives for studying the notion of intersectionality in the accumulation of inequalities. While we used it to reveal such accumulations of inequality in the household position of young adults, it may also be used for studying other contexts in which intersectionality may make a social and political difference.

NOTE

*   The ideas presented in this chapter are based on a project funded within the third programme on Policy Research Centres – Domain Equality Policies, financed by the Flemish Government. The data analysis has been conducted for the sole purpose of this chapter.

REFERENCES

Arnett, J.J. (2000), 'Emerging adulthood: a theory of development from the late teens through the twenties', *American Psychologist*, 55 (5), 469. doi:10.1037/0003-066x.55.5.469.

Billari, F.C. and A.C. Liefbroer (2010), 'Towards a new pattern of transition to adulthood?', *Advances in Life Course Research*. doi:j.alcr.2010.10.003.

Breiman, L. (2001), 'Statistical modeling: the two cultures', *Statistical Science*, 16 (3), 199–231, doi:10.1214/ss/1009213726.

Breiman, L., J. Friedman, R. Olshen and C. Stone (1984), *Classification and Regression Trees*, Belmont, CA: Wadsworth Publishing Company.

Choo, H.Y. and M.M. Ferree (2010), 'Practicing intersectionality in sociological research: a critical analysis of inclusions, interactions, and institutions in the study of inequalities', *Sociological Theory*, 28 (2), 129–149. doi:10.1111/j.1467-9558.2010.01370.x.

Collins, P.H. (1990), *Black Feminist Thought: Knowledge, Consciousness, and the Politics of Empowerment*, New York: Routledge.

Crenshaw, K. (1991), 'Mapping the margins: intersectionality, identity politics, and violence against women of color', *Stanford Law Review*, 43 (6), 1241. doi:10.2307/1229039.

Davis, K. (2008), 'Intersectionality as buzzword: a sociology of science perspective on what makes a feminist theory successful', *Feminist Theory*, 9 (1), 67–85. doi:10.1177/1464700108086364.

Furstenberg, F.F. (2008), 'The intersections of social class and the transition to adulthood', *New Directions for Child in Adolescent Development*, 119 (119), 1–10. doi:10.1002/cd.205.

Hancock, A.-M. (2007), 'When multiplication doesn't equal quick addition', *Perspectives on Politics*, 5 (1), 63–79. doi:10.1017/s1537592707070065.

Hankivsky, O. and R. Cormier (2011), 'Intersectionality and public policy: some lessons from existing models', *Political Research Quarterly*, 64 (1), 217–229. doi:10.1177/1065912910376385.

Hobcraft, J. and W. Sigle-Rushton (2008), 'Identifying patterns of resilience using classification trees', *Social Policy and Society*, 8 (1), 87. doi:10.1017/s1474746408004612.

Hothorn, T., K. Hornik and A. Zeileis (2006), 'Unbiased recursive partitioning: a conditional inference framework', *Journal of Computational and Graphical Statistics*, 15 (3), 651–674. doi:10.1198/106186006x133933.

Hothorn, T., K. Hornik and A. Zeileis (2015), 'ctree Conditional Inference Trees', https://cran.r-project.org/web/packages/partykit/vignettes/ctree.pdf.

Jordan-Zachary, J.S. (2007), 'Let men be men: a gendered analysis of black ideological response to familial policies', *National Political Science Review*, 11, 177–192.

McCall, L. (2005), 'The complexity of intersectionality', *Signs: Journal of Women in Culture and Society*, 30 (3), 1771–1800. doi:10.1086/426800.

Meier, P., D. Mortelmans and C. Defever (forthcoming), 'Intersectional policies? A reflection using the example of intersecting inequalities in transition to early adulthood', *DiGest*, in review.

Nash, J.C. (2008), 'Re-thinking intersectionality', *Feminist Review*, 89, 1–15. doi:10.1057/fr.2008.4.

Phoenix, A. and P. Pattynama (2006), 'Intersectionality', *European Journal of Women's Studies*, 13 (3), 187–192. doi:10.1177/1350506806065751.

Purdie-Vaughns, V. and R.P. Eibach (2008), 'Intersectional invisibility: the distinctive advantages and disadvantages of multiple subordinate-group identities', *Sex Roles*, 59 (5–6), 377–391. doi:10.1007/s11199-008-9424-4.

Rindfuss, R.R. (1991), 'The young adult in years: diversity, structural change, and fertility', *Demography*, 28 (4), 493–512. doi:10.2307/2061419.

Settersten, R.A. (2008), 'Social policy and the transition to adulthood: toward stronger institutions and individual capacities', in R.A. Settersten and F.F. Furstenberg (eds), *On the Frontier of Adulthood: Theory, Research and Public Policy*, Chicago, IL: University of Chicago Press, pp. 534–560.

Shanahan, M.J. (2000), 'Pathways to adulthood in changing societies: variability and mechanisms in life course perspective', *Annual Review of Sociology*, 26, 667–692. doi:10.1146/annurev.soc.26.1.667.

Sigle-Rushton, W. (2014), 'Essentially quantified? Towards a more feminist modeling strategy', in M. Evans, C. Hemmings, M. Henry, H. Johnstone, S. Madhok, A. Plomien et al. (eds), *The SAGE Handbook of Feminist Theory*, London: Sage Publishing, pp. 431–445.

Singer, B., C.D. Ryff, D. Carr and W.J. Magee (1998), 'Linking life histories and mental health: a person-centered strategy', *Sociological Methodology*, 28 (1), 1–51. doi:10.1111/0081-1750.00041.

Therneau, T.M. and E.J. Atkinson (1997), 'An introduction to recursive partitioning using the RPART routines', 61, Technical Report, Mayo Foundation.

Warner, L.R. (2008), 'A best practices guide to intersectional approaches in psychological research', *Sex Roles*, 59 (5–6), 454–463. doi:10.1007/s11199-008-9504-5.

Weldon, L. (2008), 'Intersectionality', in A.G. Mazur and G. Goertz (eds), *Politics, Gender, and Concepts. Theory and Methodology*, New York: Cambridge University Press, pp. 193–218.

Young, I.M. (2004), 'Gender as seriality: thinking about women as a social collective', *Signs: Journal of Women in Culture and Society*, 19 (3), 713. doi:10.1086/494918.

Zhang, H. and B. Singer (2013), *Recursive Partitioning in the Health Sciences*, New York: Springer Science & Business Media.

5. From the kitchen table to the other: results of ethnographic research on undocumented mothers' parenting practices creating feelings at home

Tine Brouckaert*

INTRODUCTION

The case study of ten single undocumented mothers (that is, immigrants who entered Europe without registration by authorities or who overstayed their visas), who do not comply with normative models of parenting within the Belgian nation-state, provides a useful epistemic starting point from which to explore participation and membership in a community beyond its classically conceived features of formal rights and obligations. In general, for groups living at the limits of society, inequality and exclusion have increased over the past decade. For many people, strategies based on an economic model have failed to bring about potentials for an inclusive citizenship. This has led to the search for new approaches that look at citizenship contributions beyond the public realm. Feminists (Dietz 1985; Lister 2003), amongst others, have pointed out a gendered exclusion from citizenship linked to the public–private divide that identifies men's roles as being in the public domain of politics and paid employment, and women's roles in caring and child-rearing in the home. In its various understandings, maternalism seeks recognition for the citizenship potential of mothering. Nevertheless, from a feminist perspective it remains controversial for its essentializing tendencies and universalist pretensions. This chapter argues that the instilling of 'feelings of home' is an important element of citizenship. While 'feelings of home' have been considered significant to citizenship (Duyvendak 2009; Longman et al. 2013), the connection of these feelings in relation to maternal work in the private sphere remains unexplored when it comes to people excluded from citizenship. This chapter reveals that the remembrance of home is instilled through ritualized maternal practices. These everyday practices are often assessed as trivial due to their banality and routine; however, in this chapter, these practices appear to be essential in the process of education towards citizenship insofar as they provide the primary form of attachment, the basis of identity. Moreover, they strongly determine the sentiments of connection and solidarity with others in society. The following section describes the methodology of this study and the methodological process. Through the main body of this text, responses will be formulated to the question: 'What does feeling at home mean in a situation of irregularity?' Concrete cases of fieldwork include an initial study of material conditions at home, followed by an analysis based on interviews and participatory observations. The chapter shows how home is a feeling that may refer to daily mothering practices of life. It then shows how these repetitive maternal practices are central to the collective (cultural) identity and may have the potential to resist discrimination that minorities experience in the public domain. Finally, it shows the creative and innovative potential of maternal practices, before drawing conclusions.

METHODOLOGY

This study is based on a small-scale, in-depth ethnographic study of the lives of ten undocumented single migrant mothers who were interviewed and accompanied closely in their daily activities between October 2008 and January 2013. The women who feature in this study come from various backgrounds. At the time of the study they resided in Belgium (in the cities of Ghent and Antwerp in the region of Flanders) and France (the cities of Saint-Etienne and Lyon). These women, who were willing to participate in the study, were located through various organizations (non-governmental organizations working with refugees) and social demonstrations that claimed a collective regularization.[1] Their reason for migrating to the West was to find a better future for themselves and/or their child(ren), who were born either in the country of origin or on European territory. The single mothers' ages ranged from 24 to 60 years old. They came from different racial, ethnic, class and religious backgrounds, and the number of their children ranged from one to five, a number which shifted during the fieldwork period due to additional births. At the start of the study, these women were all '*sans papiers*' (Raissiguier 2010), living in a status of so-called illegality (Balibar and Wallerstein 1991) in Belgium and France. As refugees, the women had arrived in Belgium or France alone or with their children but without any immediate family, social network or community to rely upon. Hence, they share their womanhood, their single motherhood and their undocumented migrant status as being their 'master status'

(Hughes 1994). Yet from an intersectional perspective,[2] all of them can be positioned differently on the dominant axes of social economic and educational capital. Rather than claiming to be representative of all undocumented migrant mothers, this qualitative study claims to offer insight into the everyday lives of migrant mothers without formal citizenship status in all their facets and diversity. Even if similarities between the women appear, their life stories must be seen as reflecting unique individual experiences. In any case, these women and their children are seen by the dominant society as legal and cultural outsiders, being cast into a marginalized position due to being economically deprived and the fact that racism is still structurally embedded in European, Belgian and French everyday life. Methodologically, the study draws on feminist standpoint epistemology (Harding 2004; Collins 2000), intersectional theory (Lykke 2010) and critical multiculturalism (McDowell and Fang 2007).

As the researcher who carried out the fieldwork, I am positioned in a privileged position vis-à-vis the participants. My citizenship status, educational and physical characteristics are generally considered as dominant characteristics in the global and social context in which this research takes place. I am a highly educated, white, Belgian national.

The ten women were monitored closely in their daily activities over a period of three years. The activities and practices that the ethnographer shared were varied, such as bringing and picking up children to and from school, going to social services, shops, refugee organizations, accompanying the women and translating for them in their contacts with lawyers, the police, the courts, and so on. However, most of the time spent together was in their own homes. In the case of fieldwork abroad (that is, France), the research involved mainly telephone calls, online chat sessions and emailing.

Apart from participant observations, which delivered important fieldwork data, there were at least two other settings which provided valuable research data. These settings were in-depth interviews and 'sensing'. A total of 87 in-depth interviews were conducted with all participants, most of which were recorded (except for three participants who refused recording), transcribed and analysed. The analyses of the interviews conducted by the researcher were presented to the interviewees for feedback. In addition to this, three moments of 'sensing' were organized to present the collective data analysis to groups of undocumented women and staff from social organizations working with undocumented migrants.

This chapter focuses mainly on their everyday indoor activities, such as cooking, food customs, sleeping habits, storytelling, television preferences routines and daily religious practices. Because these ritualized maternal practices are inherently repetitive, they are often assessed as trivial. However, those practices will prove to be essential in the process of education because they provide the primary form of attachment, the basis of identity and, as such, they strongly determine the sentiments of connection and solidarity with others.

WHAT CAN FEELING AT HOME MEAN IN A SITUATION OF IRREGULARITY?

Due to economic constraints, undocumented mothers often share their home places with other mothers and their children who are in the same situation. This is the case with Paquita and Eva. Paquita is an undocumented mother from Bolivia, and Eva is in the same situation but comes from Colombia and recently had a child, Elvio. Their names are not displayed on the doorbell. This allows them to remain separated from the visible, public life, which often means living in fear of being arrested by the police or other authorities. Eva and Elvio share an apartment with Paquita and her daughter Zena, who was only two years old when we first met. The apartment is divided by a curtain, thus creating two separate living areas. One area is reserved for Eva and her son, who sleep together in a single bed. Paquita and Zena sleep together in a double bed on the other side of the colourful curtain. This bed serves a double purpose and is used as a sofa for the other inhabitants of the apartment and visitors, or when watching television. During my visits, I spent a lot of time watching Spanish soap operas. In the homes of some mothers of African origin I often watched the French Ivorian series *My Family*. In the house of Ella, an undocumented single mother of Cameroonian origin, the television is also used to watch Bamilikian and Ivorian dance and music DVDs. Her three-year-old son was inspired by these dance performances and perfectly imitated them in the living room. Since the time of our acquaintance, Ella has moved three times but she has always remained in the city of Antwerp. When I visited her in hospital after the birth of her third child, she confessed to me that she is so attached to the city she no longer wants to move anywhere else. Whenever she does move within the city of Antwerp, she accumulates goods, which she then trades for other, better items. Her sofa is covered with a blanket, which is meant to look like an authentic African product, despite not being one. She made her own curtains using a cheap fabric. Other than that, the rooms are mostly bare. When I noticed a jar filled with copper coins, Ella laughed and explained its purpose to me: 'Africans in Europe tend to collect these coins as savings for times of scarcity. These are used to buy life's necessities, such as food for my child, when times are difficult.'

Ella was also keen to share with me her creative approach to purchasing certain items. For instance, she tends to buy large quantities of reduced-price items and share them among her friends and family back home. She also likes to haggle, even in shops where Belgian nationals would never do such a thing. When I arrived at her house one day, she had bought an entire box of bargain bras and underpants, some of which she was very eager to give to me, and the rest of which she intended to send to her sisters in Africa. One day she had bought loads of tomatoes, which she had spread out on the kitchen table and she said: 'I like to imagine that my kitchen table is a Cameroonian marketplace, this is how we do it' (laugh).

Ethnographic descriptions of observations of the home generally accentuate the visible, material conditions of the respondent's home life. In the case of the undocumented women, this is usually fairly basic. This, of course, is directly linked to the economic positioning of the women as mothers and undocumented, single parents. In her research on the reproductive work among Moroccan migrants in Italy, Ruba Salih (2003) described the complexity of the process of building a 'haven to retreat to'. Through a captivating ethnography, she describes the position of not being a full citizen, but instead being an 'in-between' citizen of two nation-states. Although Salih believes that the two worlds to which the women in her research belonged are dynamic and changing, her analysis does not extend beyond the binary of these two worlds (Salih 2003, pp. 124–130). This chapter shows that the lived reality of Ella, Paquita and the other participants did not fit this conceptualization of home in its duality of here and there. Since leaving her home country at age 17, Ella had tried to create shelters to feel at home in several places during her migration route. This search for a home possibly continues at this very moment. The immersion in the fieldwork and the numerous participant observations, however, have shown what might seem very logical to many: that is, that an understanding of the material and visible conditions in which these mothers find themselves is not enough to fully comprehend the concept of a peaceful haven for their child(ren) and themselves. Therefore, this chapter argues that an observation of materiality alone is not a sufficient guarantee to overcome the double bipolarity between here (place of residence) and there (place of origin), and the nostalgia of yesterday and the utopia of tomorrow. A feeling of a home cannot be achieved solely by speech and via what is visible. Initial observations of home during the fieldwork did not seem to provide the data that I had envisaged. I often wondered why I continued to partake in daily banalities such as cooking, eating, and watching television and music video clips. What seemed at first to be useless and a waste of time, later turned out to be essential to attributing meaning to the concept of home. It was precisely in the underlying repetitive and routine nature of this banality that the potential meaning of home could be perceived.

THE FEELING OF HOME IS LIKE THE FEELING I HAVE FOR MY MOTHER

I asked Aïsha, an undocumented mother for almost ten years, what 'feeling at home' meant to her as a woman and as a parent. After a while, she handed me a piece of paper with the following words:

> In my life, I have two mothers, my natural birth mother and Algeria. I have the same feelings for both. I cannot leave my mother behind as I cannot leave Algeria behind. They are both a part of me. Being in Algeria, it is being at my home, it is like my big house. It is hard to criticize your mother, the same way in which it is hard to find fault with the place where you belong. At home, I don't need to cry because I feel like a stranger, because there is no racism. Home is where I belong. In Algeria I have the right to belong because there is no law indicating that I'm a stranger there. The feeling of home is like the feeling I have for my mother. However, I don't live at home and I do miss home because it is very different here. (free translation from Aïsha's French)

What fascinates me most in Aïsha's idea of home is the convergence of space and time. The memories of Algeria and of her mother are memories of the past, a past which she seems unable to let go of entirely. It is similar to what Ella describes in the previous section. Ella also had to create shelters in order to feel at home in several places during her migration route. Her first experience of home, however, was in her country of origin. This is where she experienced what mothering meant to her and this has remained a point of reference ever since.

The second aspect which struck me in Aïsha's writing is the emotional incorporation of space and time in her memories. Home is a feeling, which gives Aisha the right to belong to her primary destination. For her this means her mother and her home country, Algeria. This feeling gives her the strength not to cry because she is a foreigner. The incorporation of the maternal, the past and the socio-geographical collective identity goes beyond space and time and can only be perceived in the present moment of everyday life.

Subtle somatic incentives, included in everyday practices, are the only elements which can recall that intimate shelter called home (Connerton 1989). Thus, analysing home and belonging is only possible when connecting with feelings and sensations incorporated into ritualized, daily practices. Indeed, there is a strong link between these kinds of practices and practices of parenting or mothering observed in these undocumented migrant women. Because historically – and to a great extent still nowadays – women are in charge of providing the daily care for children and performing parenting practices, I prefer to use the term 'motherwork'

(Collins 1994) instead of the gender-neutral term 'parenting'. In this sense, it is not surprising that Aisha's maternal subjectivity is strongly connected to the intimate space that she had to leave behind. These mothering practices include the ritualized maternal bedtime routines, food preferences, storytelling, and so on. These practices might come across as routine and trivial, but they are also at the basis of the development of intimate and emotional connection (Carling et al. 2012).

Buitelaar (2009) studied these incorporated memories and feelings and established a connection with the construction of identity in second-generation women from Morocco residing in the Netherlands. During an interview, Buitelaar asked one of these women what Morocco still meant to her, to which she replied: 'Morocco to me smells like my mother.' Evoking feelings referring to experiences that lie in the past is not a new phenomenon. The passage in which Marcel Proust (1982) describes the memory of the senses triggered by his famous madeleine, is a famous one. He remembers the taste, the smell and the senses of touch in his experience and food perception; a feeling that refers to a primary experience, in search of lost time. That is why Claude Lévi-Strauss (1997, p. 28) said: '[F]ood is not only good to be eaten but also good to be thought about.' Emotions that are hidden in the daily ritual of food are generated through incentives of flavours, tastes and smells. That is why the ethnography of food is an excellent point of connection to the field of home. Ella's statement below clearly illustrates this strong connection:

> If I could go back home, that is, my home country, it wouldn't be so much to see anyone specific [Ella no longer has any close relatives there] or to do anything specific, I would just go home to walk down the streets and experience the smell and taste of food . . . and yes, it is so different, you can never make the same dish here, not even with the same hands, or with the same ingredients . . . but the most important thing is that you never stop trying.

This is exactly what the underlying meaning of mothering is about: 'to do what your mother taught you, even if it is much more difficult because of a different context' (Dominique, 43 years old). When transferred to food, this would be like preparing the same recipe, not using the exact same ingredients, yet trying to generate the same somatic experience. Memory works in a normative manner and it is also at the heart of food. These sensations and somatic practices opened up another research path whilst investigating the field of home.

TO DO WHAT YOUR MOTHER TAUGHT YOU: BETWEEN ROUTINE AND RITE

It is my task to share our story with my children! . . . They should know the history that lies behind their lives. They were not born in Europe coincidently, just like that [Ella snaps her fingers and pauses] . . . No, they were born in Europe because someone called 'Ella' arrived here without any documents and did this and that . . . The history of any life always starts with someone, right? Something? Roots, this is where we come from. It is for me to teach them that . . . But Tina, tell me honestly, an African mother who does not cook traditional African food for her children, what does she have to offer them, really? Her child will only know European cooking and would be like a black child raised by Belgians. (interview with Ella, translated from the French)

Understanding the concept of home, in other words, is understanding the mothering practices relating to food, including food preferences, food preparation, consumption and other maternal practices in the domestic environment. Because meal or food preferences not only belong to the daily practices of caring for one's self, but also involve looking after others, they belong to the realm of maternal practices. The relationship between memory and food is therefore deeply rooted. At the same time, food could be considered a return to lost time and space. In the reconstruction of home, there is an important element that refers to the position of the mother and its social, emotional and cultural meanings.

In these cases of undocumented single mothers residing in Belgium and France, an interesting question is: 'What do their food habits tell us about their maternal subjectivity in a post migrational context?' Mothering is a repetitive practice; it is a routine, but at the same time it is also a rite (Bugge and Almås 2006). Repetition and ritual reinforce themselves in the realm of mothering. It involves repeatedly trying to imitate the original act, which is close to one's primary identity. According to Butler (1999), it is through the imitation – which is always an imitation of a previous imitation – that one gives shape to one's sense of self. Repetition in this case is trying to imitate the original act, one which is based on a self-experienced primary identity. This primary identity has been shaped by first attachment and the immersion into the realm of the mother and the mothering practices. It is always an unspoken and unconscious imitation of mothering practices that have been passed on from generation to generation. As such, Ella and many others stress the importance of cooking what Ella calls typical meals for her child(ren) (as per the quotation above). Transferring specific alimentary regimes to her children means, for Ella and for the other women participants, that they not only nurture their children with a piece of their identity, but also manage, through this transferral, to heal the wounds that were caused by the suffering of their irregular migrations.

Food practices reflect lifestyle choices, opportunities and geographic trajectories experienced by anyone throughout their lifetime. Sometimes even a single dish can provide an eye-opening perspective into the culture of these people who have experienced a challenging migration, because their past and present are reflected in what they eat, what they like and consider to be good food (Parasecoli 2007, p. 22; Sutton 2001). Referring to food, Sutton develops an understanding of displacement and fragmentation among the Kalymnians in Greece during their experience of exile (Sutton 2001, pp. 73–88). It is based on Fernandez's (1986) concept of 'wholeness', used to understand the experiences of displacement and fragmentation. For Fernandez, returning to the whole (or primary identity) is a process that follows the alienation caused by colonialism and modernity. Fernandez's research occurred in a context of revitalized religious movements in West Africa, namely within the Fang Bwiti group in Gabon. It considers revitalization as an attempt to rebuild and reintegrate the past into the present.

What particularly interests me is that Fernandez uses the term 'iteration' to refer to this return. I had previously replaced iteration in this context with its synonym, repetition. These undocumented mothers have undergone a forced interruption in their sense of self, caused by (irregular) migration that complicated their emotional continuity of practices in their daily lives and strongly impacted upon their mothering practices and educational tasks. Their task of transferring daily practices and perpetuating continuity was complicated further because of the struggle for them and their child(ren) to integrate on a social, economic and legal level into their countries of residence. The mothering of the women who participated in this study made me realize that their repetitive daily practices promote a more conscious return to one's self. These repetitions and routines are undoubtedly present in everyone's daily work, more specifically that of women and men who mother. Nevertheless, whenever this repetition is abruptly interrupted, as is so often the case with forced migration, these women try to overcome this divide, and the mothering practices that attempt to resemble the original are performed with a heightened level of awareness. Consequently, these essential practices in the educational process provide the principles of identity but also of feelings of belonging and solidarity with oneself and others. These others may be present and/or absent and may be known or unknown. If indeed a return to the maternal primary identity and sense of self in relation to others is reflected in repetitive daily somatic practices (as, for example, in the realm of food), then what does this tell us about this repetitiveness in relationship to the construction of collective identities, in particular the citizenship identity?

HOME IS THE ONLY PLACE THAT CAN LIBERATE THOSE DOMINATED IN SOCIETY

In his book *Remembrance of Repasts*, David Sutton (2001) explains how food practices play a major role in the construction of collective memory. Although food has the power to construct feelings of solidarity and belonging, it also has the power to separate us from 'the other' across the boundaries of time and culture (Flandrin and Montanari 1999). Everyone can undoubtedly come up with certain stereotypes on food in relationship to national identities. The undocumented migrant women with whom I connected during the course of my fieldwork often joked about Belgian food, especially in comparison to the food of their tradition. They were all convinced that their traditional dishes taste better and make you stronger because they are prepared with 'real' and healthier ingredients. bell hooks[3] (1990, p. 46) argues that for those who are suppressed in society, a return to the whole[4] is never entirely possible in the public space. It can only be achieved at home, the only safe haven that is located at a distance from the public realm and which she refers to as 'space of the Other' (hooks 1990, p. 46). Therefore a migrant can only perform those specific daily maternal and repetitive practices in the safety of their own home, where they are allowed to become the subject. Because these practices contain values and beliefs which are essentially incompatible with a normative identity in public life, hooks claims that repetition of daily maternal practices will always be a subversive political act. Only in their own homes can the collective memories of dominated people have a chance of survival. Home therefore becomes the only realm for resistance and struggle for liberation (hooks 1990, pp. 42–47).

> resistance, at root, must mean more than resistance against war. It is a resistance against all kinds of things that are like war . . . So perhaps, resistance means opposition to being invaded, occupied, assaulted and destroyed by the system. The purpose of resistance, here, is to seek the healing of yourself in order to be able to see clearly . . . I think that communities of resistance should be places where people can return to themselves more easily, where the conditions are such that they can heal themselves more easily, where the conditions are such that they can heal themselves and recover their wholenesss. (Thich Nhat Hahn, in hooks 1990, p. 43)

In analogy to this, Paul Kershaw (2010a) states that maternal practices, for children who culturally, physically (Longman et al. 2013) or legally (Brouckaert 2013) deviate from the norm of citizenship, contain a political dimension and therefore even a citizenship potential. Experiences of ethnic minority families are not reflected in the public space, because authorities, schools, media and public institutions fail to recognize their identities. When identities of minorities are reflected in public spaces, they are considered deviant from the 'invisible' norm. They deviate in colour (non-white), religion (non-Catholic), citizenship status (undocumented) and/or gender (not male and/or not heterosexual), and so on. Basing his research on Patricia Hill Collins (1991, p. 51), Kershaw (2010a) claims that ethnic minority families tend to create a resource to resist this discrimination in the form of compensatory nursery practices. bell hooks (1990) considers the home as the prime site of resistance to postcolonial power. 'We can make homeplace that space where we return for renewal and self-recovery, where we can heal our wounds and become whole' (hooks 1990, p. 49). So far, critical debates on citizenship have denied the political potential of mothering practices because these are found in the realm of subjectivity and positioned in the private and intimate place of home (Kershaw 2010a, p. 396). Ruth Lister (2003) suggests reconsidering care as bonds and skills that are central to citizenship. In doing so, we could strengthen the emancipatory potential of citizenship. It also allows us to reject the male privilege of the concept of citizenship, which by its original definition excludes women and certain male minority statuses.

However, according to Kershaw (2010b), maternal practices deployed in the domestic space by families of ethnic or racial minorities are citizenship practices in their own right. Kershaw refers to research that was conducted by feminist sociologist Patricia Hill Collins (2000) on African American mothers in the United States. The mothers in Collins's study compensated at home by arming their children with tools that enabled them to resist the discrimination and racism they might experience in the dominant societal sphere. 'By working to ensure that their children cultivate a proud affiliation with their cultural or racial history, many ethnic minority mothers contribute to sustaining the self-definition of the collective minority identity and the collective political agency to which this self-definition gives rise' (Kershaw 2010a, p. 306). For Kershaw, reproductive and mothering practices contribute to a cultural identity that serves to empower and resist discrimination prevailing in public space. In doing so, Kershaw contributes to the understanding of how a 'lived' citizenship may challenge the perception of a traditional citizen. At the same time, Kershaw recognizes the political potential of the private space. Continuing Kershaw's intention to extend the basics of feminist theory as identified by Ruth Lister (2007, p. 55), and drawing attention to the political citizenship potential even within the private space, we now claim that this political citizenship potential should also be transferred into the emotional and somatic areas of repetitive practices.

INNOVATIVE AND CREATIVE NATURE OF REPETITIVE MOTHERING PRACTICES

In their performance of daily mothering practices, the undocumented migrant mothers in this research instill somatic memories that engender feelings of identity and belonging that go beyond the realm of their homes. If Kershaw (2005) and hooks (1990) talk about resistance by performing daily ritual practices that are opposed to the values and shared experiences of the public sphere, then I claim that this also implies a 'returning to the whole' or in other words, to 'a primary sense of self'. This return is only possible by performing maternal practices that are daily repetitions of care. However, in doing so, these practices are constantly adapted when measured against the practices of others who pretend to share the same sense of self, and also against 'the Other', namely those people from the majority framework who do not share this sense of self and the values which it entails.

Firstly, I want to mention the example of invigorating this return to the whole through shared experiences with others. The realm of food, which has the potential to strengthen a return to the self, is also a good foundation for thinking about collective identities. The story of Paquita clearly illustrates this. When Paquita was living in her home country, Bolivia, she was a devout member of the Anglican Church. However, when she arrived in the city of Antwerp and started looking for Anglican Spanish-speaking congregations, she could not find any. She soon came into contact with other Spanish-speaking people, with whom she strongly identified. These other Spanish-speaking people got together at a Catholic church in Borgerhout.[5] Although Paquita considers herself a member of this Catholic Church, she never lost her inner connection to the religion she grew up with and still refers to herself as an Anglican. She chose to have her daughter christened, and yet she has never fully embraced Catholic beliefs. When Paquita arrived in Belgium, she left her four children with her mother in Bolivia and tried to perform daily repetitive practices in the city of Antwerp in an attempt to create a sense of belonging to herself. In doing so, she performed, in a divergent way, what did not seem incompatible to her. A lot of gatherings, which were often organized by her, referred to special days at home (for example, Santa Cruz in Bolivia) and were attended by a group of people who had come from all over Latin America and were now residing in the city of Antwerp. Although there is a big difference in mothering practices and food preferences within the many traditions of Ecuador, Bolivia, Chile and Santa Domingo, during these gatherings, representatives of all these countries always referred to 'our food', 'our *patcha mama*' and 'our culture'. I claim that within a situation where one is considered a minority or an undocumented migrant, one needs to connect with others who share the same values, feelings and sensitive memories of daily incorporated practices in order to return to this primary sense of self. 'For someone to truly believe in eternity, others must share this belief because the belief that no one shares is called schizophrenia' (Pelevin 2002, p. 235). The above-mentioned shared experiences with others in a context of exile not only allow a return to the self but also intrinsically alter and reinvent this sense of primary self by unconsciously recoding deeply rooted and embodied memories.

Secondly, I want to draw attention to the context of experiences shared by the undocumented migrant women with people from the majority framework, such as myself. When I was invited to Paquita's home or to the gatherings which she frequently organized, it was clear that I was an outsider. 'You have to come to my birthday Tina and don't forget "do not eat in advance" . . . [she talks to her partner] . . . Ernest says that it is not like in Flemish homes, haha, in our homes we serve real food and not snacks' (freely translated from Spanish).

The above quotation, taken from a telephone conversation with Paquita, shows how she wants to include me in her experience of home and maternal practices, often referred to by means of food. The fact that my daughter has a black father and a white mother, which Paquita calls *mestiza*, caused her to assume that I might lack the appropriate knowledge on how to deal with this mothering context. One day, when my daughter was ill, Paquita gave me the following advice: 'Is your daughter ill? You should give her "*platanos con leche*". That is what we give our children in order to become strong and build up resistance. You know, I have to do the same with my daughter because she is also *mestiza*.'

Food and maternal daily practices as such have always been ambivalent in the exploration of the Other. On the one hand they foster the feeling of belonging to a whole, but on the other hand they also produce effects of exclusion. As such, multiple other examples arise from fieldwork that emphasizes the belonging to a cultural entity or a return to the whole after the abrupt interruption of forced migration. An outsider, belonging to the majority framework, does not share the same emotional connection to the maternal practices. I clearly did not share the same sensory embodied experiences with my participants and I did not know the unspoken stories related to those practices and habits of home. All undocumented women and their environment offered me very warm and open access to their intimate spaces of home and introduced me into their daily practices 'without speaking'. They wanted to share something with me, believing that I had never experienced the same maternal memories they share. The hierarchy that exists between the oppressed and the Other is reversed in a liberating way in this intimate sphere. Paquita and the other women in this research became experts because they introduced me into their home space. This does not mean, however, that there was no mutual influence.

Ella, an undocumented mother from Cameroon, who was always very curious about gender relationships in Europe, once stated: 'If I have to teach my children what African cooking is like, I want my partner to contribute to the household.' This quotation proves that in order to ensure continuity of shared maternal practices, one has to adapt to the context of the society that one lives in while in exile, and roles may need to change.

Despite the fact that I was seen as an outsider in the realm of food, it was a shared realm where the boundary between inclusion and exclusion was drawn. When Paquita refers to 'my home', she not only returns to the place she considers home, but also to the experience of an identity shared with others who live in exile and have gone through the same abrupt rupture in continuity. Returning to the emphasis placed by hooks (1990) and Kershaw (2005), which is to centre daily maternal practices around the public–private division as an intercultural division, I argue that we need to go beyond this division in our analyses. Based on the fieldwork experiences provided in this study, I argue that this culture-based public–private division offers an incomplete image of the maternal practices that were performed by the undocumented mothers in this study. We need to incorporate the notions of context and time. The concept of contagion plays a major role in this, both in the sense of perpetuation and in the innovative aspect thereof. 'A return to the whole' is brought about by contagion, through any contact with another body that is not contiguous (with oneself or what is familiar to oneself). Contagion is a somatic trigger caused by direct or indirect contact with the other, which aims to contaminate another body in the same situation. Experiences and feelings do not remain isolated but they move and communicate, they create relationships, they come into contact with other bodies. An individual, private act can trigger a process of contagion, including the author, the surroundings and the interpretations that are present in the social space and are disseminated in other proximities. This notion of contagion has proved to be a source of agency which also aims to mobilize external solidarities and emotions that are obtained in new configurations. These solidarities and emotions, which are not 'local' or 'national', are deployed for recognition and liberation in various areas. In addition, we must note that those mothering practices change through time and context and may be ambivalent and innovative in their outcomes.

CONCLUSIONS

Feminists, among others, have pointed out that there is a gender-based exclusion from public life, linked to the public–private dichotomy, which identifies the role of men as appropriate to the public world of politics and paid employment, and the role of women as suitable for the care and education of children at home. An analogous statement has been made from a cultural minorities perspective. For these reasons, women who are excluded not only legally but also socially and visibly from citizenship, provide a useful epistemological starting point, ideal for the exploration of their participation and membership in a community beyond the classic features of legality.

The subtle somatic incentives generated by daily maternal practices instill primary memories of the self. Therefore, the exploration of mothering practices is the only way to find the intimate shelter called home. Their maternal practices should be viewed as homemaking practices that have the potential to repair the sense of primary belonging and the sense of self after the abrupt rupture of a forced and undocumented migration. The performance of these daily mothering practices allows mothers to build intangible allegiances and solidarity within and across kinship circles and cultural and transnational boundaries. They negotiate normative discourses and create new subjectivities and identities for themselves and their children. Therefore, I argue that their motherwork is not merely limited to the private domain but extends to public and political spheres, an idea that demands a reassessment of traditional understandings of what is political.

Although these routine mothering practices have often been and are still regarded as trivial in current citizenship debates, I have come to the conclusion that those repetitive practices do not simply reproduce the same phenomena. It is the general misinterpretation and underestimation of the intimate and private spheres, typically found in neoliberal societies, that threatens the site of home with its disappearance. All daily repetitive activities and practices are creative and dynamic. Therefore, I argue that a revaluation of the realm of home and its daily maternal practices, and the recognition of its innovative and liberating potential, are essential to the education of (future) citizens in our society.

NOTES

* Special thanks go to my friend and neighbour E.E.D. for revising this chapter.
1. Collective regularization in 2009 in Belgium.
2. Intersectional theory has been an important paradigm in this work (McCall 2005) as it

conceives identities as complex and multiple, determined by gender, ethnicity, class, and so on, and as 'sites' in which the major systems of oppression in society are intersecting. As such, using intersectionality as an analytic tool implies paying attention to an apparently neutral norm of inclusion. Hence, from an intersectional perspective, women asylum seekers are an interesting group to focus on given their position in relation to the construction of national and collective identities. This chapter aims to render visible the multiple discriminations on the basis of race, class, ethnicity and gender that are linked to the reality of parenting and motherwork (Collins 1994) by using intersectionality as an analytic tool.

3. This author, bell hooks, who has taken her name from her maternal great-grandmother, Bell Blair Hooks, chooses not to use capital letters.
4. Although bell hooks does not use the term 'returning to the whole', which I use here to explain the effort of trying to imitate the original, maternal acts whereupon one deduces a sense of self or a self-experienced primary identity.
5. Borgerhout is a district within the city of Antwerp.

REFERENCES

Balibar, E. and I.M. Wallerstein (1991), *Race, Nation, Class: Ambiguous Identities*, London and New York: Verso.

Brouckaert, T. (2013), 'Accoucher la citoyenneté. Expériences et témoignages de femmes sans-papiers à propos de leur travail materne', doctoral dissertation.

Bugge, A.B. and R. Almås (2006), 'Domestic dinner representations and practices of a proper meal among young suburban mothers', *Journal of Consumer Culture*, 6 (2), 203–228.

Buitelaar, M. (2009), *Van huis uit Marokkaans: over verweven loyaliteiten van hoogopgeleide migrantendochters*, Amsterdam: Uitgeverij Bulaaq.

Butler, J. (1999), 'Bodily inscriptions, performative subversions', in J. Price and M. Shildrick (eds), *Feminist Theory and the Body: A Reader*, New York: Routledge, pp. 416–422.

Carling, J., C. Menjívar and L. Schmalzbauer (2012), 'Central themes in the study of transnational parenthood', *Journal of Ethnic and Migration Studies*, 38 (2), 191–217.

Collins, P.H. (1991), 'Black women and motherhood', in V. Held (ed.), *Justice and Care*, New York: Teachers College Press.

Collins, P.H. (1994), 'Shifting the center: race, class, and feminist theorizing about motherhood', in E.N. Glenn, G. Chang and L.R. Forcey (eds), *Mothering: Ideology, Experience, and Agency*, New York: Routledge, pp. 45–65.

Collins, P.H. (2000), 'What's going on? Black feminist thought and the politics of postmodernism', in E.A. St Pierre and W.S. Pillow (eds), *Working the Ruins: Feminist Poststructural Theory and Methods in Education*, New York: Routledge, pp. 41–73.

Connerton, P. (1989), *How Societies Remember*, Cambridge: Cambridge University Press.

Dietz, M.G. (1985), 'Citizenship with a feminist face: the problem with maternal thinking', *Political Theory*, 13 (1), 19–37.

Duyvendak, J.W. (2009), 'Thuisvoelen: een korte introductie op drie artikelen', *Sociologie*, 5 (2), 257–260.

Fernandez, J.W. (1986), *Persuasions and Performances: The Play of Tropes in Culture*, Vol. 374, Bloomington, IN: Indiana University Press.

Flandrin, J.L. and M. Montanari (1999), *A Culinary History of Food*, New York: Columbia Press (English edition by A. Sonnenfeld).

Harding, S.G. (2004), *The Feminist Standpoint Theory Reader: Intellectual and Political Controversies*, New York: Psychology Press.

hooks, b. (1990), *Yearning: Race, Gender and Cultural Politics*, Boston, MA: South End Press.

Hughes, E.C. (1994), *On Work, Race, and the Sociological Imagination*. Chicago, IL: University of Chicago Press.

Kershaw, P. (2005), *Carefair: Rethinking the Responsibilities and Rights of Citizenship*, Vancouver: UBC Press.

Kershaw, P. (2010a), 'The "private" politics in caregiving: reflections on Ruth Lister's citizenship: feminist perspectives', *Women's Studies Quarterly*, 38 (1–2), 302–312.

Kershaw, P. (2010b), 'Caregiving for identity is political: implications for citizenship theory', *Citizenship Studies*, 14 (4), 395–410.

Lévi-Strauss, C. (1997), 'The culinary triangle', in C. Counihan and P. Van Esterik (eds), *Food and Culture: A Reader*, New York: Routledge, pp. 28–35.

Lister, R. (2003), *Citizenship: Feminist Perspectives*, 2nd edn, Basingstoke: Palgrave Macmillan.

Lister, R. (2007), 'Inclusive citizenship: realizing the potential', *Citizenship Studies*, 11 (1), 49–62.

Longman, C., K. De Graeve and T. Brouckaert (2013), 'Mothering as a citizenship practice: an intersectional analysis of "carework" and "culturework" in non-normative mother-child identities', *Citizenship Studies*, 17 (3–4), 385–399.

Lykke, N. (2010), *Feminist Studies: A Guide to Intersectional Theory, Methodology and Writing*, New York: Routledge.

McCall, L. (2005), 'The complexity of intersectionality', *SIGNS: Journal of Women in Culture and Society*, 30 (31), 1771–1802.

McDowell, T. and S.R.S. Fang (2007), 'Feminist-informed critical multiculturalism considerations for family research', *Journal of Family Issues*, 28 (4), 549–566.

Parasecoli, F. (2007), 'Bootylicious: food and the female body in contemporary black pop culture', *Women's Studies Quarterly*, 35 (1–2), 110–125.

Pelevin, V. (2002), *Homo Zapiens*, New York: Penguin Books.

Proust, M. (1982), *Remembrance of Things Past*, Vol. 1, transl. C.K. Scott Moncrieff and T. Kilmartin, New York: Vintage-Random House, pp. 706–707.

Rassiguier, C. (2010), *Reinventing the Republic. Gender, Migration and Citizenship in France*, Stanford, CA: Stanford University Press.

Salih, R. (2003), *Gender in Transnationalism: Home, Longing and Belonging among Moroccan Migrant Women*, London and New York: Routledge.

Sutton, D.E. (2001), *Remembrance of Repasts: An Anthropology of Food and Memory*, New York: Berg Publishing.

PART III

Looking at children

6. What is family in the context of genetic risk?

Katie Featherstone*

INTRODUCTION

Kinship is a well-established topic of enquiry within anthropology and sociology; however, biomedical innovations have given this topic renewed significance: the relationship between biology and kinship is not straightforward. While shared genetic material may be believed to be biologically constitutive of kinship, kinship defined in social and cultural terms cannot be equated directly or unproblematically with biological relatedness. Such a lens on kinship also provides the opportunity to explore a number of analytic themes and questions from a new perspective: how do people trace their relationships and how do they express them? What does 'family' mean in everyday terms and how do people maintain those ties in practical ways? How do people make everyday practical decisions about sharing genetic risk information and beliefs with other family members?

Genetic research into the molecular basis of common, 'complex' (that is, multifactoral) diseases promises to transform the practice of medicine (Chiliback et al. 2011). For the foreseeable future, however, we will have to live with genetic technologies that provide diagnostic and predictive information about disease risk for individuals, while remaining relatively powerless to intervene. Importantly, this genetic knowledge is not just of relevance to the individual, but will also have implications for their family members, who may also be at risk of inheriting a condition, and can be informed about the potential future onset of a condition. Because information about an individual's genetic composition is relevant to other members of their extended family, this raises important questions as to how far collective respect for confidentiality can be reconciled with an individual's right of access to information about kin, information that may have direct relevance to them and their future. Family members may have legitimate interests in genetic information about their kindred and this may be particularly true for kindred where there may be a shared risk of trans-mitting or manifesting a genetic disease.

New genetic technologies therefore have potentially impor-tant consequences for social relations and self-identities (Inhorn and Birenbaum-Carmeli 2008). Biomedical phenomena are endowed with new social meanings and social phenomena are equally endowed with new biological significance (Franklin 2003; Rose 2006). The identification of a genetically inherited disease, or a risk of disease, creates a context in which health, illness, risk and susceptibility to disease are subject to definition and redefinition. New genetic technologies may thus transform everyday practi-cal understandings of inheritance, relatedness and disease, and these will in turn have consequences for our definitions of kinship, pathology and risk.

The field of anthropology has provided a body of studies examin-ing reproduction and kinship in EuroAmerica (cf. Carsten 2000, 2004; Franklin 1997, 2003; Strathern 1992a, 1992b). Biomedical innovations have given this topic a renewed significance, with a particular focus on examining the impact of assistive reproductive technologies, which are seen as embodying the influence of biotechnologies in shaping identity and family (cf. Inhorn and Birenbaum-Carmeli 2008). This field increas-ingly sees kinship as something more fluid and subject to transformation (Carsten 2000, 2004; Strathern 2005) and there is a growing body of work examining how these technologies may redefine and expand our ideas of family and relatedness (Bonaccorso 2007; Edwards 2000; Edwards and Salazar 2008).

The development of assistive reproductive technologies has led to an examination of the commercialization of parenthood (Goodwin 1992), the position of gay men and lesbian women in relation to donated gametes (Haimes and Weiner 2000; Levine 2008) and the identity of those con-ceived using these practices (Haimes 1998). Some argue that the increas-ing availability of these technologies give rise to increasing social change and challenge what it means to be a 'parent' by providing opportunities for the formation of non-traditional familial units (New 2006) produced through different patterns of social relationships, for example the proc-esses of 'kinning' whereby the transnationally adopted child is made to be kin (Howell 2007). In contrast, others suggest it has led to new forms of essentialism (cf. Franklin 1993).

However, these studies focus on examining reproductive technologies, which have very different applications to the clinical genetic technologies of diagnosis and risk assessment, and have a potentially different range of consequences. The goals of the clinical genetics service sees the deliv-ery of risk information as providing individuals with the opportunity to make informed and responsible choices about managing their (and other family members') risk, disclosure and future health (Armstrong et al. 1998; Richards 1999; Sarangi and Clarke 2002a, 2002b; Sarangi et al. 2003). Studies focusing on genetic knowledge suggest that they generate new forms of obligations (Novas and Rose 2000; Rose 2006) and a large body of literature has focused on the ways in which their patients manage the burden of responsibility and how individuals rationalize their strategies in response to genetic risk information (cf. Arribas-Ayllon et al. 2008a, 2008b; Hallowell 1999; Hallowell et al. 2003).

Yet there has been little research examining the work of family and kinship within the context of new genetic technologies. Work in this area has predominantly examined the experience of individuals who have attended a clinical genetics service and received predictive information on their current or future disease status on the basis of clinical data or molecular tests (cf. Sivell et al. 2008). Few studies examining these themes have been based on the examination of kinship or family (Featherstone et al. 2006; Geelen et al. 2011; Gregory et al. 2007; Sobel and Cowan 2000). This must extend to examine the disclosure practices and exchange of genetic information among kin where it may be withheld or shared as part of the wider network of social relationships and information exchange that constitutes practical family membership. We need to examine who constitutes kin, what the dynamics of information exchange are and how individuals negotiate practical decision-making within the context of genetic information and risk.

This chapter examines the experiences of individuals attending a clinical genetics service and their wider kindred, following the flow of information through one family: not only the experience of those who attend the clinic, but that of wider family members who may also be at risk, but do not attend themselves. The approach in this chapter is to apply the well-established principle that the interview data should be treated as narrative accounts of family relatedness and inheritance, which can be examined to consider what kind of biographical and social work they accomplish. This analysis is therefore based on the understandings that family and kinship are accomplished or performed, and are constructed through the biographical and autobiographical work people do. Importantly, these are not performances about 'families' or 'relatedness' that exist independently of such biographical work. In a fundamental sense they constitute or produce the relationships and the families; the work of family and kinship are accomplished through self-presentation and these accounts are occasioned performances for a number of different audiences. For example, the clinical team, other family members and the researcher will each be presented with a different performance of 'family' and 'family communication'.

This chapter focuses on interviews with one extended 'kindred'[1] to examine the narrative forms that accomplish family within the context of genetic risk information. These include the construction of the life course, age and generational differences; the performance of moral character and personality types; and the embedding of the self in accounts of relatedness, through the performance of memory and emotion.

METHODS

This study is based on fieldwork carried out within a clinical genetics service that is based in a major United Kingdom teaching hospital (Featherstone et al. 2006). To explore the dynamics of family and genetic disclosure found across the sample, the chapter describes the biographical narratives of ten members of one kindred who are affected by an inherited degenerative condition.

This disorder does not follow the classical patterns of Mendelian inheritance, but is passed on through mitochondrial inheritance – so-called matrilineal inheritance: the condition is only transmitted by women, who pass it on to their children (both male and female). Men can inherit the condition, but cannot transmit it to their children. There is a wide phenotypic variability among mitochondrial conditions such as this, which is characterized by muscle weakness, wasting and pain, tiredness and fatigue. Additionally, large and disfiguring lipomas (benign lumps that form due to an overgrowth of fat cells and can form anywhere on the body where there are fat cells) can develop on the body. Genetic testing is available for this condition; however, mothers pass it on to their children, so essentially this indicates which members of the kindred will be affected. Any test carried out will only confirm diagnosis, but will not reveal the severity of the condition, the way it will affect the individual or the time of onset.

The proband Veronica and her three sisters (all in their late forties and early fifties), Lindsey, Maggie and Suzanne, had all been diagnosed with the condition at the genetics clinic and are at different stages of disease progression. Their mother and one sister died of the condition (although they did not receive a clinical diagnosis). The next generation (all in their twenties) includes Veronica's two daughters Jenny and Angie, Maggie's daughter Susan, Lindsey's daughter Sally, and Carrie, whose mother died of the condition; they were also interviewed. All but one of the women in this second generation (Angie) has young children. Doug, Lindsey's partner, was the only male member of the kindred we were able to interview. Because snowball sampling was relied upon to follow the information flow through the family, it was not possible to obtain access to other male members of the kin. All interviewed (apart from Doug, who is connected by marriage) and a large number of the extended kindred will have inherited the condition from their mothers; however, to what extent they will be affected or the likely time of onset of the condition is not known. No treatment or intervention is currently available for this condition.

The data are based on interview transcripts using a semi-structured checklist of topics to guide the discussion to ensure that similar issues were discussed, but discussions were open-ended and encouraged the respondents to express other issues of importance. All interviews were carried out, audio-taped and transcribed verbatim by the author, and analysis took the form of narrative analysis. The author also carried out early analysis and produced detailed accounts of emergent themes. Data presented has been kept as verbatim as possible, to illustrate findings and allow the reader to judge interpretations. All names have been changed to preserve anonymity.

FINDINGS

This kindred were described by the clinical genetics team within their weekly team meetings as an 'open family' who were 'quite happy to come to clinic together'. They were presented to the author as a large kindred from their clinical caseload that could be enrolled as an example of effective communication and disclosure of genetic information. From the perspective of the clinical team, the effective transmission of genetic information from the proband through to the wider kindred has been accomplished successfully.

However, it is necessary to problematize this account of the kindred as 'open'. Family and kinship work are accomplished through self-presentation and narrative accounts which are occasioned performances for different audiences: for example, the performance of 'family' and 'family communication' for the clinical team will differ from the performance given to other family members, the author and so on. Using these kindred as a case study, this chapter will examine the accounts of family, communication and disclosure presented to the author.

BELIEFS ABOUT INHERITANCE

The kindred presented a number of theories that explain where the condition may have originated and how it has been transmitted through the family. In doing so, members of this kindred described both the substance where the condition resides and various routes that are attributed to its transmission. This is not to suggest that they harboured a literal belief in such routes and substances, but that they used well-established idioms commonly employed to express the principles of inheritance, rather than the terms employed within biomedical theories of inheritance.

Substance and Routes of Transmission

'Blood' was described by a number of the kindred as a route of transmission. For example, Jenny recalls how 'bad blood' and the 'bad family bloodline' was often referred to during discussions within the family to describe why this happened to them, as well as the mechanism by which the condition has been transmitted through their family 'line'. This account of 'bad blood' was not just the focus of the family lore relating to the specific condition, but was also associated with the transmission of the wide range of other health problems observed within members of the kin over a number of generations. This is part of the process of looking for patterns of health and illness to make sense of where the condition originated and why it affects their family.

> *Suzanne*: Like they wouldn't have remembered the auntie, but I remember her. My mother always used to say it's the bad blood on both her parents' side, she always said that. Because my grandfather used to have these lumps on his head and all like these cysts you know and they cut them off but they said no they weren't cysts the ones the girls had, hormones or some bloody thing.

Importantly, establishing the condition as being in the blood is interpreted as an indication that the condition is ever-present in all family members. However, the question remains as to whether it will remain dormant (this is a late onset condition) or whether it will express itself and affect an individual:

> *Veronica*: Yeah, we came out and it was basically sort of a case of 'Well you've got it in your blood but it's just whether it actually comes out or not'.

Such beliefs are integrated into understandings of who is at risk, and the processes of disclosure and surveillance, which will be discussed further below.

Sides of the Family

The condition was often described within families as originating on and being transmitted through one 'side' of the family. This was the case in this family, and here Maggie describes her belief that she has identified a pattern of inheritance within the family, seeing it as originating from her mother's 'side', as it seems not to have affected other branches of her family. For example, she believes her uncle and cousins are unaffected, but that the female descendants of her mother are affected, with the age of onset appearing to occur earlier with each generation:

> Maggie: Er none of them have shown any, my mother's brother's children they seem to be all right. It seems to be the women in the family, my mother's, my mother's side, seem to be at younger ages getting this. . . . But er, like Dr — said it doesn't, doesn't come out in the male.

GENDER DIFFERENCES

Many of the kindred strongly identified gender differences in the way in which the condition was transmitted among their kin, and this had implications for who was believed to be at risk. Within this kindred, women were believed to be more at risk. This reflects the pattern of the visibility of the condition at this point within the kin; as Jenny notes, 'it's more in the woman' – so far, none of the men appear to have developed symptoms or signs that may indicate the onset of the condition:

> *Jenny*: They've told her that it's more in the woman and like she can't pass it, she could pass it onto R—, that's my mother's son but he couldn't pass it onto his children. Because they've got one brother and there's nothing wrong with him, but my mother and aunts, all of them after shopping they're just, she could sleep all night if we left her there. And if she goes up the stairs quick she's out of breath and she's got to lie on the bed and like making her bed, she finds that hard.

Looking to the Past to Identify the Origins of the Condition

An important part of the process for individuals and families in making sense of how the condition is inherited is the scrutiny of the past in the attempt to identify its origins and where the condition started in their family. Such beliefs about where the condition originated are passed on to other family members and become part of family lore, the oral history of how and why the condition manifested itself within this kindred: why it happened to them. For example, Suzanne, in reflecting on where the condition has come from, evokes a sinister image of her grandmother's sister, 'the lady in black' who was 'all screwed up' and 'twisted':

> *Suzanne*: When I think back and I remember an aunt I was telling them, it was my grandmother's sister. Oh and she couldn't speak and she was all screwed up and I really remember her and she was always in black, I used to be frightened

to death of her and her speech an' all. In fact some days I look at Maggie [her sister] and I think oh my God you're like Auntie A— you know, but you wouldn't dare say it because they wouldn't have known her. I mean she died when I was quite, well 10 or 11. I vaguely remember her then you know because I remember this lady in black and oh she was so twisted.

Importantly, although this process is part of making sense of the condition and why it has affected their family, it is a key part of identifying who is at risk within the family now and who will be at risk in future generations. Suzanne goes on to suggest that the condition originated and 'stemmed from' an aunt and since then has been passed on to the women within the family, and that this pattern of inheritance will ostensibly continue 'all the way down' through successive generations of women:

> *Suzanne*: I remember this auntie vividly and I often think, I wonder if it really stemmed from there because that was my mother's sister, so it was obviously in the line all the way down.

Thus, both the condition and the stories of its origin are passed down through the kin and through 'the line'. These beliefs inform their decisions about disclosure, who is at risk and who needs to be informed.

PRACTICES OF DISCLOSURE

As has been noted, assumptions were often made by the clinic about the nature of disclosure within families and what constitutes 'family' in the context of genetic information. The clinical perspective implied the unproblematic transfer of information about the potential risk of inheriting a genetic condition. In contrast, the experience of disclosure within families within the study, and within this extended family, were found to be much more complex. Veronica (the family member who first attended the clinic) reports that she and her family are 'open' and that she is an 'open book', and reports that most of her kindred know about the condition:

> *Veronica*: Well we're all pretty open anyway you know. If I, I tend to be an open book though if I've got a problem I tell everybody and I say what's what like.

It would, however, be unrealistic to assume that within such an 'open' family there are overt episodes of sharing or transmitting genetic information. The disclosure of genetic information within this kin does not consist of a number of specific instances of communication, where information is unproblematically provided to a willing recipient. As Veronica's daughter

Jenny explains, it is a process that has no clear boundaries and is always partial in nature. In contrast to her mother's account, Jenny sees this differently.

> *Jenny*: It's funny isn't it, like we're a close family but then things like that you don't talk about then.

Jenny adds that all her knowledge of the condition has been obtained by overhearing her mother and aunts talking together, and when her mother occasionally mentions aspects of the condition to her. She is aware that her knowledge is partial and reports that they have never discussed the condition in any depth:

> *Jenny*: No, no. I think they probably don't know any more than what I know about her. Like you know picking up bits of conversation if I'm in the room or not really being in on the conversation they don't, they do know a little bit . . . yeah just picking up little bits . . . No never, even when my mother [Veronica] first found out like it weren't sort of like 'Sit down, I've got something to tell you', it was just sort of going up there for a cup of tea and you know you're popping in anyway and then just, she just was saying a little bit about it.

More widely within the kin, discussions about the condition were often reported as partial and it is important to note that the actual condition was never named by any of the kin, but referred to as 'it' or 'this thing'. This may be because knowledge of the condition is part of a wider set of shared and tacit everyday knowledge within the kindred:

> *Sally*: You know but none of them ever know the name, they always say 'Maybe you've got what I've got', they don't know what the hell it's called, they don't name it, well I don't know if they know the name themselves do they you know, because I haven't got a clue what that name is.

> *Lindsey*: But they don't, no they don't, they don't name it by name any time they mention it you know they just say like 'What we've got'.

In the process of disclosure, individuals often incorporated a number of devices such as humour to disguise their concerns that a family member may be presenting early signs of the condition. This is linked to surveillance. Veronica believes her daughter is experiencing the early symptoms of the condition. However, despite this concern, Veronica tells us that they are only able to discuss this fear briefly and through the use of humour:

> *Veronica*: Well as I say joking again I said, she said 'I hope I haven't got what you've got', she said 'I'm not going to end up in a wheelchair, all lumps over me',

and I said 'Well', I said 'You know I can't help that, it's not my fault'. But she does suffer with a lot of pain in her legs and swelling and all, which my mother's feet and legs always swollen. And yours did yesterday didn't it? [to Jenny]

It is also used as a way of disclosing their concern through what appear to be casual remarks such as 'I hope you haven't got what I've got', yet which are suffused with high levels of fear and anxiety.

BELIEFS INFORMING DISCLOSURE AND WHO IS FAMILY IN THE CONTEXT OF GENETIC RISK

The kin held a number of beliefs about who is at risk of developing the condition and who needs to be informed. As has been seen, the focus of concern within this kindred was the women in the family; the men were generally not considered to be at risk of developing the condition. Some stated that it cannot be 'passed on' to the men in the family:

Jenny: She did say one day but I can't remember, but it can't be passed onto boys, can it?

Even when family members thought that the condition could be 'passed on' to male members of the family, this did not mean that they believed they would be affected. The large number of women within the family who appear to be showing visible signs of the condition (tiredness and exhaustion are key early signs of onset) and the absence of any cases of men affected by the condition so far appears to be interpreted as evidence that the men may have inherited the condition, but in some benign way. Suzanne expresses this belief and states that although her son Ryan may be 'carrying' the condition, this does not mean that he will develop it:

Suzanne: But I think it's Ryan [son] I'll do it for, to see if she you know because there's always something every day that, the sons are carrying it or something, this is Veronica now see but I don't want to listen to her.

This has implications for who within the kin is considered to be at risk. For example, Veronica suggests that because of the pattern of inheritance she can see, some family members do not need to be worried about it, or even informed. She rationalizes that they are not at risk because she believed that the condition only affected those on her mothers 'side' of the family and so far that 'side' appears to be unaffected. However, there is minimal contact with these members of the family; they are not in close or regular contact.

Veronica: But they, their kids haven't got it, not that we know of anyway.
Interviewer: So have, is that, that kind of your mother's, your mother's aunt or . . .
Veronica: I think it was on my mother's side.

Thus, beliefs about who is at risk for developing the condition are informed by beliefs about the routes and substance through which the condition can be inherited and the pattern of inheritance, and signs and symptoms of the condition displayed visibly so far within the kindred.

MUTUAL SURVEILLANCE

These practices of partial or non-disclosure of genetic risk are in the context of high levels of mutual surveillance in which family members are continually inspected, compared and scrutinized for signs that indicate the inheritance and the development of this condition. This surveillance includes surveillance of the self. Such family work is also part of the process of identifying where the condition has come from and looking for signs that they can associate with risk and susceptibility in order to predict and project its future trajectory within themselves and members of their kin.

The Performance of Memory

There appears to be an ongoing comparison of the self with both previous and current generations, inspecting them for signs of the condition. Maggie and her daughter Susan exemplify this work in their assessment of who is at risk. Throughout her account, Maggie describes her surveillance of her kindred and of her ability to see the patterns of inheritance and to read the subtle signs of who is affected by 'it' in the family. She believes that although they have not attended the clinic or been diagnosed, it is affecting her daughter and nieces; she can 'see it':

> *Maggie*: But my, my nieces, none of them they, Sally and Penny haven't had the tests, but I can see it there you know there's something not hitting home right.

Maggie had observed her mother's experience, and recalls the manifestation and development of the condition in her and compares it to her own experience of the onset of the condition. She describes the similarities to how it affects her and also the ways in which she responds and manages her illness. Her description also implies a similar disease progression; the condition led to her mother using a wheelchair, that may be her future trajectory:

Maggie: But a lot of the things my mother used to say, 'Oh I can't go out today, if you put me in the wheelchair we'll just go to the shops'. And she'd 'Oh stop now because everything is spinning', and that's exactly how I feel and I think to myself now I know how she felt. There we are.

Susan has also observed her mother's (Maggie) manifestation and development of the condition and believes that she is likely to follow the same pattern of onset as her mother and her aunts. She also describes her fear of the future and her expectation that even though she has decided not to have the predictive genetic test, her inheritance of the condition is inevitable. She has an expectation of a similar age of onset as her mother:

Susan: We have to sit there and think oh well we're 40 we're going to get this, we're going to get that by the time we're 40. I don't want to end up like this. But I will, won't I, waiting for it to happen, that's why I don't want to know. So I'll have the blood test but I don't want to know.

Surveillance as a Form of Partial Disclosure

Their accounts are suffused with explicit accounts of surveillance; the close inspection of other family members, using comments about their health and their observations of their behaviour and health status (both emotional and physical) to imply onset. There appears to be a continual comparison between and across the generations for any slight physical and emotional sign that may indicate their risk of the condition, the onset or the disease stage they have reached:

Maggie: And I notice with my brother's girls now, I mean they're only 18 and 14 but there is something there. I mean perhaps I'm being an old witch or something . . . but it is, it's there you know you can see it kicking off. Their mothers don't notice it, but I, whether it's because I'm an older generation and I've seen so much I'm thinking you know it is there . . . But I can see it in a lot of them, in all of the nieces and nephews, it's something I notice. One of them will come and say 'Oh I feel knackered today', and I think oh well it's your age. But then when you take stock and watch them how they move about and some of the little things they do I think oh there's something there like.

These acts of surveillance constitute the social reality of the family; the tacit and hidden search for signs of this condition is how they define their family and how their family is constituted. The kin communicate via the subtle (and not so subtle) introduction of information about the condition into the consciousness; through mutual surveillance and commentaries on similarities or differences between individuals and their worries and concerns about who is or is not at risk, who is encouraged to attend the clinic, who becomes the current focus of their health concerns and should be 'worried about'. The following extract between Maggie and her daughter Susan demonstrates the way in which the physical signs and emotional behaviour of family members are used as indicators of the underlying condition. Surveillance of others is often silent; however, in the interview below, when Susan suggests she is unaffected, Maggie applauds her positive attitude (although this is in a tone that implies disbelief) and immediately comments on her depression at a young age, suggesting that this may be associated with the possible onset of the condition:

Susan: I don't think I've got anything wrong with me.
Maggie: Well that's nice, that's nice to know you've got that attitude.
Susan: I don't think I have to be honest with you.
Maggie: Not even with the depressions as young as you are?
Susan: Yeah but that could be . . . it could be yeah. But when I went to my counsellor the first time, she said didn't she, because my uncle had died and my auntie and she said 'Your problem is you're frightened for your mother'. Well they did say that was the root of it, because of your, well the illness. Not because of you yourself but I didn't go back after that, I just went on tablets.

The narratives presented by this mother and daughter are suffused with explicit accounts of surveillance: the close inspection of each other and of their own bodies. There appears to be a continual comparison across the generations for signs that might indicate their risk of the condition (for the younger generation) or the disease stage they have reached (for the older generation).

Similarly, Susan goes on to describe how her mother and aunts continually comment on her health, particularly her tiredness and depression, suggesting that these were signs and early symptoms of the condition and linking it explicitly to how the condition initially manifested in them:

Susan: They reckon like the sleeping, I can fall asleep easy, they reckon that's a symptom and because I'm on Prozac anti depressant. But it's nothing to do with all that you know it's the past and that isn't it . . . They're going 'Oh it's this. It could be to do with this', and 'See we used to have that', and I'm thinking 'Oh you know at the end of the day I don't want to know'. I would like to know if I've got it but I don't want to sort of like dwell on everything. You know you have like a bad day 'Oh it's the illness', do you know what I mean, I'd end up making myself worse.

RESPONSIBILITY AND DISCLOSURE

At the level of family, such accounts also inform the moral and ethical work that individuals such as Maggie perform. She integrates her beliefs about who is likely to be affected with theories of moral character and personality type – who she believes can and cannot cope with the condition, or information about their potential risk status – and uses this to inform her rationalizations of non-disclosure of genetic information:

> *Maggie*: No, so er no, not with Peter [her son in his twenties], I hope not anyway because I don't think he'd take it the same way as the rest of us you know.
> *Interviewer*: Why is that?
> *Maggie*: Because he hasn't got that er, he hasn't, he hasn't got the attitude for it. He's not that way inclined, he'd be one of these things of if you said 'You've got this wrong with you', he'd go and sit in a corner and wait for it to happen like. He's not very up and at it at all.

Similarly, Lindsey has not spoken to her son about the condition. She suggests that he is the type of person who would not want to know and she adds that she would also find it difficult to talk to him about the condition. However, she believes that he is aware of 'something going on' in the family and he knew his grandmother, who died of the condition. She is not as concerned about the men in the family and is reassured that he cannot pass it on to his son:

> *Interviewer*: Has he told you about it, has he said [anything] about this?
> *Lindsey*: No he just knows there's something going on like but he's not exactly sure what. He knew my mother was in a wheelchair like and pushed her about and that, but no not really.
> *Interviewer*: Do you think, do you get the feeling he'd want to know or . . .
> *Lindsey*: Yeah R— is come day, go day, nothing bothers R— (laughs). It's funny it's hard to talk to him somehow. You know I call him and I'll say about five minutes to him and that's about it. But he wouldn't pass it onto his child and he had a boy after so I was glad they had a boy.

Focus on Molecular Testing

Discussions of risk among the kindred tended to focus on the molecular test as the key way to identify whether they will develop the condition. This focus is noteworthy; all the mothers interviewed will almost inevitably have passed on to their children at least some of the abnormal mitochondria. The molecular test provides a confirmation; however, it will not provide the likely age of onset or the severity of the condition:

> *Angie*: You know so. I don't know if I want to know really to be honest you know to go and have the tests and like I say there's nothing that can be done so you'd just worry and you know then I mean God if I have got it you know. But you can have the gene, it doesn't necessarily mean that you're going to be . . .

Thus the predictive 'blood test' appears to be a valuable mechanism for the focus of disclosure, but also becomes a barrier to further discussions about the condition and further assessment of their risk status. When used to inform family members, any discussion of a predictive test promotes the belief that there is a different pattern of inheritance with only a 50 per cent risk of developing the condition. The communication between Maggie and her daughter Susan, for instance, demonstrates the ways in which discussion of the condition runs the potential 'risk' of breaking down the communication channels within the close kin:

Maggie: Right-o then.
Susan: Veronica wants me to have it done.
Maggie: Our Veronica [sister]
Susan: I think she wants everyone to be ill.
Maggie: No, she wants everybody to know exactly what's going on.
Susan: Yeah but you don't want to know. It's different for you lot because you've got it, but like us lot don't want to know because we'll be waiting for it to happen by the time we're 40.
Susan: There's only Veronica she shouts at me. Because you know you block it out so much and she shouts. That's why I said 'Alright I'll go', you know to keep the peace.
Interviewer: So you feel you're bullied a bit into . . .
Susan: No I want to find out, but I don't. I want to find out well because of Mum and that but I don't want to know because it's my 40th birthday. But it's all 40 it hit you lot isn't it, so by the time you're coming to 40 you'll be thinking oh here we go.
Maggie: They reckon life begins at 40, what the hell went wrong for us lot (laughs). There we are such is life.

This also demonstrates that discussion of risk and disclosure about the condition also comes at a price: individuals disclosing this risk do so with a clear expectation that family members respond appropriately. Thus, disclosure was often accompanied by pressure to contact the clinical service and have the predictive test.

DISCUSSION

This case study of one kindred can help to capture and to crystallize the themes the author and colleagues have been exploring on a wider basis, namely, the way in which surveillance informs beliefs about inheritance and what informs and influences the practical everyday ethics of disclosure of genetic risk (Featherstone et al. 2006). This kindred had developed a number of theories to explain where the condition had 'come from' and the path of transmission. There appeared to be a continual process of surveillance of a series of pasts and futures that were scrutinized and made sense of in the present in order to identify who was at risk. These acts of surveillance constituted the reality of this family; living with the condition or its threat was unspoken and hidden (Zerubavel 2006). Disclosure, even within this 'open' family, did not consist of overt episodes of 'sharing'. Instead, disclosure was tacit and partial in nature and informed by a number of beliefs, which meant that those who were believed to be at risk did not necessarily correspond with the biomedical model. Thus, even though these women, their sons and their brothers will inherit the condition to some extent, the focus of their concern remained the next generation of women within their kin.

The experiences of this extended family demonstrate how these practices of surveillance were embedded in the everyday realities of everyday practical kinship. These practices were enrolled to help define, limit and draw boundaries around their family, and this was part of a wider need to control the flow of this risk information, not only in terms of who was informed, but also in terms of managing responses to this knowledge. Members of this extended kin all expressed extremely high levels of anxiety in recounting the dilemmas they faced, not only in disclosing such information, but also in managing the future (Arribas-Ayllon et al. 2011).

The dominant focus for social scientists, clinical geneticists and bioethicists has been the examination of the retrospective experiences and deliberations of individuals who attend specialist clinical services, and within the context of a clinical model of disclosure of risk information via discrete packages of information. However, as this kindred exemplifies, genetic knowledge is embedded in pre-existing family relationships (Featherstone et al. 2006; Geelen et al. 2011) and in the everyday frameworks of family life (Chiliback et al. 2011). Few studies have recognized the importance of examining these phenomena as social processes rather than decision-making moments (Atkinson et al. 2013). The significance of this will only increase as the field of genetics and genomics extends its gaze to include the identification of the genetic factors associated with a wide spectrum of common multifactorial conditions (cf. Arribas-Ayllon et al. 2010).

NOTES

* Orcid reference: orcid.org/0000-0003-4999-8425.
1. 'Kindred' can be defined as a 'social group or category consisting of an individual's circle of relatives, or that range of a person's relatives accorded special cultural recognition' (Keesing 1975, p. 150).

REFERENCES

Armstrong, D., S. Michie and T. Marteau (1998), 'Revealed identity: a study of the process of genetic counselling', *Social Science and Medicine*, 47 (11), 1653–1658.

Arribas-Ayllon, M., A. Bartlett and K. Featherstone (2010), 'Complexity and accountability: the witches' brew of psychiatric genetics', *Social Studies of Science*, August, 40 (4), 499–524.

Arribas-Ayllon, M., K. Featherstone and P. Atkinson (2011), 'The practical ethics of genetic responsibility: non-disclosure and the autonomy of affect', *Social Theory and Health*, 9 (1), 3–23.

Arribas-Ayllon, M., S. Sarangi and A. Clarke (2008a), 'Managing self-responsibility through other-oriented blame: family accounts of genetic testing', *Social Science and Medicine*, 66 (7), 1521–1532.

Arribas-Ayllon, M., S. Sarangi and A. Clarke (2008b), 'The micropolitics of responsibility vis-à-vis autonomy: parental accounts of childhood genetic testing and (non)disclosure', *Sociology of Health and Illness*, 30 (2), 255–271.

Atkinson, P., K. Featherstone and M. Gregory (2013), 'Kinscapes, genescapes and timescapes: families living with genetic risk', *Sociology of Health and Illness*, 35 (8), 1227–1241.

Bonaccorso, M. (2007), *Conceiving Kinship: Procreation, Family and Assisted Conception in South Europe*, Oxford: Berghahn Books.

Carsten, J. (2000), 'Introduction: cultures of relatedness', in J. Carsten (ed.), *Cultures of Relatedness: New Approaches to the Study of Kinship*, Cambridge: Cambridge University Press, pp. 1–36.

Carsten, J. (2004), *After Kinship*, Cambridge: Cambridge University Press.

Chiliback, G., M. Lock and M. Sehdev (2011), 'Postgenomics, uncertain futures, and the familiarization of susceptibility genes', *Social Science and Medicine*, 72 (11), 1768–1775.

Edwards, J. (2000), *Born and Bred: Idioms of Kinship and New Reproductive Technologies in England*, Oxford: Oxford University Press.

Edwards, J. and C. Salazar (eds) (2008), *European Kinship in the Age of Biotechnology*, Oxford: Berghahn Books.

Featherstone, K., P. Atkinson, A. Bharadwaj and A. Clarke (2006), *Risky Relations: Family, Kinship and the New Genetics*, Oxford: Berg.

Franklin, S. (1993), 'Essentialism, which essentialism? Some implications of reproductive and genetic techno-science', *Journal of Homosexuality*, 24 (3–4), 27–40.

Franklin, S. (1997), *Embodied Progress: A Cultural Account of Assisted Conception*, London: Routledge.

Franklin, S. (2003), 'Rethinking nature/culture: anthropology and the new genetics', *Anthropological Theory*, 3 (1), 65–86.

Geelen, E., I. Van Hoyweghen and K. Horstman (2011), 'Making genetics not so important: family work in dealing with familial hypertrophic cardiomyopathy', *Social Science and Medicine*, 72 (11), 1752–1759.

Goodwin, A. (1992), 'Determination of legal parentage in egg donation, embryo transplantation, and gestational surrogacy arrangements', *Family Law Quarterly*, 26, 275.

Gregory, M., P. Boddington, R. Dimond, P. Atkinson, A. Clarke and P. Collins

(2007), 'Communicating about haemophilia: the importance of context and of experience', *Haemophilia*, 13 (2), 189–198.

Haimes, E. (1998), 'The making of "the DI child": changing representations of people conceived through donor insemination', in K. Daniels and E. Haimes (eds), *Donor Insemination: International Social Science Perspectives*, Cambridge: Cambridge University Press, pp. 53–75.

Haimes, E. and K. Weiner (2000), '"Everybody's got a dad . . .": issues for lesbian families in the management of donor insemination', *Sociology of Health and Illness*, 22 (4), 477–499.

Hallowell, N. (1999), 'Doing the right thing: genetic risk and responsibility', *Sociology of Health and Illness*, 21 (5), 597–621.

Hallowell, N., C. Foster, R. Eeles, A. Ardern-Jones, V. Murday and M. Watson (2003), 'Balancing autonomy and responsibility: the ethics of generating and disclosing genetic information', *Journal of Medical Ethics*, 29 (2), 74–83.

Howell, S. (2007), *The Kinning of Foreigners: Transnational Adoption in a Global Perspective*, Oxford: Berghahn Books.

Inhorn, M.C. and D. Birenbaum-Carmeli (2008), 'Assisted reproductive technologies and culture change', *Annual Review of Anthropology*, 37, 177–196.

Keesing, R. (1975), *Kin Groups and Social Structure*, New York: Holt, Rinehart & Winston.

Levine, N.E. (2008), 'Alternative kinship, marriage, and reproduction', *Annual Review of Anthropology*, 37, 375–389.

New, J.G. (2006), '"Aren't you lucky you have two mamas?": redefining parenthood in light of evolving reproductive technologies and social change', *Chicago-Kent Law Review*, 81, 773.

Novas, C. and N. Rose (2000), 'Genetic risk and the birth of the somatic individual', *Economy and Society*, 29 (4), 485–513.

Richards, M.P.M. (1999), 'Genetic counselling for those with a family history of breast or ovarian cancer: current practice and ethical issues', *Acta Oncologica*, 38, 559–565.

Rose, N. (2006), *The Politics of Life Itself: Biomedicine, Power, and Subjectivity in the Twenty-First Century*, Princeton, NJ: Princeton University Press.

Sarangi, S. and A. Clarke (2002a), 'Zones of expertise and the management of uncertainty in genetics risk communication', *Research on Language and Social Interaction*, 35, 139–171.

Sarangi, S and A. Clarke (2002b), 'Constructing an account by contrast in counselling for childhood genetic testing', *Social Science and Medicine*, 54, 295–308.

Sarangi, S., A. Clarke, K. Bennert and L. Howell (2003), 'Categorisation practices across professional boundaries: some analytic insights from genetic counselling', in S. Sarangi and T. van Leeuwen (eds), *Applied Linguistics and Communities of Practice*, London: Continuum, pp. 150–168.

Sivell, S., G. Elwyn, C.L. Gaff, A.J. Clarke, R. Iredale, C. Shaw, J. Dundon, H. Thornton and A. Edwards (2008), 'How risk is perceived, constructed and interpreted by clients in clinical genetics, and the effects on decision making: systematic review', *Journal of Genetic Counseling*, 17 (1), 30–63.

Sobel, S. and D.B. Cowan (2000), 'Impact of genetic testing for Huntington disease on the family system', *American Journal of Medical Genetics*, 90 (1), 49–59.

Strathern, M. (1992a), *Reproducing the Future: Essays on Anthropology, Kinship and the New Reproductive Technologies*, Manchester: Manchester University Press.

Strathern, M. (1992b), *After Nature: English Kinship in the Late Twentieth Century*, Cambridge: Cambridge University Press.

Strathern, M. (2005), *Kinship, Law and the Unexpected: Relatives Are Always a Surprise*, Cambridge: Cambridge University Press.

Zerubavel, E. (2006), *The Elephant in the Room: Silence and Denial in Everyday Life*, Oxford: Oxford University Press.

7. The educational gradient of maternal employment patterns in 11 European countries

David De Wachter, Karel Neels, Jonas Wood and Jorik Vergauwen

INTRODUCTION

Over the last two decades the share of mothers returning to work after childbirth has increased rapidly in Europe (OECD 2011). Nevertheless, the presence of a young child still acts as a barrier to female employment. Most women temporarily retreat from the labour market after childbirth or cut back on working hours. When the children get older, most women take up work again and/or increase working hours (Neels and Theunynck 2012; Stier and Lewin-Epstein 2001; Uunk et al. 2005; Van Lancker and Ghysels 2010). The share of mothers in employment varies considerably between countries (Eurostat 2011; OECD 2007). Scholars have attributed this variation to cross-national differences in family policy (OECD 2011), family culture (Jappens and Van Bavel 2013; Van Lancker and Ghysels 2010) and heterogeneity in the socio-economic composition of the population (Uunk et al. 2005). Few demographic studies have focused on educational variation in the effect of childbirth on maternal employment (De Wachter and Neels 2011) and how this varies among European countries (Neels and Theunynck 2012). Most scholars implicitly assume that childbirth affects maternal employment to the same extent in all educational groups (Pettit and Hook 2005). This assumption may not be valid. First, the opportunity costs of leaving the labour force vary greatly between educational groups (Becker 1981; Mincer 1963). Second, there is evidence of a strong educational gradient in the uptake of family policy, particularly regarding the use of formal childcare (De Wachter and Neels 2011; Ghysels and Van Lancker 2011; Neels and Theunynck 2012; OECD 2007). Third, educational groups have different opinions as to whether it is appropriate for a mother to combine the care for a small child with paid employment (Kalmijn 2003; Neels and Theunynck 2012). These factors are likely also relevant for explaining educational differences in the choice between part-time and full-time work among women who decide to remain active on the labour market after childbirth. Differential labour market outcomes among working mothers is another topic that has not drawn much attention in the demographic literature, as most research efforts have gone to explaining whether or not women remain active in the labour force (Neels and Theunynck 2012; Pettit and Hook 2005).

This chapter re-examines maternal employment patterns in 11 European countries. We further investigate whether cross-national differences in childcare use can explain country variation in maternal employment. The chapter adds to the literature by looking at educational differentials in maternal employment patterns and selective entry into part-time and full-time employment. It also contributes to policy research by analysing the association between maternal employment and both formal and informal childcare. So far, the majority of studies have only considered the association with formal childcare, whereas the association with informal childcare has rarely been studied. We apply multilevel multinomial regression analysis to micro-data from the first round of the Generations and Gender Survey, which is supplemented with contextual information on use of formal and informal childcare from the European Union Statistics on Income and Living Conditions (EU-SILC) (Eurostat 2015). The results indicate that cross-national differences in female employment are smaller among childless women than among women who have a child. The number of children and particularly the age of the youngest child in the household are strongly associated with maternal employment, but the size and the sign of the association are different for full-time and part-time work. The association further varies between educational groups and also between countries. Cross-national differences in maternal employment are partially explained by country differences in childcare use. Cross-national variation in formal childcare is more strongly associated with maternal employment than cross-national variation in informal childcare. Finally, both formal and informal childcare are positively associated with full-time and part-time employment in all educational groups, with the size of the association being more articulated among highly educated women.

EDUCATIONAL DIFFERENTIALS IN MATERNAL EMPLOYMENT

During the 1950s and 1960s women in Western countries had few possibilities to combine the roles of mother and worker (Brewster and Rindfuss 2000; Liefbroer and Corijn 1999). The incompatibility was reduced when

European governments started supporting women in the combination of work and family, for instance by providing publicly funded childcare and by offering parents the possibility to take up parental leave (Brewster and Rindfuss 2000; Thévenon 2011). Other measures that contributed to an increase in maternal employment were the introduction of flexible work arrangements such as part-time work (Plantenga and Remery 2010). Gender role systems also became more permissive vis-à-vis mothers in paid employment, although some social stigma remained about mothers who combine the care for a small child with full-time employment (O'Reilly et al. 2013). The overall outcomes of these developments were that women were less inclined to leave the labour force after childbirth, and that they came back at increasingly shorter intervals (OECD 2011). Maternal employment was not only seen as a way to sustain household income and to fulfil increasing consumption aspirations, but it was also seen by the European Union as a means to combat poverty and to achieve sustained economic growth (Elborgh-Woytek et al. 2013; European Commission 2011; OECD 2007; Tomlinson et al. 2009).

Despite the fact that many of the barriers of maternal employment have been lifted or lowered, studies have shown that the transition to a dual earner family has not been uniform across socio-economic groups and is marked by a strong educational gradient (Cantillon et al. 2001; Evertsson et al. 2009; Van Lancker and Ghysels 2013). Not only are low-educated women less likely to enter a career track than more highly educated women, differences between educational groups become particularly pronounced after women have made the transition into parenthood (Gutiérrez-Domènech 2005). Mothers with low education levels are much more likely to exit the labour force after childbirth and/or to reduce their working hours (De Wachter and Neels 2011; Neels and Theunynck 2012). In the literature the lower maternal employment rates of low-educated women have been related to lower financial incentives to remain active in the labour market after childbirth, more traditional gender roles, less frequent use of childcare, and selection into part-time jobs with lower career prospects. These factors furthermore show considerable variation between countries (OECD 2011).

Micro-Level Explanations

Research on the employment–fertility nexus has been dominated by Becker's new home economics. It predicts that highly educated women are less likely to withdraw from the labour market after childbirth because they have invested more in the acquisition of human capital and the development of a career (Becker 1981). Highly educated women time the arrival of a child so that it has a minimal impact on their future career (Gustafsson 2001; Kreyenfeld 2010; Liefbroer and Corijn 1999). They will go back to work soon after having taken maternity leave because a pro-longed absence from the labour market entails a depreciation of job skills, missed promotions, slower career advancement and reductions in lifetime earnings (Dex and Joshi 1999; Muresan and Hoem 2010; Tomlinson et al. 2009). Furthermore, employers may interpret an extended absence from the labour force as a sign of lower work commitment (Corell et al. 2007; OECD 2011). For these reasons, highly educated women will also be less inclined to take full advantage of maternity and parental leaves (Gustafsson 2001; OECD 2011). Their stronger connection to the labour market also results from the fact that they receive higher financial returns from their labour supply (Becker 1981; OECD 2013). Higher wages and income enables them to substitute time spent on parental obligations with paid alternatives such as formal childcare or home help (Dex and Joshi 1999; Macunovich 1996).

For women with lower education levels the opportunity costs of leaving the labour force after childbirth are lower because they have less favourable career prospects. Jobs of low-educated women are often less interesting, lower paid and characterized by less favourable working conditions, irreg-ular working hours, weekend work, and so on (OECD 2013). The lower remuneration they receive for their labour also gives them fewer possibili-ties to pay for formal childcare, even though public childcare support in most countries favours low-income groups (OECD 2011). Consequently, if the income difference between remaining active or withdrawing from the labour market is small, low-educated women will be less inclined to keep working after childbirth (Buchholz et al. 2009). Continued female employment raises family income, which implies that some low-income households will no longer be able to qualify for certain welfare benefits. In these households it may thus be more economically advantageous for women to be unemployed than to work (OECD 2007). Scholars further suggest that women who have few prospects of reducing uncertainty in life through career building, and who are confronted with higher risks of long-term exclusion from the labour market, may choose the alternative career of motherhood (European Commission 2011; Friedman et al. 1994; Meron and Widmer 2002; Vikat 2004). They will also be more inclined to make full use of maternity and parental leaves and less likely to return to the labour market afterwards (Neyer 2005). Finally, maternal employment among low-educated groups is discouraged by an increased risk of in-work poverty: being poor while being employed (OECD 2011).

Microeconomic theory only provides a partial explanation for edu-cational variation in maternal employment. Studies suggest that lower

employment rates among low-educated women are also due to more conservative attitudes regarding the combination of work and family. Using
data from the Generations and Gender Survey, Neels and Theunynck
(2012) show that the share of women agreeing with the proposition that
female labour force participation is harmful for a pre-school child is much
lower among highly educated groups than among low-educated groups.
The study also shows considerable variation between countries: women
in Scandinavian countries are much less inclined to accept this proposition than women in Continental and particularly Eastern and Central
European countries. The finding of more positive attitudes towards maternal employment among highly educated groups is in line with the results
of previous research (e.g. Kalmijn 2003; Konietzka and Kreyenfeld 2010;
Scott 1999). A second explanation for lower employment rates among
low-educated mothers is that they (and their partners) are more likely to
approve a traditional division of household and labour tasks (Crompton
and Lyonette 2005; Marks et al. 2009). This is further amplified after
they have made the transition into marriage and parenthood (Dribe and
Stanfors 2009). Highly educated women, however, are more likely to form
partnerships with highly educated men (Domański and Przybysz 2007).
The latter have been shown to hold more progressive attitudes towards
their partners' employment than low-educated men, and they are also
more prepared to do their share of the household work and care responsibilities (Poortman and van der Lippe 2009).

Family Policies

The increase in maternal employment is closely intertwined with the emergence of family policies. Since the 1970s, European countries have set up
governmental programmes to support women in the combination of work
and family (Esping-Andersen 2009; Gauthier 2002). These programmes
have multiple objectives: to increase fertility, sustain female employment
and promote gender equality (Luci and Thévenon 2012; Thévenon 2011).
Families with children receive direct support through cash benefits (for
example, family and child allowances) and indirect support through work-
related measures (for example, childcare and parental leave) and tax breaks
(Gauthier 2007; OECD 2011). Public spending on childcare services in
particular has increased significantly since the mid-1990s (Jensen 2009;
OECD 2011) since it is regarded as a crucial precondition for sustained
maternal employment (Castles 2003; Matysiak and Steinmetz 2008).
    The design and objectives of family policies vary greatly among
European countries (Thévenon 2011). This is because family policies are
deeply embedded in family culture (Billari 2004; Esping-Andersen 2009;

Fux 2008; Mayer 2001). Family policies in Scandinavian countries aim at supporting the individual in achieving a work–life balance (Crompton and Lyonette 2006). These policies are also directed towards egalitarian gender roles inside and outside the labour force (Duvander et al. 2010). Maternal employment is supported through the provision of quality, affordable and widely available public childcare (Datta Gupta et al. 2008). Moreover, Norwegian policies have also indirectly supported maternal employment by granting access to welfare state provisions based on work experience before parenthood (Lappegård and Rønsen 2005). Family policies in continental European countries aim to support the family rather than the individual, although there is large variation between countries (e.g. Thévenon 2011). Policies in Belgium and France have more followed the Scandinavian model, in the sense that they have invested strongly in public childcare and parental leave (Klüsener et al. 2013; Neyer 2005). On the other hand, policies in Germany and Austria have favoured the male breadwinner model (Gottfried and O'Reilly 2002; Klüsener et al. 2013). Although recent reforms have brought family policies in German-speaking countries more in line with the Scandinavian model (Rindfuss et al. 2010), there is still a lack of public childcare, particularly for children under the age of three (Andersson et al. 2009; Del Boca 2015; Hoem et al. 2001). In Southern European countries, family policies developed later than in other parts of Europe and are characterized by relatively limited public childcare support for women with young children (Baizan 2009; Del Boca 2002). In these countries, women frequently rely on informal networks, such as childcare provided by grandparents (Jappens and Van Bavel 2013). Before the dissolution of the Soviet Union, Central and Eastern European countries combined high fertility with high female employment due to strong state support for working mothers (Frejka 2008). The transition to a market economy, however, went together with rising economic uncertainty and financial cutbacks in family policy. The funding of public childcare services in particular was considerably reduced (Aassve et al. 2006; Frejka 2008; Szelewa and Polakowski 2008). Unlike Southern European countries the lack of public support is not compensated by informal childcare use (Neels and Theunynck 2012).

The expansion of family policies in Europe has not benefited all women to the same extent (Gauthier 2007; Neyer and Andersson 2008; Van Lancker and Ghysels 2010, 2013). Part of the variation in maternal employment rates between educational groups is due to differential take-up of family policies. Research shows that highly educated women are more likely to use formal (and informal) childcare than low-educated women and that they are also more likely to take parental leave (De Wachter and Neels 2011; Lapuerta et al. 2011; Neels and Theunynck 2012). On the one hand, educational differentials arise because highly educated women have more need for these amenities. On the other hand, highly educated women are also better informed on how to make use of them (Storms 1995; Van Lancker and Ghysels 2013). Consequently, educational differentials in use of childcare and (in taking) parental leave have also been found when analyses are restricted to women who are working (Ghysels and Van Lancker 2009). In contrast to childcare, there is more ambiguity about the utility of parental leave to sustain maternal employment (Thévenon 2011; Thévenon and Solaz 2013). This is the case, for instance, in countries where parental leave payments have a fixed rate, such as in France, Belgium and Austria (OECD 2011). This lowers the incentives for highly educated women to take parental leave for longer periods because it raises opportunity costs, and also because they can rely on paid childcare (McDonald 2006; Thévenon and Solaz 2013). Fixed-rate benefits, on the other hand, encourage longer leave among women with lower incomes. The overall outcome is that more highly educated women are more likely to take up parental leave than low-educated women, whereas the latter are more likely to stay on leave for extended periods (OECD 2011).

In all European countries, women with lower educational levels are less likely to make use of childcare and parental leave, but the size of the educational gradient varies between countries. Policies in Scandinavian countries have generally been more successful in targeting different social strata, resulting in lower educational differentials (Eeckhaut et al. 2014; Evertsson et al. 2009). Of the Continental countries, France, Belgium and Germany are characterized by uneven usage, whereas differentials are smaller in Austria (Ghysels and Van Lancker 2011; Neels and Theunynck 2012). In Eastern Europe, educational differentials are generally lower, but so is the availability of public childcare (Ghysels and Van Lancker 2011). In general, educational variation in maternal employment is lowest in countries with weak support for families with children (Fondazione G. Brodolini 2006).

Part-Time Work

The increase in maternal employment is to an important extent driven by more frequent part-time work (Fondazione G. Brodolini 2006). When part-time work emerged during the 1970s it was seen as a way for mothers to take care of family and children while maintaining a link with the labour market (Bernhardt 1986; Hakim 2003; Joshi et al. 1996). Part-time work forms part of an increasing range of flexible work schemes and it is by far the most prevalent (Vere 2007). Contrary to popular belief, part-time work arose from the demand of employers for a more flexible workforce. The question of whether part-time work could improve the work–life balance among women was of secondary importance (OECD 2011; Tomlinson 2007; Vere 2007). Many researchers have pointed to the duality surrounding part-time work. On the one hand, part-time work gives women the opportunity to ease the role incompatibility between motherhood and employment. On the other hand, part-time work has been associated with lower wages, less job protection, limited opportunities for career advancement, fewer employment benefits and lower positions in the labour market (Blossfeld and Hakim 1997; European Commission 2011; Vere 2007; Wright and Hinde 1991). Even though progress has been made in the equal treatment of part-time and full-time workers (OECD 2011), part-time work often entails a secondary position on the labour market and has also been criticized for reinforcing gender roles (Begall and Mills 2011; Fondazione G. Brodolini 2006; OECD 2012). Some authors therefore argue that full-time work is a better indicator of gender equality than the share of women in employment (Konietzka and Kreyenfeld 2010).

Even though there is some debate as to whether the choice for part-time work is a coping strategy to balance household and market work or an adaptive strategy that is more in line with the preference of women for both activities (Rose 2001; Wierda-Boer et al. 2008), the evidence suggests that the majority of women in part-time employment have voluntarily chosen this position and are happy with it (Begall and Mills 2011; OECD 2011). Using data for the United Kingdom, Connolly and Gregory (2010) show that for some women, part-time work is a temporary position until they return to full-time work, whereas for others part-time work is a more permanent position that is often alternated with spells of unemployment. Educational attainment is a likely factor determining whether women see part-time work as temporary or more permanent. Given that highly educated mothers have high career aspirations (Kreyenfeld 2010), it is unlikely that they will consider part-time work an attractive (long-term) career path. Consequently, they will be more inclined to take up full-time work again shortly after childbirth (De Wachter and Neels 2011). Low-educated women, on the other hand, disproportionally find themselves in part-time work after childbirth and are more likely to end up in inactivity (De Wachter and Neels 2011; Neels and Theunynck 2012). As such, part-time work among more vulnerable groups does not allow them to remain attached to the labour market (OECD 2011). A partial explanation is that low-educated women more frequently have temporary contracts (European Commission 2011; OECD 2002). Compared to highly educated women in part-time employment they also have less control over the timing and scheduling of their work (Vere 2007). As such, part-time work among low-educated women thus may not always improve work–life compatibility.

Although women in most European countries have statutory rights to apply for part-time work (OECD 2011), estimates show that there are considerable cross-national differences in the share of women working part-time. Part-time work is popular in the Netherlands, Belgium, Denmark, Germany, Austria, the United Kingdom, Ireland, Sweden and Norway (OECD 2007, 2011). On the other hand, part-time employment rates are very low in Eastern and Southern Europe (Del Boca 2002; OECD 2011). In Southern European countries the lack of part-time work opportunities has not only been related to lower female employment, but also to sustained levels of below-replacement fertility (Del Boca 2002). But even in countries where part-time work is common, there are substantial cross-national differences regarding the implications for further career development (Tomlinson et al. 2009). In liberal welfare regimes such as the United Kingdom, part-time work is often a dead-end street, offering limited career prospects. In social democratic welfare regimes such as Sweden, qualitative differences between part-time work and full-time work are lower and mothers are encouraged to return to full-time work. In conservative welfare regimes such as Germany, part-time work reinforces the gendered division of labour and thus indirectly sustains the male breadwinner model (Stier and Lewin-Epstein 2001).

AIM OF THE CHAPTER AND RESEARCH HYPOTHESES

This chapter investigates the educational gradient of full-time and part-time employment among mothers in 11 European countries. We test the following research hypotheses:

Hypothesis 1: We expect important country variation in maternal employment patterns for highly educated women, since countries differ strongly in the opportunities for women to combine work and family. We expect maternal employment to be higher in Scandinavian countries and continental European countries such as France and Belgium, which have invested heavily in family policies (H1A). We expect country variation to be smaller for low-educated women, given that their labour force participation is less likely to be dependent on the availability of public childcare or the possibility of taking parental leave (H1B).

Hypothesis 2: Women with children are expected to be more frequently full-time employed in countries where social policies support women in the combination of work and family (H2A). Although educational differentials in the selection into full-time and part-time work are expected to be smaller in these countries, highly educated women are expected to disproportionally choose full-time work, whereas low-educated women are expected to more frequently choose part-time work or to become unemployed or inactive (H2B).

Hypothesis 3: Cross-national variation in maternal employment is expected to become smaller if we control for cross-national variation in the use of formal and informal childcare (H3A). We expect the reduction in the cross-national variation to be more pronounced among highly educated women since they are more likely to be confronted with the work–family conflict (H3B).

DATA

The analyses make use of data from the first round of the Generations and Gender Survey (GGS).[1] The GGS is an initiative aimed at comparative research about demographic changes in Europe. A focal point is how micro- and macro-level variables affect individual behaviour in various domains such as household and union formation, labour market participation, relations between partners and relations between parents and children. The comparative nature of the GGS is expressed by the GGS contextual database which holds country-specific information on characteristics of the overall labour market, demographics and social policy. In comparison with other surveys, the GGS benefits from a relatively large sample size with a target sample of about 10 000 individuals per country. Currently first round data are available for 16 countries: Australia, Austria, Belgium, Bulgaria, Estonia, France, Georgia, Germany, Hungary, Italy, Lithuania, the Netherlands, Norway, Poland, Romania and the Russian Federation. Data collection occurred between 2002 and 2008 among individuals aged 18–79. The aim of the GGS is to set up a longitudinal research design, but currently second round data are only available for seven countries.

Selection of Countries

In this chapter we limit the analyses to 11 European countries, excluding those with missing or insufficiently detailed information on household composition and activity status. Estonia is excluded from the analyses since household members aged under 15 are merged into one age group, making it impossible to identify households with (very) young children. Poland is not retained in the analyses, since no distinction can be made between full-time and part-time employment. Finally, Russia and Georgia are also excluded because there is no information available in the EU-SILC database about the use of formal and informal childcare.[2]

Research Population

The research population consists of women aged 20–49 at the time of the survey. This age range delineates the 'busy years' where women will complete their education, leave the parental home, form partnerships, have children and get established in the labour market. We set the upper age limit at 49 so that our sample is less likely to contain women who retire early and are no longer on the job market (Neels and Theunynck 2012). We further limit the sample to women who have completed their education, since educational enrolment is strongly negatively correlated with household formation and labour force participation (e.g. Blossfeld and Huinink 1991; Lappegård and Rønsen 2005).

Variables

Micro-level variables

The dependent variable is activity status that is based on the self-assessment of individuals. We identify three categories: (1) full-time employment; (2) part-time employment; (3) and unemployed or inactive. The last category will be the reference category throughout the analyses. The independent variables are the age of the respondent, level of education, partnership status, number of children in the household and age of the youngest child in the household. Age is operationalized as a second-order polynomial to allow for a non-linear association with activity status. Level of education is divided into three categories based on the International Standard Classification of Education (ISCED) classification: (1) low education (at most lower secondary education); (2) medium education (secondary education); and (3) high education (short or long-term tertiary education). Partnership status has two categories: (1) cohabiting with a partner; and (2) not cohabiting with a partner. Number of children in the household and age of the youngest child in the household[3] are operationalized as a combination variable with five categories: (1) no children residing in the household; (2) one or two children residing in the household with the youngest child being less than 3 years old; (3) one or two children residing in the household with the age of the youngest child aged between 3 and 5; (4) one or two children residing in the household with the youngest child being at least 6 years old; and (5) three or more children in the household irrespective of the age of the youngest child.[4]

Macro-level variables

We also include country-specific information on the use of formal and informal childcare. Formal childcare is operationalized as the percentage of children less than three years old who are enrolled in formal childcare. Informal childcare is operationalized as the percentage of children less than three years old who use other types of care than formal childcare arrangements. Both variables are drawn from the EU-SILC[5] (Eurostat 2015). For Germany, France, Norway, Austria, Belgium and Lithuania the reference year for the variables relating to childcare corresponds to the year in which the majority of the GGS surveys were conducted in the respective country. For Germany and France the reference year is 2005, for Lithuania it is 2006, for Norway it is 2007, and for Belgium and Austria it is 2008. For the remaining countries, the reference year for the variables relating to childcare lies as close as possible to the year in which the survey was conducted. For Bulgaria the reference year for the variables about childcare is 2006, whereas the survey was conducted in 2004. For Hungary the reference year is 2005, whereas the survey was conducted in 2004 For Italy and the Netherlands the reference year is 2005, whereas the surveys were conducted in 2003. Finally, for Romania the reference year is 2007, whereas the survey was conducted in 2005.

METHODS

We use a two-level multinomial logit model to estimate the probability of full-time and part-time employment for an individual woman i living in country j. Because we only have a small number of countries we used Markov chain Monte Carlo (MCMC) estimation methods instead of maximum likelihood-based estimation methods (Browne 2012). For a response variable with three categories the multilevel multinomial model has two equations. On the one hand it contrasts the log-odds of full-time employment (superscript [1] in the equation below) against the log-odds of being unemployed or inactive (superscript [3]). On the other hand it contrasts the log-odds of part-time employment (superscript [2]) against the log-odds of being unemployed or inactive. We allow only the coefficients of the variable number of children and age of the youngest child in the household to vary between countries. Because it was not possible to estimate the unstructured variance–covariance matrix, we estimated only the variances of the intercepts and the variances of the categories of the combination variable number of children and age of the youngest child in the household (that is, the diagonal values of the variance–covariance matrix below). All the covariances in the matrix are assumed to be zero.[6]

We further stratified the model by level of education (De Wachter and Neels 2011; McDonald 2013; Neels and De Wachter 2010). As such, the model is defined for each educational group:[7]

$Log(odds^{(1)}/odds^{(3)}) = B_{0j} + B_1age_{ij} + B_2age^2_{ij} + B_3partner_{ij} + B_{4j}onetwokid\_le2_{ij} + B_{5j}onetwokid\_ge3le5_{ij} + B_{6j}onetwokid\_ge3le5_{ij} + B_{7j}threekid_{ij} + B_8formal\_le2_j + B_9informal\_le2_j$

$Log(odds^{(2)}/odds^{(3)}) = B_{10j} + B_{11}age_{ij} + B_{12}age^2_{ij} + B_{13}partner_{ij} + B_{14j}onetwokid\_le2_{ij} + B_{15j}onetwokid\_ge3le5_{ij} + B_{16j}onetwokid\_ge3le5_{ij} + B_{17j}threekid_{ij} + B_{18}formal\_le2_j + B_{19}informal\_le2_j$

$$B_{0j} = B_0 + v_{0j} \qquad\qquad B_{10j} = B_{10} + v_{10j}$$

$$B_{4j} = B_4 + v_{4j} \qquad\qquad B_{14j} = B_{14} + v_{14j}$$

$$B_{5j} = B_5 + v_{5j} \qquad\qquad B_{15j} = B_{15} + v_{15j}$$

$$B_{6j} = B_6 + v_{6j} \qquad\qquad B_{16j} = B_{16} + v_{16j}$$

$$B_{7j} = B_7 + v_{7j} \qquad\qquad B_{17j} = B_{17} + v_{17j}$$

$$
\begin{pmatrix} v_{0j} \\ v_{4j} \\ v_{5j} \\ v_{6j} \\ v_{7j} \\ v_{10j} \\ v_{14j} \\ v_{15j} \\ v_{16j} \\ v_{17j} \end{pmatrix} \sim N \left\{ \begin{pmatrix} 0 \\ 0 \\ 0 \\ 0 \\ 0 \\ 0 \\ 0 \\ 0 \\ 0 \\ 0 \end{pmatrix}, \begin{pmatrix} \sigma^2_{v\,0} \\ 0 & \sigma^2_{v\,4} \\ 0 & 0 & \sigma^2_{v\,5} \\ 0 & 0 & 0 & \sigma^2_{v\,6} \\ 0 & 0 & 0 & 0 & \sigma^2_{v\,7} \\ 0 & 0 & 0 & 0 & 0 & \sigma^2_{v\,10} \\ 0 & 0 & 0 & 0 & 0 & 0 & \sigma^2_{v\,14} \\ 0 & 0 & 0 & 0 & 0 & 0 & 0 & \sigma^2_{v\,15} \\ 0 & 0 & 0 & 0 & 0 & 0 & 0 & 0 & \sigma^2_{v\,16} \\ 0 & 0 & 0 & 0 & 0 & 0 & 0 & 0 & 0 & \sigma^2_{v\,17} \end{pmatrix} \right\}
$$

RESULTS

The results section consists of three subsections. First, we analyse the cross-national variation in female employment patterns. Second, we discuss the results of the multivariate analyses where we estimate the association between age, level of education, partnership status, the number of children and the age of the youngest child in the household, and full-time and part-time employment. Third, we check whether cross-national differences in the use of formal and informal childcare can explain cross-national differences in activity status.

Between-Country Variation in Female Employment Patterns

We start the analyses with a two-level variance components model with no predictor variables (that is, a null model). In this model we only allow the intercepts to vary between countries. We estimated separate null models for each educational group and for each category of the combination variable representing the number of children in the household and the age of the youngest child in the household. Figures 7.1 and 7.2 display the best linear unbiased predictors of the random country effects (BLUPs or empirical Bayes estimates) for full-time and part-time employment. For each null model, the BLUPs give an indication of the deviation of the average employment rate in a particular country relative to the employment rate in the 'average European country': in our case, the deviation of the mean employment rate in one country vis-à-vis the estimate of the grand mean over the 11 countries in the dataset. The average European country in the graphs is depicted at the value of zero on the vertical axis. The graphs reveal important cross-national variation in activity status with the variation being higher for part-time employment than for full-time employment.

By level of education
Considering cross-national variation in female employment by level of education (Figure 7.1), the results show that women living in Germany, Austria and the Netherlands are less likely to work full-time than women in other countries (particularly among highly and medium-educated women) and more likely to work part-time. Norway stands out as a country with high full-time and part-time employment rates among all educational groups and especially among low- and medium-educated women. France and Italy occupy an intermediate position with full-time and part-time employment rates, balancing around the European average. Women living in Belgium occupy an intermediate position with respect to full-time work, but lie at the higher end of the distribution for part-time work (particularly among highly educated groups). Finally, Central and Eastern European countries stand out as countries with more frequent full-time employment among medium-educated women and (to a lesser extent) highly educated

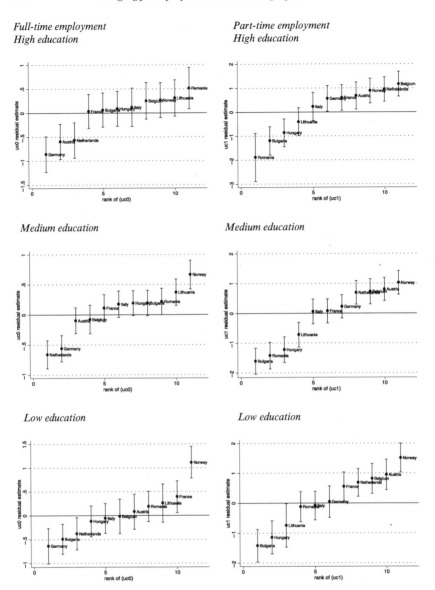

Source: GGS first round (Bulgaria, Germany, France, Italy, Netherlands, Romania, Norway, Austria, Belgium, Lithuania, Hungary). Calculations by authors.

Figure 7.1   *Best linear unbiased predictors of the random country effects (logit scale) for full-time and part-time employment, stratified by level of education*

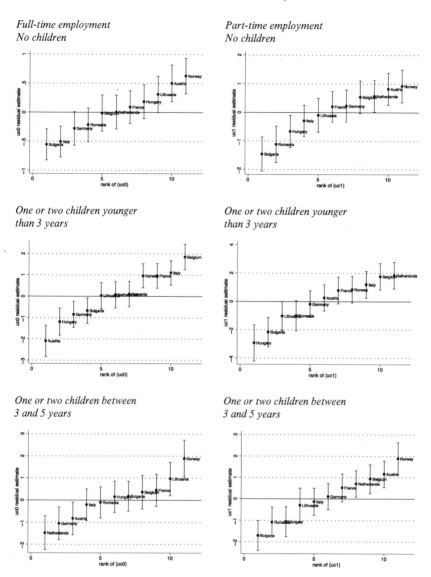

Source: GGS first round (Bulgaria, Germany, France, Italy, Netherlands, Romania, Norway, Austria, Belgium, Lithuania, Hungary). Calculations by authors.

Figure 7.2   *Best linear unbiased predictors of the random country effects (logit scale) for full-time and part-time employment, stratified by number of children and age of the youngest child in the household*

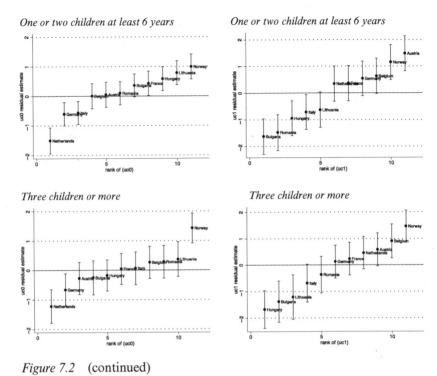

Figure 7.2   (continued)

women. Regardless of educational attainment, women living in these countries are the least likely to work part-time.

By number of children and age of the youngest child
Turning to the random country effects according to the number of children and the age of the youngest child in the household (Figure 7.2), an important finding is that the between-country variability in full-time and part-time employment is smaller among childless women than among mothers. It suggests that before the onset of childbearing the labour market outcomes of women are to a greater extent determined by individual-level characteristics (age, education, and so on) and to a lesser extent by overall characteristics of the labour market or family policy. Childless women in Norway and Austria report full-time employment rates significantly above the European average, whereas childless women in Bulgaria and Italy report rates below the European average. Country differentials are more pronounced with respect to part-time employment, with rates being highest in Norway, Austria and the Netherlands, and lowest in Bulgaria, Romania and Hungary.

Cross-national differences in female employment are clearly more pronounced in households where the youngest child is less than three years old. Women living in Belgium, Italy, France and Norway are more likely to remain full-time employed shortly after childbirth compared to women living in Hungary, Bulgaria and the German-speaking countries. Central and Eastern European countries are on the lower end of the distribution for part-time work, suggesting that women in these countries are more likely to work full-time than part-time if they remain active on the labour market. Germany and Austria occupy intermediate positions for part-time work, suggesting that women in these countries remain connected to the labour market but reduce their work hours when there are young children present in the household. Belgium and the Netherlands stand out with part-time employment rates that are clearly higher than in the other European countries.

In households where the youngest child is 3–5 years old, full-time employment rates are highest in Norway and Lithuania. Women living in France and Belgium now occupy an intermediate position, together with the Central and Eastern European countries. The German-speaking countries and the Netherlands record full-time employment rates significantly below the European average. Except for Germany, women in the latter group of countries are clearly more likely to work part-time compared to the average European mother.

In households where the youngest child is at least six years old, Norway, France and the Central and Eastern European countries record the highest full-time employment rates. Possible explanations for the return to full-time employment among women in Central and Eastern European countries is that part-time jobs are scarce or that it is necessary for the woman to revert back to full-time work in order to sustain household income (Neels and Theunynck 2012). Austria and Norway stand out as countries with very high proportions of part-time employment.

Finally, a similar pattern emerges for women with three or more children, but the distribution of the country effects is less clearly delineated (particularly for full-time employment). This is likely the result of the more heterogeneous composition of this group.

Multivariate Analysis: The Association between Age, Education, Partnership Status, Number and Age of Children, and Full-Time and Part-Time Employment

Fixed effects

In a subsequent step we add individual-level predictor variables to the null models. We stratify the models according to level of education in order to allow the coefficients of age, partnership status, number of children and age of the youngest child in the household to vary between educational groups. As indicated in the model specification we only model random coefficients for the combination variable number of children and age of the youngest child in the household, allowing the coefficient of this covariate to vary across countries. The estimates of the fixed effects of the multivariate model are presented in Table 7.1.

For both full-time and part-time employment, the coefficient of the first-order term of age is positive while the coefficient of the second-order term of age is negative, suggesting that the probability of full-time and part-time employment increases with age and that the rate of increase levels off as women get older. The association between partnership status and full-time employment varies by level of education. Among low-educated women there is no association between partnership status and full-time employment. Among women with medium and high levels of education a partner is associated with a lower probability of full-time employment but the association is only significant for women with medium levels of education. The finding that the presence of a partner is not negatively associated with full-time employment among low-educated women may indicate that female labour force participation in these households is necessary in order to sustain household income. Turning to the association between partnership status and part-time employment, the association is positive, significant and about the same size for all educational groups. The findings suggest that the male breadwinner model in Europe has not completely vanished: when a partner is present in the household, women are more likely to reduce their labour supply or decide to work part-time.

The number of children and the age of the youngest child in the household are strongly associated with female employment, but the size and the sign of the association varies for full-time and part-time work. As expected, the presence of children aged less than three is associated with a much lower probability of full-time work. The negative association is about the same size for all educational groups. The latter finding is important because it suggests that the combination of work and family is as likely an issue for low-educated women as it is for highly educated women. Furthermore, part-time employment is negatively associated with the presence of young children, which suggests that parenthood even decreases the likelihood of being part-time employed. As expected, the association between parenthood and part-time employment is less pronounced than for full-time employment, although it is still strongly negative and significant. The overall conclusion is that the presence of a young child in the household is negatively associated with female employment, even when it concerns part-time work.

In line with previous research, maternal employment rates are higher in

Table 7.1 Multilevel multinomial logit models of activity status (contrasts are full-time versus unemployed/inactive and part-time versus unemployed/inactive) by educational level, women aged 20–49

	Low education			Medium education			High education		
	Logit	s.e.	Sig.	Logit	s.e.	Sig.	Logit	s.e.	Sig.
Full-time work									
Constant	0.111	0.198		1.601	0.117	***	2.419	0.221	***
Age (1st order term)	0.011	0.004	**	0.012	0.003	***	0.025	0.006	***
Age (2nd order term)	-0.001	0.000	**	-0.002	0.000	***	-0.002	0.001	*
Has no partner	–	–	–	–	–	–	–	–	–
Has a partner	0.007	0.075	–	-0.137	0.048	**	-0.093	0.084	–
No children	–	–	–	–	–	–	–	–	–
1 or 2 children, youngest <3 yrs	-1.896	0.254	***	-2.806	0.509	***	-2.240	0.409	***
1 or 2 children, youngest 3–5 yrs	-0.675	0.202	**	-1.033	0.333	**	-0.828	0.284	**
1 or 2 children, youngest >5 yrs	-0.342	0.167	*	-0.686	0.209	***	-0.467	0.286	*
3 children or more	-1.325	0.199	***	-1.937	0.266	***	-2.262	0.187	***

Table 7.1 (continued)

Part-time work	Low education			Medium education			High education		
	Logit	s.e.	Sig.	Logit	s.e.	Sig.	Logit	s.e.	Sig.
Constant	-1.079	0.331	***	-0.623	0.176	***	-0.282	0.413	
Age (1st order term)	0.000	0.005		0.012	0.004	**	0.025	0.007	***
Age (2nd order term)	-0.001	0.001	*	-0.001	0.000	**	-0.001	0.001	–
Has no partner	–	–	–	–	–	–	–	–	–
Has a partner	0.258	0.089	**	0.195	0.066	**	0.328	0.109	***
No children	–	–	–	–	–	–	–	–	–
1 or 2 children, youngest <3 yrs	-1.040	0.320	***	-1.198	0.296	***	-1.107	0.444	***
1 or 2 children, youngest 3–5 yrs	-0.174	0.181		0.279	0.105	**	0.156	0.182	
1 or 2 children, youngest >5 yrs	0.290	0.129	*	0.238	0.160		0.235	0.180	
3 children or more	-0.277	0.185		-0.575	0.171	**	-0.678	0.159	***

Notes:
Age is centred at 36.3 years (grand mean).
Significance levels: * p <0.05, ** p <0.01, *** p <0.001.

Source: GGS first round (Bulgaria, Germany, France, Italy, the Netherlands, Romania, Norway, Austria, Belgium, Lithuania, Hungary). Calculations by authors.

160

households where the youngest child is aged three and older. In households where the youngest child is aged three to five, the negative association between parenthood and full-time employment is about two-thirds smaller than in households where the youngest child is younger than three years. The probability of full-time employment increases further in households where the youngest child is at least six years old, although it still remains below the level of childless women. The findings thus suggest that entry into parenthood leaves a permanent footprint on full-time employment. The opposite pattern becomes apparent when we look at the association between parenthood and part-time employment.

Random effects

Table 7.2 displays the estimates of the variance components of the multilevel model. The variance components give an indication of the

Table 7.2 Variance–covariance matrix of the multilevel multinomial logit models in Table 7.1

	Level of education		
	Low	Medium	High
Variance–covariance matrix: Country level			
Variance intercepts: Full-time	0.344	0.154	0.327
Variance coefficient 1 or 2 children, youngest <3 yrs: Full-time	0.420	2.623	1.921
Variance coefficient 1 or 2 children, youngest 3–5 yrs: Full-time	0.300	1.127	0.702
Variance coefficient 1 or 2 children, youngest >5 yrs: Full-time	0.324	0.567	0.736
Variance coefficient 3 children or more: Full-time	0.358	0.938	0.143
Variance intercepts: Part-time	1.156	0.998	1.139
Variance coefficient 1 or 2 children, youngest <3 yrs: Part-time	0.967	1.463	1.694
Variance coefficient 1 or 2 children, youngest 3–5 yrs: Part-time	0.076	0.017	0.066
Variance coefficient 1 or 2 children, youngest >5 yrs: Part-time	0.055	0.179	0.070
Variance coefficient 3 children or more: Part-time	0.123	0.156	0.027

Source: GGS first round (Bulgaria, Germany, France, Italy, the Netherlands, Romania, Norway, Austria, Belgium, Lithuania, Hungary). Calculations by authors.

country variation in the association between parenthood and female employment. In line with expectations, the estimates of the variance components for full-time work are larger for medium- and highly educated mothers than for low-educated mothers. It suggests that the possibilities for mothers with higher levels of education to combine work and family strongly depend upon the country in which they live. Country variation in full-time employment is particularly large for medium- and highly educated women who live in households with children less than three years old.

In order to assess how the association between parenthood and female activity status varies by education in the respective countries, we have calculated the predicted probability of being full-time employed and part-time employed for women with high and low levels of education. The probabilities are calculated for women aged 37 who live with a partner.

As expected, highly educated women are more likely to be full-time employed than low-educated women (Figure 7.3a). Educational differentials are already very marked among childless women, with highly educated women being about 1.5 to 2.5 times more likely to work full-time than low-educated women. In households where the youngest child is less than three years old, the probability of full-time employment is much lower than among childless women. Among more highly educated groups there is considerable country variation, with full-time employment being more common in Belgium, Italy, Romania, France and Norway, whereas rates are clearly lower in the Netherlands and the German-speaking countries. Among low-educated groups, full-time employment rates are higher in Norway than in the other countries. Educational differentials in full-time employment are least articulated in Norway, the Netherlands and Austria. In Norway and the Netherlands, highly educated women are, respectively, 1.8 and 2.5 times more likely to be employed full-time than low-educated women. In Austria low-educated women are more likely than highly educated women to work full-time but it should be noted that the probability of working full-time is very low for both educational groups. In contrast to Norway, smaller educational differentials in the Netherlands and Austria are due to the fact that highly educated mothers in these countries are clearly less likely to be employed full-time. In comparison, highly educated women in Italy and Belgium are about 3.5 times more likely to work full-time than low-educated women, and 5.2 times more likely in Romania. In households where the youngest child is three to five years old, full-time employment rates are higher than in households with children less than three years old. Among highly educated women, the return to full-time employment is very common in the Central and Eastern European countries. Italy, Norway, France and Belgium form an intermediate group of

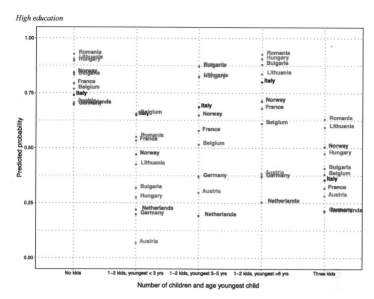

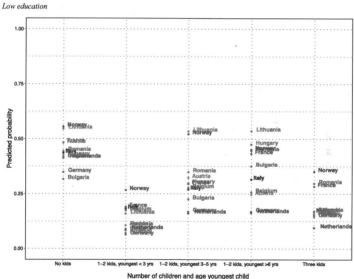

Source: GGS first round (Bulgaria, Germany, France, Italy, Netherlands, Romania, Norway, Austria, Belgium, Lithuania, Hungary). Calculations by authors.

Figure 7.3a   Best linear unbiased predictors of random country effects (probabilities scale) for full-time employment, stratified by level of education, women aged 37 years, living with a partner

countries, whereas full-time employment is clearly lower in the German-speaking countries and the Netherlands. Among low-educated mothers the rate of return to full-time work is clearly higher in Norway and Lithuania. Apart from Bulgaria, educational differentials are smaller than in households with children less than three years old. This suggests that the return to full-time employment is somewhat more pronounced among low-educated women. Educational differentials are smallest in Norway, Germany, Austria and the Netherlands, and now also in Belgium, France and Lithuania. Although the return to full-time employment is very pronounced among highly educated women in Central and Eastern Europe, it should be noted that this likely reflects a more select group of highly educated women who have made the step into parenthood and are able to combine it with a professional career. This explanation may hold for Italy as well, since the country combines frequent full-time employment among highly educated mothers with low levels of period fertility. This picture contrasts with Scandinavian countries such as Norway, where high fertility is associated with high female employment (Neels and Theunynck 2012). A similar picture emerges for households where the youngest child is at least six years old.

Turning to part-time employment, the general picture is that in most countries both low- and highly educated mothers have a similar probability of being employed part-time (Figure 7.3b). The likelihood of part-time employment is generally higher in households where children are older. Furthermore, both low- and highly educated mothers are more likely to work full-time than part-time. The latter results suggest that even though low-educated women more often work full-time than part-time, the share of part-time workers in the active population is higher among low-educated groups than among highly educated groups. The results also suggest that educational differentials in maternal employment are more strongly the result of variations in full-time employment than variations in part-time employment (Neels and Theunynck 2012). The main exceptions to the aforementioned pattern are Germany, Austria and the Netherlands. In these countries, highly educated mothers are not only more likely to work part-time than low-educated mothers, but they are also more likely to work part-time than full-time.

The Association between Childcare Use and Full-Time and Part-Time Employment

The last question we address is whether the association between childcare use and maternal employment varies by education, and whether cross-national differences in childcare use can explain cross-national differences

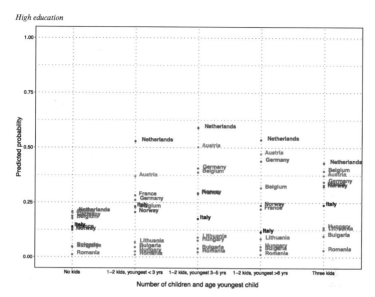

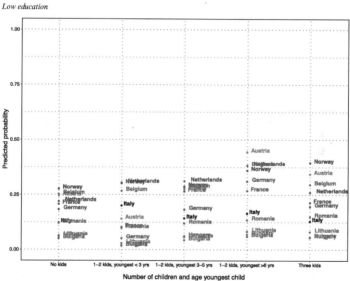

Source: GGS first round (Bulgaria, Germany, France, Italy, Netherlands, Romania, Norway, Austria, Belgium, Lithuania, Hungary). Calculations by authors.

Figure 7.3b   *Best linear unbiased predictors of random country effects (probabilities scale) for part-time employment, stratified by level of education, women aged 37 years, living with a partner*

Table 7.3   Use of childcare (national percentages): average enrolment rate
of children not yet three years of age in formal childcare and
percentage of children using informal childcare during a typical
week

Country	% using formal childcare	% using informal childcare
Bulgaria	16	32
Germany	16	27
France	32	31
Hungary	7	46
Italy	25	33
Netherlands	40	52
Romania	6	45
Norway	32	11
Austria	6	26
Belgium	43	24
Lithuania	5	21
Country average	20	32

Note: The reference year for France, Germany, Hungary, Italy and the Netherlands is
2005. For Lithuania and Bulgaria the reference year is 2006. For France and Romania the
reference year is 2007. For Belgium and Austria the reference year is 2008.

Source: EU-SILC (Bulgaria, Germany, France, Italy, the Netherlands, Romania, Norway,
Austria, Belgium, Lithuania, Hungary). Calculations by authors.

in the association between parenthood and maternal employment. Table 7.3
displays the use of formal and informal childcare. There are important differences between countries: reliance on formal childcare is high in France,
Norway, Belgium and the Netherlands. The average enrolment rate in these
countries ranges from 32 to 43 per cent. Use of formal childcare is low in
Central and Eastern Europe, with figures lying between 5 and 16 per cent.
Enrolment rates are also low in the German-speaking countries: 16 per
cent in Germany and 6 per cent in Austria. Italy, previously characterized
by low childcare availability, now occupies a middle position, with 25 per
cent enrolment. There are important differences between countries with
respect to the use of informal childcare: figures range from 45 and 52 per
cent in Romania and the Netherlands, respectively, to 11 and 21 per cent in
Norway and Lithuania, respectively.

   In Table 7.4 we add cross-level interaction terms between the use
of formal and informal childcare, on the one hand, and the combination variable number and age of the youngest child, on the other hand.
Unfortunately, it was not possible to use the same operationalization as in

Table 7.4 *Multilevel multinomial logit models of activity status (contrasts are full-time versus unemployed/inactive and part-time versus unemployed/inactive) by educational level, women aged 20–49*

Model	Low education						Medium education						High education					
	(1)			(2)			(3)			(4)			(5)			(6)		
	Logit	s.e.	Sig.	Logit	s.e.	Sig.	Logit	s.e.	Sig.	Logit	s.e.	Sig.	Logit	s.e.	Sig.	Logit	s.e.	Sig.
Full-time work																		
Constant	-0.253	0.182		-0.171	0.165		1.109	0.154	***	1.178	0.147	***	2.108	0.174	***	2.132	0.126	***
Age (1st order term)	0.007	0.004		0.007	0.004	*	-0.001	0.003		-0.001	0.003		-0.006	0.005		-0.006	0.005	
Age (2nd order term)	0.000	0.000		0.000	0.000		0.000	0.000		0.000	0.000		-0.002	0.001	**	-0.002	0.001	**
Has a partner	-0.122	0.068	*	-0.136	0.066	*	-0.367	0.043	***	-0.369	0.047	***	-0.268	0.077	***	-0.259	0.073	***
Child youngest <3 yrs	-1.859	0.272	***	-1.900	0.251	***	-2.213	0.317	***	-2.109	0.337	***	-1.992	0.342	***	-2.270	0.329	***
Formal care*Child youngest <3 yrs				0.037	0.019	*				0.063	0.028	*				0.085	0.028	***
Informal care*Child youngest <3 yrs				-0.012	0.020					0.008	0.027					0.014	0.023	

Table 7.4 (continued)

Model	Low education						Medium education						High education					
	(1)			(2)			(3)			(4)			(5)			(6)		
	Logit	s.e.	Sig.	Logit	s.e.	Sig.	Logit	s.e.	Sig.	Logit	s.e.	Sig.	Logit	s.e.	Sig.	Logit	s.e.	Sig.
Part-time work																		
Constant	−1.189	0.300	***	−1.093	0.211	***	−0.618	0.322	***	−0.313	0.340		0.399	0.279		−0.100	0.267	
Age (1st order term)	0.004	0.005		0.004	0.005		0.017	0.004	***	0.017	0.004	***	0.026	0.006	***	0.026	0.006	***
Age (2nd order term)	−0.002	0.001	**	−0.002	0.001	**	−0.002	0.000	***	−0.003	0.000	***	−0.003	0.001	***	−0.003	0.001	***
Has a partner	0.282	0.092	**	0.281	0.087	**	0.296	0.057	***	0.281	0.063	***	0.429	0.096	***	0.448	0.090	***
Child youngest <3 yrs	−1.118	0.280	***	−1.317	0.401	***	−1.472	0.435	***	−1.445	0.267	***	−1.445	0.334	***	−1.555	0.351	***
Formal care*Child youngest <3 yrs				0.028	0.022					0.049	0.026	*				0.064	0.024	***
Informal care*Child youngest <3 yrs				0.019	0.032					0.027	0.032					0.009	0.030	

Notes:
Age is centred at 36.3 years (grand mean). Formal and informal childcare are centred at 20 and 32 per cent, respectively.
Significance levels: * p <0.05, ** p <0.01, *** p <0.001.

Source: GGS first round (Bulgaria, Germany, France, Italy, the Netherlands, Romania, Norway, Austria, Belgium, Lithuania, Hungary). Calculations by authors.

168

Table 7.5   Variance–covariance matrix of the multilevel multinomial logit models in Table 7.4

| | Level of education | | | | | |
| | Low | | Medium | | High | |
	(1)	(2)	(3)	(4)	(5)	(6)
Variance–covariance matrix: Country level						
Variance intercepts: Full-time	0.321	0.314	0.268	0.273	0.405	0.396

Variance coeff. children,
  youngest <3 yrs:
  Full-time
	0.531	0.340	1.876	1.349	1.972	1.077

Variance intercepts: Part-time	1.122	1.038	1.344	1.294	1.355	1.046

Variance coeff. children,
  youngest <3 yrs:
  Part-time
	0.524	0.818	1.729	1.173	1.399	0.952

Source: GGS first round (Bulgaria, Germany, France, Italy, Netherlands, Romania, Norway, Austria, Belgium, Lithuania, Hungary). Calculations by authors.

the previous models. The variable number and age of the youngest child is now categorized as a dichotomy, with a category for mothers with children less than three years old and a category representing all other women in the sample. The results indicate that childcare use is positively associated with full-time and part-time employment for all educational groups. The association is stronger for formal than for informal childcare, and as expected, the size of the association increases with level of education.

Finally, Table 7.5 displays the estimates of the variance components for the models without and with cross-level interaction terms. If we compare the estimates for women with children less than three years old, we see that the inclusion of the cross-level interaction terms has reduced the size of the variance components. This indicates that cross-national differences in the association between parenthood and maternal employment are partially explained by cross-national differences in childcare use. The reduction in the cross-national variance is more pronounced among highly educated women with regard to full-time work, whereas the reduction in the cross-national variance is more pronounced among both medium- and highly educated women with regard to part-time work.

CONCLUSION

This chapter has re-examined the association between parenthood and maternal employment. In line with previous research, the results show that women strongly reduce their work hours shortly after childbirth and that female employment is higher in households where children are older. There are, however, large educational differences in the proportion of women who remain active in the labour force after childbirth, and whether they work full-time or part-time. In all countries, highly educated mothers are much more likely than low-educated mothers to remain employed after childbirth. In accordance with hypothesis 1A we find that country differentials in maternal employment rates are quite pronounced among highly educated women. This indicates that countries differ strongly in the opportunities for highly educated women to combine work and family. Full-time and part-time employment among mothers of very young children is consistently higher in countries with well-developed family policies. In line with hypothesis 1B, country variation in maternal employment is less articulated among low-educated women than among highly educated women. The lower country variation among low-educated groups is likely associated with the fact that their labour force participation is less dependent on family policy.

In line with hypothesis 2A, mothers more frequently work full-time in countries with strong public support for families with children, such as Norway, France and Belgium. Contrary to expectations, similar results are found in Central and Eastern Europe, where public support for families is comparatively weaker. However, in Norway, France and Belgium the lower penalty of childbirth on full-time employment is likely to reflect better opportunities for women to combine work and family, given that these countries have period total fertility rates close to the replacement level. In Central and Eastern Europe (and also Italy), on the other hand, the lower penalty of childbirth on full-time employment is likely to reflect higher work–family conflict given that these countries have period total fertility rates that lie considerably below the replacement level. In these countries women are likely to reduce fertility because they have fewer opportunities to work part-time, public childcare is less readily available and/or full-time employment is needed to sustain household income. The results (partially) corroborate hypothesis 2B, which predicts that educational differentials in maternal employment are smaller in countries with strong public support for families with children. Norway stands out with frequent full-time (and part-time) employment after childbirth and also lower educational differentials in female employment. In Belgium and France, however, public policies have benefited highly educated groups more strongly than low-educated groups, resulting in larger educational differentials in maternal employment than in Norway. Although both low- and highly educated mothers more frequently work full-time than part-time, the share of women who choose part-time work over full-time work is higher among low-educated groups. The major exceptions to this pattern are the Netherlands, Austria and Germany. In these countries, highly educated mothers are more likely to work part-time than low-educated mothers. A possible explanation is that qualitative differences between part-time and full-time jobs are smaller in these countries. An alternative explanation is that highly educated women in these countries can afford to reduce their hours because their partners' incomes are higher and/or family policies favour one-income households.

Corroborating hypothesis 3A, cross-national differences in maternal employment can be partially explained by differential use of childcare. The results also show that use of formal childcare is more strongly associated with maternal employment compared with informal childcare. It suggests that informal childcare complements but cannot substitute for formal childcare. In line with hypothesis 3B, the reduction in cross-national differences in maternal employment after controlling for childcare use is more pronounced among highly educated women. At the same time, controlling for childcare use also resulted in a reduction in the cross-national differences in full-time employment among low-educated women. It suggests that access to childcare in order to stimulate maternal employment is important for low-educated women as well. However, in all European countries, highly educated women are more likely to make use of childcare than low-educated women (Ghysels and Van Lancker 2011).

The chapter used data from the first round of the Generations and Gender Survey. Data collection took place before 2009 and the results therefore largely pertain to the period before the onset of the latest economic crisis. In the past few years, there has been a substantial increase in economic uncertainty, with rising unemployment levels, more frequent temporary work, and so on (Sobotka et al. 2011). Moreover, the crisis has disproportionally affected sectors where many low-educated women are employed (Konietzka and Kreyenfeld 2010). The economic crisis has also introduced austerity in family policies with cutbacks in public spending on childcare (OECD 2011). As such, the country and educational differentials found in this chapter are likely to show increasing diversity to the extent that countries and socio-economic groups have responded differently to the challenges imposed by the economic crisis.

An important limitation of our study is that we only had access to cross-sectional data. Therefore it was not possible to study maternal employment from a life course perspective. The latter requires detailed retrospective information on the maternity and employment histories of women. Currently, these data are available in the second round of the Generations and Gender Survey but only for seven countries.

NOTES

1. See http://www.ggp-i.org.
2. An additional reason to exclude Georgia from the analyses is that this country has very low female labour force participation rates. In multilevel regression models the country consistently came out as an outlier, which suggests that it should be studied individually.
3. We do not make the distinction between biological children, stepchildren and foster children.
4. We tried a more detailed operationalization of the combination variable with separate categories for households with one and two children. Unfortunately sample sizes are too small to estimate reliable variance components in multilevel models where the effects of these covariates are allowed to vary between countries (see below). We choose a less detailed operationalization of the variable number of children in the household and for a more detailed categorization of the variable age of the youngest child in the household since additional analyses showed that the variation between countries in terms of activity status is greater for the age of the youngest child than it is for the number of children in the household.
5. Individual-level information on the uptake of formal and informal childcare was not available in the GGS for all countries. Hence, we had to rely on aggregate-level data from the EU-SILC.
6. We estimated additional models where we tried to estimate the other covariances. The values of the covariances that could be estimated were sometimes different from zero. The reason not to retain them in the current analysis is twofold. First, we wanted to compare models that have the same structure of the variance–covariance matrix. Second, estimation of the covariances did not (much) affect the estimates of the variance components of the intercepts and the categories of the combination variable number of children and age of the youngest child in the household.
7. We tried to fit a single model where level of education on the one hand, and the combination variable number and age of the youngest child on the other hand, were included as main effects together with interaction terms between the categories of both variables. Although this could have raised statistical power, it was not possible with the data to allow both the main effects of the variables and their interaction terms to vary between countries. Therefore we stratified the model according to level of education. In Figures 7.3a and 7.3b we will plot the predicted probabilities of full-time and part-time employment so that we can have an idea of the magnitude of the education effect.

REFERENCES

Aassve, A., F.C. Billari and Z. Spéder (2006), 'Societal transition, policy changes and family formation: evidence from Hungary', *European Journal of Population*, 22, 127–152.

Andersson, G., M. Kreyenfeld and T. Mika (2009), 'Welfare state context, female earnings and childbearing', MPIDR Working Paper WP 2009-026.

Baizan, P. (2009), 'Regional child care availability and fertility decisions in Spain', *Demographic Research*, 21 (27), 803–842.

Becker, G.S. (1981), *A Treatise on the Family*, Cambridge, MA: Harvard University Press.

Begall, K. and M. Mills (2011), 'The impact of subjective work control, job strain and work–family conflict on fertility intentions: a European comparison', *European Journal of Population*, 27, 433–456.

Bernhardt, E.M. (1986), 'Women's home attachment at first birth', *European Journal of Population*, 2, 5–29.

Billari, F. (2004), 'Becoming an adult in Europe: a macro(/micro)-demographic perspective', *Demographic Research*, (Special Volume) 3, 15–44.

Blossfeld, H. and C. Hakim (1997), *Between Equalization and Marginalization: Woman Working Part-time in Europe and the United States of America*, New York: Oxford University Press.

Blossfeld, H. and J. Huinink (1991), 'Human capital investments or norms of role transition? How women's schooling and career affect the process of family formation', *American Journal of Sociology*, 97 (1), 143–168.

Brewster, K.L. and R.R. Rindfuss (2000), 'Fertility and women's employment in industrialized nations', *Annual Review of Sociology*, 26, 271–296.

Browne, W.J. (2012), 'MCMC Estimation in MLwiN, v2.26', Centre for Multilevel Modelling, University of Bristol.

Buchholz, S., D. Hofäcker, M. Mills, H. Blossfeld, K. Kuz and H. Hofmeister (2009), 'Life courses in the globalization process: the development of social inequalities in modern societies', *European Sociological Review*, 25 (1), 53–71.

Cantillon, B., J. Ghysels, N. Mussche and R. van Dam (2001), 'Female employment differences, poverty and care provisions', *European Societies*, 3, 447–469.

Castles, F.G. (2003), 'The world turned upside down: below replacement fertility, changing preferences and family-friendly public policy in 21 OECD countries', *Journal of European Social Policy*, 13 (3), 209–227.

Connolly, S. and M. Gregory (2010), 'Dual tracks: part-time work in life-cycle employment for British women', *Journal of Population Economics*, 23 (3), 907–931.

Correll, S.J., S. Benard and I. Paik (2007), 'Getting a job: is there a motherhood penalty?', *American Journal of Sociology*, 112 (5), 1297–1338.

Crompton, R. and C. Lyonette (2005), 'The new gender essentialism – domestic and family "choices" and their relation to attitudes', *British Journal of Sociology*, 56, 601–620.

Crompton, R. and C. Lyonette (2006), 'Work–Life "Balance" in Europe', *Acta Sociologica*, 49 (4), 379–393.

Datta Gupta, N., N. Smith and M. Verner (2008), 'Child care and parental leave in the Nordic countries: a model to aspire to?', *Review of Economics of the Household*, 6 (1), 65–89.

De Wachter, D. and K. Neels (2011), 'Educational differentials in fertility intentions and outcomes: family formation in Flanders in the early 1990s', *Vienna Yearbook of Population Research*, 9, 227–258.

Del Boca, D. (2002), 'The effect of child care and part time opportunities on participation and fertility decisions in Italy', *Journal of Population Economics*, 15 (3), 549–573.

Del Boca, D. (2015), 'Child care arrangements and labor supply', IDB Working Paper Series, No. IDB-WP-569.

Dex, S. and H. Joshi (1999), 'Careers and motherhood: policies for compatibility', *Cambridge Journal of Economics*, 23 (5), 641–659.

Domański, H. and D. Przybysz (2007), 'Educational homogamy in 22 European countries', *European Societies*, 9 (4), 495–526.

Dribe, M. and M. Stanfors (2009), 'Does parenthood strengthen a traditional household division of labor? Evidence from Sweden', *Journal of Marriage and Family*, 71, 33–45.

Duvander, A.Z., T. Lappegård and G. Andersson (2010), 'Family policy and fertility: fathers' and mothers' use of parental leave and continued childbearing in Norway and Sweden', *Journal of European Social Policy*, 20 (1), 45–57.

Eeckhaut, M.C.W., M.A. Stanfors and B. Van de Putte (2014), 'Educational heterogamy and the division of paid labour in the family: a comparison of present-day Belgium and Sweden', *European Sociological Review*, 30 (1), 64–75.

Elborgh-Woytek, K., M. Newiak, K. Kochhar, S. Fabrizio, K. Kpodar, P. Wingender, B. Clements and G. Schwartz (2013), 'Women, work, and the economy: macroeconomic gains from gender equity', IMF Staff Discussion Note SDN/13/10.

Esping-Andersen, G. (2009), *The Incomplete Revolution: Adapting Welfare States to Women's New Roles*, Cambridge: Polity Press.

European Commission (2011), *Employment and Social Developments in Europe 2011*, Luxembourg: Publications Office of the European Union.

Eurostat (2011), 'Women and men in the EU seen through figures', Eurostat newsrelease, STAT/11/36.

Eurostat (2015), 'Eurostat Database', accessed 24 September 2015 at http://ec.europa.eu/eurostat/data/database.

Evertsson, M., P. England, I. Mooi-Reci, J. Hermsen, J. de Bruijn and D. Cotter (2009), 'Is gender inequality greater at lower or higher educational levels? Common patterns in the Netherlands, Sweden, and the United States', *Social Politics: International Studies in Gender, State and Society*, 16 (2), 210–241.

Fondazione, G. Brodolini (2006), 'Achieving the Europe 2020 Employment Target', background note for session I: Equal Economic Independence: The Contribution of Women to Achieving the Europe 2020 targets, conference on Equality between Women and Men, European Commission, DG Justice, 19–20 September, Brussels.

Frejka, T. (2008), 'Overview chapter 5: determinants of family formation and childbearing during the societal transition in Central and Eastern Europe', *Demographic Research*, 19 (7), 139–170.

Friedman, D., M. Hechter and S. Kanazawa (1994), 'A theory of the value of children', *Demography*, 31 (3), 375–401.

Fux, B. (2008), 'Pathways of welfare and population-related policies: towards a multidimensional typology of welfare state regimes in Eastern and Western Europe', in C. Höhn, D. Avramov and I. Kotowska (eds), *People, Population Change and Policies: Lessons from the Population Policy Acceptance Study – Volume 1*, Berlin: Springer, pp. 59–90.

Gauthier, A.H. (2002), 'Family policies in industrialized countries: is there convergence?', *Population-E*, 57 (3), 447–474.

Gauthier, A.H. (2007), 'The impact of family policies on fertility in industrialized countries: a review of the literature', *Population Research and Policy Review*, 26, 323–346.

Ghysels, J. and W. Van Lancker (2009), 'Het Matteüseffect onder de loep: over het ongelijke gebruik van kinderopvang in Vlaanderen', Berichten working paper, Antwerpen: Universiteit Antwerpen, Centrum voor Sociaal Beleid UFSIA.

Ghysels, J. and W. Van Lancker (2011), 'The unequal benefits of activation: an analysis of the social distribution of family policy among families with young children', *Journal of European Social Policy*, 21 (5), 472–485.

Gottfried, H. and J. O'Reilly (2002), 'Reregulating breadwinner models in socially conservative welfare systems: comparing Germany and Japan', *Social Politics*, 9 (1), 29–59.

Gustafsson, S. (2001), 'Optimal age at motherhood: theoretical and empirical considerations on postponement of maternity in Europe', *Journal of Population Economics*, 14 (2), 225–247.

Gutiérez-Domènech, M. (2005), 'Employment after motherhood: a European comparison', *Labour Economics*, 12 (1), 99–123.

Hakim, C. (2003), 'A new approach to explaining fertility patterns: preference theory', *Population and Development Review*, 29 (3), 349–374.

Hoem, J.M., A. Prskawetz and G. Neyer (2001), 'Autonomy or conservative adjustment? The effect of public policies and educational attainment on third births in Austria, 1975–96', *Population Studies*, 55, 249–261.

Jappens, M. and J. Van Bavel (2013), 'Regional family norms and child care by grandparents in Europe', *Demographic Research*, 27 (4), 85–120.

Jensen, C. (2009), 'Institutions and the politics of childcare services', *Journal of European Social Policy*, 19 (7), 7–18.

Joshi, H., S. Macran and S. Dex (1996), 'Employment after childbearing and women's subsequent labour force participation: evidence from the British 1958 birth cohort', *Journal of Population Economics*, 9, 325–348.

Kalmijn, M. (2003), 'Country differences in sex-role attitudes: cultural and economic explanations', in W. Arts, J. Hagenaars and L. Halman (eds), *The Cultural Diversity of European Unity*, Leiden: Brill, pp. 311–337.

Klüsener, S., K. Neels and M. Kreyenfeld (2013), 'Family policies and the Western European fertility divide: insights from a natural experiment in Belgium', *Population and Development Review*, 39 (4), 587–610.

Konietzka, D. and M. Kreyenfeld (2010), 'The growing educational divide in mothers' employment: an investigation based on the German micro-censuses 1976–2004', *Work, Employment and Society*, 24 (2), 260–278.

Kreyenfeld, M. (2010), 'Uncertainties in female employment careers and the postponement of parenthood in Germany', *European Sociological Review*, 26 (3), 351–366.

Lappegård, T. and M. Rønsen (2005), 'The multifaceted impact of education on entry into motherhood', *European Journal of Population*, 21 (1), 31–49.

Lapuerta, I., P. Baizan and M.J. González (2011), 'Individual and institutional constraints: an analysis of parental leave use and duration in Spain', *Population Research and Policy Review*, 30, 185–210.

Liefbroer, A.C. and M. Corijn (1999), 'Who, what, where, and when? Specifying the impact of educational attainment and labour force participation on family formation', *European Journal of Population*, 15, 45–75.

Luci, A. and O. Thévenon (2012), 'The impact of family policy packages on fertility trends in developed countries', Ined: Documents de Travail (174).

McDonald, P. (2006), 'Low fertility and the state: the efficacy of policy', *Population and Development Review*, 32 (3), 485–510.

McDonald, P. (2013), 'Societal foundations for explaining low fertility: gender equity', *Demographic Research*, 28 (34), 981–994.

Macunovich, D.J. (1996), 'Relative income and price of time: exploring their effects on US fertility and female labor force participation', *Population and Development Review*, 22, 223–257.

Marks, J., L. Chun Bun and S.M. McHale (2009), 'Family patterns of gender role attitudes', *Sex Roles*, 61 (3–4), 221–234.

Matysiak, A. and S. Steinmetz (2008), 'Finding their way? Female employment patterns in West Germany, East Germany, and Poland', *European Sociological Review*, 24 (3), 331–345.

Mayer, K.U. (2001), 'The paradox of global social change and national path dependencies: life course patterns in advanced societies', in A.E. Woodward and M. Kohli (eds), *Inclusions–Exclusions*, Routledge: London, pp. 89–110.

Meron, M. and I. Widmer (2002), 'Unemployment leads women to postpone the birth of their first child' (transl. by D. Shapiro), *Population-E*, 57 (2), 301–330.

Mincer, J. (1963), 'Market prices, opportunity costs, and income effects', in C. Christ (ed.), *Measurement in Economics*, Stanford, CA: Stanford University Press, pp. 67–82.

Muresan, C. and J.M. Hoem (2010), 'The negative educational gradients in Romanian fertility', *Demographic Research*, 22 (4), 95–114.

Neels, K. and D. De Wachter (2010), 'Postponement and recuperation of Belgian fertility: how are they related to rising female educational attainment?', *Vienna Yearbook of Population Research*, 8 (Special Issue on Education and Demography), 77–106.

Neels, K. and Z. Theunynck (2012), 'Gezinsvorming en vrouwelijke arbeidsparticipatie: de opleidingsgradiënt van voltijds werk en attitudes ten aanzien van gezin en werk in 10 Europese landen', *Tijdschrift voor Sociologie*, 3–4, 428–461.

Neyer, G. (2005), 'Family policies in Western Europe: fertility policies at the intersection of gender, employment and care policies', *Österreichische Zeitschrift für Politikwissenschaft*, 34, 91–102.

Neyer, G. and G. Andersson (2008), 'Consequences of family policies on childbearing behavior: effects or artifacts?', *Population and Development Review*, 34 (4), 699–724.

OECD (2002), *OECD Employment Outlook 2002*, Paris: OECD Publishing.

OECD (2007), 'Matching work and family commitments. Issues, outcomes, policy objectives and recommendations', in *Babies and Bosses, Reconciling Work and Family Life: A Synthesis of Findings for OECD Countries*, OECD Publishing.

OECD (2011), *Doing Better for Families*, OECD Publishing, accessed 22 October 2015 at http://dx.doi.org/10.1787/9789264098732-en.

OECD (2012), *Closing the Gender Gap: Act Now*, OECD Publishing, accessed 22 October 2015 at http://dx.doi.org/10.1787/9789264179370-en.

OECD (2013), *Education at a Glance 2013*, OECD Indicators, OECD Publishing, accessed 22 October 2015 at http://dx.doi.org/10.1787/eag-2013-en.

O'Reilly, J., T. Nazio and J.M. Rocher (2013), 'Compromising conventions: attitudes of dissonance and indifference toward full-time maternal employment in Denmark, Spain, Poland and the UK', *Work, Employment and Society*, 28 (2), 168–188.

Pettit, B. and J. Hook (2005), 'The structure of women's employment in comparative perspective', *Social Forces*, 84 (2), 779–801.

Plantenga, J. and C. Remery (2010), *Flexible Working Time Arrangements and Gender Equality. A Comparative Review of 30 European Countries*, Luxembourg: Publications Office of the European Union.

Poortman, A.-R. and T. van der Lippe (2009), 'Attitudes toward housework and child care and the gendered division of labor', *Journal of Marriage and Family*, 71 (3), 526–541.

Rindfuss, R.R., D.K.G. Guilkey, S.P. Morgan and Ø. Kravdal (2010), 'Child-care availability and fertility in Norway', *Population and Development Review*, 36 (4), 725–748.

Rose, M. (2001), 'Closing down a work career: housework, employment plans, and women's work attitudes', ESRC Project on Employment Trajectories, Careers, and Work Rationale, Working Paper 1, Bath: Department of Social and Policy Sciences, University of Bath.

Scott, J. (1999), 'European attitudes towards maternal employment', *International Journal of Sociology and Social Policy*, 19 (9–11), 144–177.

Sobotka, T., V. Skirbekk and D. Philipov (2011), 'Economic recession and fertility in the developed world', *Population and Development Review*, 37 (2), 267–306.

Stier, H. and N. Lewin-Epstein (2001), 'Welfare regimes, family-supportive policies, and women's employment along the life-course', *American Journal of Sociology*, 106, 1731–1760.

Storms, B. (1995), 'Het matteüs-effect in de kinderopvang', *Berichten*, Antwerpen: Universiteit Antwerpen, Centrum voor Sociaal Beleid UFSIA.

Szelewa, D. and M.P. Polakowski (2008), 'Who cares? Changing patterns of childcare in Central and Eastern Europe', *Journal of European Social Policy*, 18 (2), 115–131.

Thévenon, O. (2011), 'Family policies in OECD countries: a comparative analysis', *Population and Development Review*, 37 (11), 57–87.

Thévenon, O. and A. Solaz (2013), 'Labour market effects of parental leave policies in OECD countries', OECD Social, Employment and Migration Working Papers, No. 141, OECD Publishing, accessed at http://dx.doi.org/10.1787/5k8xb6hw1wjf-en.

Tomlinson, J. (2007), 'Employment regulation, welfare and gender regimes: a comparative analysis of women's working-time patterns and work–life balance in the UK and the US', *International Journal of Human Resource Management*, 18 (3), 401–415.

Tomlinson, J., W. Olsen and K. Purdam (2009), 'Women returners and potential returners: employment profiles and labour market opportunities – A case study of the United Kingdom', *European Sociological Review*, 25 (3), 349–363.

Uunk, W., M. Kalmijn and R. Muffels (2005), 'The impact of young children on women's labour supply. A reassessment of institutional effects in Europe', *Acta Sociologica*, 48 (1), 41–62.

Van Lancker, W. and J. Ghysels (2010), 'Female employment, institutions and the role of reference groups: a multilevel analysis of 22 European countries', CSB Working Paper, no. 10/02.

Van Lancker, W. and J. Ghysels (2013), 'Wie heeft profijt van het overheidsbeleid?', *Mens & Maatschappij*, 88 (1), 5–32.

Vere, J.P. (2007), '"Having it all" no longer: fertility, female labor supply, and the new life choices of generation X', *Demography*, 44 (4), 821–828.

Vikat, A. (2004), 'Women's labor force attachment and childbearing in Finland', *Demographic Research*, (Special Volume) 3, 177–212.

Wierda-Boer, H.H., J.R.M. Gerris and A.A. Vermulst (2008), 'Adaptive strategies, gender ideology, and work-family balance among Dutch dual earners', *Journal of Marriage and Family*, 70, 1004–1014.

Wright, R.E and P.R.A. Hinde (1991), 'The dynamics of full-time and part-time female labour force participation in Great Britain', *European Journal of Population*, 7, 201–230.

8. Fatherhood and men's second union formation: Norway, France and Hungary, 1980s–2000s

Lívia Murinkó and Ivett Szalma*

INTRODUCTION

As part of the past decades' profound changes in partnership behaviour, more and more people are experiencing the dissolution of their first stable relationship and entering the 're-partnering market', and many of them already have children. In this context, re-partnering offers a burgeoning area of research that could help us to understand the implications of demographic change for family life (Sweeney 2010). The aim of this chapter is to investigate how the effect of fatherhood on the re-partnering of men has changed since the 1980s in three European societies: Hungary, France and Norway.

Most studies on re-partnering focus only on women and disregard men. It is usually women who are the main caregivers, and data on female fertility and partnerships are often more readily available, more complete and accurate than those on males (Beaujouan 2011; Breton and Prioux 2009; Meggiolaro and Ongaro 2010). Moreover, it is mostly the women who live with the children after separation or divorce (de Graaf and Kalmijn 2003; Poortman 2007; Wu and Schimmele 2005).

In this chapter we focus on men for two main reasons. Firstly, men's and fathers' involvement in family life and childcare has been documented as having increased in a number of societies, while women's growing participation in the labour market has challenged the traditional gendered division of family responsibilities (Cabrera et al. 2000; Williams 2008). Secondly, many divorced or separated fathers do not live with their children, with probably different effects on men's demographic behaviour after separation than on women's. This question is especially relevant because sole maternal child custody is no longer the only option, and more and more couples choose joint physical custody after union dissolution (Elrod and Dale 2008). As a result, more men will co-reside with their children at least on a part-time basis. In the case of joint physical custody, both parents spend equal or substantial amounts of time with their children, so children have ongoing close contact with both parents (Bauserman 2002).

Regarding change over time, prior studies have found that the general rate of re-marriage has decreased, partly because many people establish a 'living apart together' (LAT) or a non-married cohabiting union as their next relationship, and partly because more people stay single (Spijker and Solsona 2012). Most of these studies looked at marriages. Since patterns of union formation have changed over time and the rate of non-marital childbearing has dramatically increased, we also take into consideration re-partnering after a cohabiting partnership and cohabitations as second unions. Moreover, most studies only refer to one point in time (e.g., Beaujouan 2012; de Graaf and Kalmijn 2003). In order to get a more comprehensive view on changes in the re-partnering of men, we examine the period between 1980 and 2008. Moreover, focusing on three countries also makes it possible to consider changes in contextual-level constructions, which may lead to different outcomes in research on men's re-partnering.

The following section provides the main theoretical considerations and empirical studies on men's re-partnering, and then we present our hypotheses. Subsequently we describe the relevant country contexts, introduce our data and methods, and finally we move on to presenting and discussing the empirical findings.

BACKGROUND AND HYPOTHESES

Parenthood status, custody and living arrangements are crucial aspects when looking at the re-partnering behaviour of men and women (de Graaf and Kalmijn 2003; Ivanova et al. 2013). Previous empirical results are not conclusive regarding the impact of fatherhood status on re-partnering. Some studies found no relationship between having children and the re-partnering of men in Canada (Wu 1994), France, Germany, Romania and the Russian Federation (Ivanova et al. 2013). Others found a negative association in the United States (US) (Sweeney 1997), the Netherlands (de Graaf and Kalmijn 2003; Poortman 2007) and Norway (Ivanova et al. 2013). Studies that differentiate between having co-resident and non-resident children showed that probably it is not parenthood itself but the presence of children in the household that slows down re-partnering (Bernhardt and Goldscheider 2002 for Sweden; Földházi 2010 for Hungary; Beaujouan 2012 for France; Ivanova et al. 2013 for France, Germany, Norway, Romania and Russia). A number of studies concluded that fathers re-partner faster than non-fathers. Stewart et al. (2003) found a positive association between having and being involved with non-resident children and the formation of non-marital unions in the US; Wu and Schimmele (2005) found the same in Canada. Goldscheider and Sassler (2006) for Sweden, and Barre (2003) for France, found a positive relationship between men having co-resident children and union formation. In the United Kingdom, having co-resident children aged 12 or younger seems to make the re-partnering of separated fathers easier (Di Nallo 2015).

Considering the contrasting implications of co-resident and non-resident fatherhood for re-partnering, it is not surprising that the empirical results are not conclusive. These mixed results may also be due to the different methods, the different conceptualizations of union and parenthood status, and the different contextual background of the examined countries; furthermore, the role of fatherhood may also have changed over time (Sullivan et al. 2014).

This chapter examines the question of how the effect of fatherhood on the re-partnering of men has changed in France, Hungary and Norway since the 1980s. Our approach is new in the sense that we focus on men, take a comparative perspective, look at change over time, consider both cohabiting and marital unions, and also differentiate between (part- or full-time) residential and non-residential fatherhood.

We develop our hypotheses for five different groups of men. Firstly we look at the most general group: all men who have experienced a union dissolution by the age of 50 (see the 'Data and Methods' section below for a detailed description of our sample). Secondly, we compare men who were childless at the end of their first union and men who already had at least one child. And thirdly, we further differentiate between two subgroups of fathers: those who have only non-resident children, and those who live together with at least one of their children on a part- or full-time basis. We are interested in how the probability of re-partnering has changed for these five groups since the 1980s.

Need, attractiveness and opportunity are three general arguments that help us to understand re-partnering behaviour (Becker 1981; de Graaf and Kalmijn 2003; Goldscheider and Waite 1986; Oppenheimer 1988). According to this approach, re-partnering depends on: (1) the person's emotional, financial or social need for a new partner; (2) the attractiveness of the individual for potential partners; and (3) their opportunities to meet possible mates.

We use the considerations of need, attractiveness and opportunity to formulate our expectations regarding the changing effect of fatherhood and the changing probability of re-partnering for the five different subgroups of men. In Table 8.1 we present the probably most important drivers for the five groups and the three considerations that may explain

Table 8.1   *Expected changes in the effect of fatherhood and the probability*
to re-partner for different subgroups of men since the
1980s, based on the considerations of need, opportunity and
attractiveness

	Need	Opportunity	Attractiveness	Expected change in the probability to re-partner since the 1980s
Men in general	Singlehood and childlessness have become more accepted; men develop skills for housework and childcare → decreasing need	The number of single and divorced/ separated women has increased, larger re-partnering market → increasing opportunity	No change	No change
Childless men	Singlehood and childlessness have become more accepted; men develop skills for housework and child care → decreasing need	The same as for men in general	No change	No change
Fathers	Singlehood and childlessness are more accepted; men develop skills for housework and childcare; the role of being a father has become more important in men's life → decreasing need	Increasing number of single women; more interactions at children's activities or at school → increasing opportunity Increasing involvement with children → decreasing opportunity	Being already a father as a sign of child- and family-centred attitudes and fecundity → increasing attractiveness	No change

Table 8.1 (continued)

	Need	Opportunity	Attractiveness	Expected change in the probability to re-partner since the 1980s
Father with only non-resident children	The same as for fathers in general	The same as for fathers in general	Involved fatherhood as the new expectation → decreasing attractiveness	Decreasing probability to re-partner
Fathers with co-resident children	The same as for fathers in general	Increasing number of single women; more interactions at children's activities or at school; online dating; increasing help from the welfare state and widely available childcare institutions → increasing opportunity Increasing involvement with children → decreasing opportunity	Being perceived as a 'good father', involved fatherhood → increasing attractiveness	Increasing probability to re-partner

changes over time in re-partnering. Since we cannot directly measure and test how the needs, the opportunities and the attractiveness of men have changed (at least not with the available data), we have formulated one hypothesis for each group. The last column of Table 8.1 shows what we expect for each group of men, based on how their need, opportunity and attractiveness may have changed. When formulating our expectations, we give about equal weight to all the three considerations (for example, if one of the considerations suggests increasing probability, one suggests decreasing probability, and one suggests that there has been no change, we expect that the trends balance each other and no change has taken place on the whole). For the sake of simplicity, we expect that changes are linear, and the 1980s is the reference period.

We have to note that the function of Table 8.1 is not to provide a full list of factors that have influenced changes in the re-partnering of men in the past three decades. Our aim is to offer an overview and to illustrate the complex nature of the phenomenon and the usefulness of distinguishing between different subgroups of men and the arguments of need, opportunity and attractiveness. Here we only list factors that may be relevant for most European societies. Other contextual factors and country-specific arguments are discussed in the next section.

The first basic argument is that people enter a union because it improves their emotional, financial or social well-being, and the greater their need in these respects, the more likely they are to re-partner. Financial need is probably less relevant for the re-partnering decisions of men than women due to the gender role expectation that men should provide for themselves (Spéder 2011). Moreover, single fathers work full-time more often and are less likely to live in poor or materially deprived households than single mothers (Chzhen and Bradshaw 2012).

We assume that the need to re-partner has decreased in all groups of men due to several reasons. Alternative living arrangements, such as being single or living apart together, have become more common and more accepted in recent decades (Lesthaeghe 2010), thus probably fewer men re-partner only to comply with social norms and expectations. The prevalence and social acceptance of childlessness have also increased (Merz and Liefbroer 2012), so the need to re-partner in order to become a father might have decreased as well. The role of being a father has become more important in the lives of many men, maybe in some cases taking priority over a new union, thus decreasing the emotional need to re-partner. A new partner may be viewed as a source of extra demands and a disruption in the relationship between father and children (Lampard and Peggs 1999). Some studies show that divorced parents living with children prefer LAT relationships: they might try to avoid disrupting the environment with which their resident children are familiar (Beaujouan et al. 2009; Levin 2004; Reimondos et al. 2011). Studies that consider longitudinal trends in men's and women's time on housework and childcare show a slow convergence between the two sexes (Bianchi et al. 2000; Neilson and Stanfors 2014). Since men have become more likely to develop the necessary skills for reconciling the responsibilities of paid work, household tasks and childcare, their need for re-partnering may have decreased.

The second argument is that the probability of re-partnering depends on the opportunity to meet potential partners. Some factors would suggest that men's and fathers' re-partnering opportunities have decreased, while other factors point at increasing opportunities. The re-partnering market may be less effective for separated or divorced people because the number of single people decreases with age and the number of social contacts decline following divorce (Kalmijn and Uunk 2007), even though separated men may increase their interactions with possible mates through other channels.

The number of single people at later ages is limited, especially for women seeking a new partner, because men often partner with somewhat younger women, and at later ages there are more women than men (de Graaf and Kalmijn 2003; Wu and Schimmele 2005). However, more and more people terminate their first unions, so the number of people searching for new partners (the 're-partnering market') has increased in all of the examined countries, especially for men, which expands men's opportunities to find a new partner (de Graaf and Kalmijn 2003; Ivanova et al. 2013; Spijker and Solsona 2012). Since the number of single mothers has increased more than the number of single fathers, fathers may have a comparative advantage after divorce or separation because they are less likely to have a strong preference against re-partnering with lone mothers, thus further enlarging their potential pool of new partners (South 1991).

Compared to younger singles, separated men are probably less involved in traditional marriage markets such as schools, voluntary associations and leisure locations. However, separated fathers may expand their opportunities to meet potential partners (probably other parents) by participating in their children's activities or interactions in the children's school. Moreover, new marriage markets have emerged such as online dating, in which divorced people are more likely to be involved. Some studies show that online dating is especially beneficial for people who face a slim marriage market, for example, gays, lesbians and middle-aged persons (Rosenfeld and Thomas 2012). We assume that it is especially fathers with co-resident children who may benefit from the new opportunities such as children's activities and online dating.

Re-partnering is probably more difficult for divorced and separated fathers with co-resident children than for their childless counterparts, because they might go out less often, especially when the children are still young and the parent is more involved with the care of the children (Munch et al. 1997). Parenthood may negatively affect fathers' chances of re-partnering, even if they do not live with the children. However, the increasing supply of childcare facilities makes it easier for fathers with small children (especially for those with co-resident children) to re-partner.

Widely available childcare institutions may help re-partnering by allowing parents more time as well as functioning as possible places to meet potential partners.

The third argument is that re-partnering prospects depend on how attractive a person is to the opposite sex.[1] We believe that it is especially fathers who have experienced changes in their perceived attractiveness. Fatherhood may have two contradictory effects on attractiveness. On the one hand, it reflects the man's experience with and interest in children. Being perceived as a 'good father' (or being able to father a child) increases men's attractiveness for potential partners (Goldscheider and Sassler 2006; Prioux 2006; Stewart et al. 2003; Wu and Schimmele 2005). Fathers whose children reside with them demonstrate the highest level of involvement (Stewart et al. 2003). Having children might also make a man more attractive in cases when the prospective female partner is over her fertility age and childless but would like to be a parent (Lampard and Peggs 1999). The attractiveness of divorced fathers has probably also increased because public opinion has become more permissive towards divorce and separation when young children are involved and divorced people are less and less stigmatized (Liefbroer and Fokkema 2008; Scott 2006). Conversely, it is possible that fathers who do not live with their children after separation, at least on a part-time basis, fail to live up to the emerging expectation of involved fatherhood and thus have become less attractive on the re-partnering market. If shared residential custody of children is a widely available option for separated parents, not taking this option may also decrease attractiveness.

Potential partners may be less interested in someone who already has children, either because prior children can serve as a source of conflict in the new relationship, or because such a person is less likely to want to have additional children (Meggiolaro and Ongaro 2008). A potential partner may also expect the child to be a financial burden and a competitor for the attention, affection and time of the partner (Stewart et al. 2003). Rearing children requires substantial time and financial investment, especially from those parents who live with their young children (Becker 1981; Gauthier and Hatzius 1997; Ongaro et al. 2009; Zagheni and Zannella 2013).

Based on the above considerations, we formulated five hypotheses for the different categories of separated and divorced men in order to get a more accurate picture of the changes in their situation:

H1. We expect that the probability of re-partnering has not changed for men in general. Men may need a new partner less in the new millennium than they did one or two decades ago, because many men have become less reliant on a female partner to do the housework and the need to re-partner to fulfil social expectations has probably also decreased. The emotional need for a new partner and men's general attractiveness probably have not changed. We suppose that men's opportunities to meet potential partners have increased because of the expanding re-partnering market. All in all, we expect no change in this group because men's decreasing need and increasing opportunities may have cancelled each other out.

H2. We expect that the probability of re-partnering has not changed for childless men. The argumentation is the same as for men in general (see H1).

H3. We assume that the probability of re-partnering has not changed in the case of fathers in general. Besides the previously discussed arguments, a few additional factors may play a role. The centrality of the father role in men's lives and the increasing involvement in childcare may have a negative effect on re-partnering, while the increased participation in child-related activities and higher attractiveness of fathers in general may have a positive effect. Overall, we suppose that these opposing effects balance out.

H4. The probability of re-partnering for fathers with only non-resident children is expected to decrease because of their decreasing attractiveness. If involved fatherhood is the new expectation and shared residential custody of children is a widely available option for separated parents, this group may seem less attractive for potential partners.

H5. We expect that the probability of re-partnering for fathers with co-resident children has increased owing to positive changes in their attractiveness and opportunity. They may benefit from the same changes that have been disadvantageous for fathers with only non-resident children. Moreover, the availability of alternative dating options and childcare institutions may have a positive impact on the opportunities to meet potential partners especially for this group.

OVERVIEW OF THE COUNTRY CONTEXTS

In this section, we briefly overview some relevant contextual factors that may help in understanding how men's re-partnering differs in the three examined societies, and what changes have taken place in the past decades. First of all, the partnership behaviour and the re-partnering market have changed since the 1980s. The institution of marriage has undergone significant changes, such as postponement, decreasing marriage rates and increasing divorce rates all over Europe (Spijker and Solsona 2012). Between 1980 and 2008 the crude marriage rate dropped from 7.5 to 3.6 per 1000 population in Hungary, from 6.2 to 3.9 in France and from 5.4 to 4.8 in Norway. In the 1980s, the total divorce rate was higher in Hungary (0.29, that is, 29 per cent of marriages) than in France (0.22) and Norway (0.24). Following a gradual increase, divorce rates were similar (0.45–0.47) in all three of the countries in 2007, and more than half of them involved children. The gender asymmetry related to divorce has increased in all three countries among people in their thirties: the number of divorced men compared to divorced women has decreased, thus the situation has become more favourable for men. However, the remarriage rates of the divorced population have decreased since the 1980s and around 25–30 per cent of divorced men remarried in the three countries in 2006 (Spijker and Solsona 2012). We have no statistical data on the rate of re-partnering after cohabitation, in spite of the spread of cohabitation in all of the three countries. This new partnership form started to increase among young people in the 1970s in Norway (Noack 2001) and France (Martin and Théry 2001), and only in the 1990s in Hungary (Spéder 2005).

Fertility rates and childbearing intentions may also influence men's re-partnering in several ways. There might be higher social expectation on childless men to re-partner than on fathers in a pro-natalist society with a low childlessness rate. Total fertility rate was above 1.8 children per woman in France and Hungary and it was only 1.68 in Norway in 1985. During the 1990s fertility dropped sharply in Hungary while it only slightly decreased in France and even increased in Norway. After 2000 it further increased in Norway and France but kept decreasing in Hungary. As a result, fertility in France and Norway is among the highest in Europe, with 1.99 and 1.96 total fertility rates in 2008, respectively, whereas Hungary, with its 1.35 total fertility rate, belongs to the low-fertility countries (OECD 2011b). Childlessness and non-marital births are somewhat less common in Hungary than in the other two countries in 2010 (OECD 2011b), but in the 1980s and 1990s the childlessness rate was similarly low in all three countries.

Not only is the rate of childlessness lower in Hungary than in France and Norway, but the acceptance of voluntary childlessness also differs. The approval of voluntary childlessness is lower in Eastern European countries, including Hungary (with a disapproval rate of more than 50 per cent), than in Western European countries, including Norway and France (Merz and Liefbroer 2012). In a given society the level of acceptance of childlessness may influence the re-partnering needs of childless persons.

Gender equality may also play a role. In spite of the fact that dual earner families are common in all three of the countries, the dual carer model is widespread only in Norway (Letablier 2013; Róbert et al. 2001). In a society where the traditional family model is dominant, men are more expected to be involved in the labour market and to have higher wages than women. Norway is one of the countries with the smallest difference between the two genders, while Hungary is among those countries where women are considerably less equal than men, and France is situated in-between (UNDP 2014). Norway is a special case because family policy actively encourages and supports men's participation in childcare and fathers are expected to play a more active role in their children's upbringing (Ellingsæter et al. 2013). In contrast, the traditional family model is still dominant in Hungary (Hobson and Fahlén 2009; Murinkó 2014; Oláh 2011; Saxonberg and Sirovatka 2006; Szalma 2010).

Some aspects of family policies may also be crucial in view of re-partnering, such as the availability of childcare services, which can alleviate single parents' situation by providing them more time for work or themselves. In Norway and France there is almost universal enrolment in formal childcare for pre-school children. In Hungary the enrolment of children aged under three is only 10.9 per cent but it is 86.7 per cent for children aged between three and five (OECD 2011b). Coverage declined in Hungary gradually after 1983, dropped sharply during the early 1990s, and a steady improvement started only in the early 2000s (Blaskó and Gábos 2012). Meanwhile, in France and Norway childcare facilities have gradually developed since the beginning of the 1980s (European Commission 2009).

In the case of separated parents, regulations concerning child custody and maintenance can also be important factors in the re-partnering process. The latest regulations in all three countries declare that both parents are regarded to be of equal importance for the child, and decisions should be made in the best interest of the child. No difference is made between married and non-married parents. While joint legal custody is regularly awarded, courts prefer joint physical custody arrangements only if all the necessary conditions are fulfilled and if parents are able to come to an agreement; however, the great majority of decisions in all three countries still place children in the full physical custody of the mother. Regulations that explicitly favour joint physical custody came into force in 2002 in France, in 2004 in Norway, and only in March 2014 in Hungary (Council of Europe 2014). Until the beginning of the new millennium the main pattern in all three countries was that the child stayed with the mother after parental separation. As a result, only a small proportion of single-parent households include the father and his child(ren): this rate was higher in Norway (18 per cent) than in France (14.7 per cent) and Hungary (12.6 per cent) in 2010 (OECD 2011b).[2] The proportion of children placed in alternating residences is around 10 per cent in Norway (4 per cent in 1996, and 10 per cent in 2004) and France (1 per cent in 1996, and 11 per cent in 2005) (Boele-Woelki et al. 2005; Council of Europe 2014), but negligible in Hungary (Weiss and Szeibert 2014). The share of parental and court decisions on joint physical custody and the actual proportion of fathers and children in this arrangement are expected to increase.

In all three countries, non-custodial parents have to contribute to the cost of raising a child by making child support payments during the entire period examined. In Norway, a public child support agency plays the leading role in setting payment rates according to rigid formulas. In France and Hungary courts register the agreements of the parents and make a decision if parents cannot reach an agreement. Courts operate with discretion and use informal guidelines (OECD 2011b). There is considerable difference in the proportion of non-widowed single-parent families receiving child support in the three countries: it was 81 per cent in Norway, 46 per cent in France, and 40 per cent in Hungary in 2000 (OECD 2011b). The proportion of single parents receiving support payments has increased in most Organisation for Economic Co-operation and Development (OECD) countries since the 1990s, with the exceptions of France and Hungary (OECD 2011b). The share of child support payment received, as a percentage of disposable income, was 14 per cent in France, 7 per cent in Norway and 5 per cent in Hungary on average at the beginning of the new millennium. Three per cent of French and Hungarian, and 9 per cent of Norwegian families make child support payments, and on average these payments amount to 7 per cent of their disposable income in Hungary, 8 per cent in Norway and 2 per cent in France (OECD 2011a, p. 231). In most countries child support amounts are reduced or stopped when care is shared (equally) between resident and non-resident parents (OECD 2011a, p. 228). In France, having a new partner and 'new' children are taken into account as additional expenses of the non-resident parent, whereas in Norway only the new partner is considered; however, these factors are often not considered in practice if the parents have relatively high earnings (Skinner et al. 2007). No such information is available for Hungary due to the marginality of shared parenting after separation.

Finally, the general economic circumstances may also influence the re-partnering market in a given country. For instance, economic hardships such as recession, high and/or rising unemployment, or cuts in social welfare spending may worsen the situation of single people, especially parents, decreasing their attractiveness and opportunities on the re-marriage market but increasing their need to form a new union to alleviate the hardships.

Gross domestic product (GDP) per capita has been highest in Norway, followed by France and Hungary, since the 1980s. Norway has experienced the most rapid GDP growth in the past decades, while in Hungary the 1990s were characterized by a sharp drop and then stagnation (IMF 2015). In Hungary unemployment was virtually non-existent in the 1980s but has been relatively high since then, similar to the level in France since the 1990s (IMF 2015). As a result of both the economic circumstances and the interventions of the welfare state, the risk of poverty in 2007 (operationalized as having income after social transfers which is below the poverty threshold) for single people living with at least one dependent child was highest in Hungary, followed by France, then Norway (Eurostat 2012).

These differences between the three examined countries and the different paths of their development probably affect how the need, opportunity and attractiveness of men and fathers have changed. However, it is hard to assess how these changing differences will manifest in the re-partnering behaviour of men in the three countries. Therefore we do not formulate country-specific hypotheses at this point, but will refer back to these differences when discussing our results.

DATA AND METHODS

For the empirical analysis, we use data from the first wave of the Generations and Gender Survey (GGS) for France (2005), Norway (2007–2008) and Hungary (2004–2005) (UNECE 2005).[3] The country surveys comprise nationally representative samples of the population aged 18–79, focusing on family, fertility, partnerships, health, ageing and related attitudes. The dataset includes complete fertility and partnership histories with monthly information. Individual weights adjust the distributions by gender, age and place of residence.

The sample that we used for the analysis includes men aged 50 or less[4] whose first (heterosexual) relationship ended in 1980 or later. The risk period starts at the end of the first union and it ends when the second union is formed or when the respondent is interviewed. The number of cases is summarized in Table 8.2. It is important to note that the number of cases or events is relatively low in the case of some variables, thus their regression coefficients should be treated with caution.

In our study, partnership is defined as either marriage or unmarried cohabitation that lasted for at least three months.[5] Living apart together and other possible partnership forms are not taken into account. Partnership dissolution is defined as either when the couple stopped living together or when they officially got divorced, whichever happened earlier. When looking at re-partnering, so far most studies have disregarded

Table 8.2   Number of cases

	Original sample size	Analysis sample, number of:		
		Persons	Events	Person-months
France	10079	884	355	6676
Hungary	13540	884	368	5165
Norway	14481	1641	854	11054

Source: Generations and Gender Survey, Wave 1, data for France (2005), Norway (2007–2008) and Hungary (2004–2005), authors' calculations.

people whose first long-term union was non-marital and/or who did not get married with their second partner (for exceptions, see Beaujouan 2012; Wu and Schimmele 2005). Releasing these restrictions is an important contribution to the literature, considering that about every second child is born outside marriage in the three examined countries (OECD 2011b).

Our main explanatory variable is the parenthood status of the male respondent.[6] In the regression models we use two parenthood status variables. The first one differentiates between fathers and childless men. This is a time-constant variable and only accounts for those children who were born during the first relationship of the men, or at most, eight months after the union ended. The second parenthood status variable further differentiates between cases (time periods) when at least one of the children is co-resident either full-time or part-time, and cases when all children live somewhere else. If parents share physical child custody after separation, both parents report that they live together with the child, so children are considered as also living with the father in these cases, and they divide their time between both parents.[7] The second parental status variable is dynamic in the sense that we keep track of children entering or leaving the father's household. However, the number of children born to the father is not allowed to change during the examined period.

In the analysis the co-residence of father and child means that the child lives with the father either full-time (sole physical custody) or part-time (joint physical custody). The dataset does not allow us to make further differentiation within this category and the number of cases would not make such a more detailed analysis possible. Moreover, shared physical custody is not the majority in any of the countries (Bjarnason and Arnarsson 2011). In spite of the fact that fathers might still spend less time with their children than mothers in the case of shared physical custody, children have a better and more frequent relationship with their father and better outcomes in general if the parents share physical custody than if the children stay only with the mother (Bauserman 2002; Bjarnason and Arnarsson 2011; Nielsen 2011). As Toulemon and Pennec (2010) have pointed out, some parents – especially fathers – are reluctant to report that the child also lives with the other parent (half of the children who are reported to live with the father actually share residence between the parents in France). It means that the dividing line between full-time and part-time co-residence between father and children may be hard to distinguish.

We suppose that the major line of distinction is between fathers who have no physical custody and those who live with their children either on a part-time or a full-time basis. The latter group may also include a few widowers (5–10 per cent in our sample), and cases where the mother has relinquished custody due to major financial difficulties, personal problems or health reasons (Thompson and Laible 1999).

Three sets of models were tested. The first set looks at how the general probability of re-partnering has changed for men; thus these models include no interaction between period and fatherhood status and the dummy parenthood status variable is used only as a control. The second set of models tests if the effect of fatherhood on re-partnering has changed; consequently the dummy parenthood status variable is interacted with period. And finally, the third set of models differentiates between men with co-resident and only non-resident children to see if these groups are affected and have changed differently. Event history analysis with piece-wise exponential models is used.

The other control variables are the same in all the models. They include period (calendar year) and age of the man at the end of the first union, time since the end of the first relationship (dynamic variable), length and type of the first partnership, whether the union ended with the death of the partner, and the level of education of the respondent.[8] Independent variables are summarized in Table 8.3.

RESULTS

During the empirical analysis, first we looked at the characteristics of men after their first relationship dissolved. The descriptive results show that about half of the men whose first stable relationship ended have children; this rate is the highest in Hungary (Figure 8.1). The ratio of men with only non-resident children is lowest in Norway (9 per cent) and highest in Hungary (32 per cent). After their first relationship ended, 25 per cent of the separated or divorced men in France, 26 per cent in Hungary and 37 per cent in Norway lived together with at least one of their children, either full-time or part-time. If we only consider the two groups of fathers,

Table 8.3   Exposure and occurrence table of the independent variables by country

	France		Hungary		Norway	
	Person-month	Event	Person-month	Event	Person-month	Event
Parenthood status						
No children	35 045	203	25 736	195	65 446	460
At least one co-resident child	9632	58	11 223	76	27 302	243
Only non-resident child(ren)	17 273	94	24 991	97	23 814	150
Period at the end of the first union						
1980–1989	26 747	118	31 373	164	48 642	272
1990–1999	28 016	180	25 513	155	50 652	408
2000–2008	7188	56	5065	50	17 268	173
Age at the end of the first union						
<25	16 568	100	14 033	126	29 556	237
25–29	16 477	110	16 700	110	34 381	275
30–34	14 495	74	16 391	61	23 309	163
35–39	8141	34	7489	43	17 667	94
40–49	6269	37	7337	27	11 649	85
Time since the end of the first union						
<1 year	9667	99	9461	145	18 473	164
1–2 years	7865	82	7497	81	15 165	187
2–3 years	6613	45	6276	36	12 501	130
3–5 years	14 303	91	14 190	69	27 169	235
5+ years	23 503	38	24 526	37	43 254	137
Length of first partnership						
0–6 years	37 121	202	34 147	238	75 031	555
7+ years	24 829	153	27 803	130	41 532	298
Type of first partnership						
Cohabitation	36 917	215	17 025	135	71 367	520
Cohabitation then marriage	14 255	86	7264	42	31 118	235
Direct marriage	10 778	54	37 662	191	14 077	99
First partner died						
Yes	1636	11	3697	24	2368	10
No	60 314	344	58 253	345	114 195	844
Level of education						
Primary	15 774	68	11 457	56	32 632	199
Secondary	30 548	179	40 308	237	40 454	327
Tertiary	15 628	108	10 186	75	43 477	328

Source: Generations and Gender Survey, Wave 1, data for France (2005), Norway (2007–2008) and Hungary (2004–2005), authors' calculations.

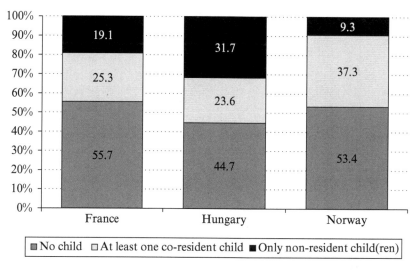

Source: Generations and Gender Survey, Wave 1, data for France (2005), Norway (2007–2008) and Hungary (2004–2005), authors' calculations.

Figure 8.1   Fatherhood status of men at the end of the first union

co-residential parenting is the most common in Norway, where 80 per cent of fathers live with their children right after separation. The corresponding figures are 57 per cent and 43 per cent in France and Hungary, respectively. These percentages decrease as time passes after the dissolution of the union, because children may leave the parental household as they grow up. In some cases, parents continue to live in the same dwelling for some time after separation because of a housing shortage or because it takes time to sell the common house. Moreover, the living or custodial arrangements may also change because of a new union of any of the parents, a residential move, or some other change in the circumstances or preferences of the child or the parents (Maccoby and Mnookin 1992).

Table 8.4 shows the main characteristics of men aged below 50 after the dissolution of their first union by parental status. Generally the groups of fathers with co-resident or non-resident children are quite similar to each other in all the three countries, while childless men are typically younger and more educated than fathers, and their first union was shorter and usually cohabitation. Childless men were on average 27–28 years old when their first union ended, while fathers were aged around 34–36. On average, first unions lasted for 7–8 years, even though the distribution is large. In Hungary, 71 per cent of these relationships were marriages, while

Table 8.4   Characteristics of men at the end of the first union by fatherhood status and country

	No child	At least one co-resident child	Only non-resident child(ren)	Total
France				
Age (years, mean)	27.8	36.1	34.6	31.1
Length of the first union (years, mean)	4.0	12.6	10.3	7.3
1st union was marriage (%)	19.3	72.9	65.0	41.6
1st partner died (%)	2.3	9.4	1.6	4.0
Number of children (mean)	–	1.86	1.74	1.80
Age of the youngest child (mean)	–	7.2	5.7	6.5
Education: primary (%)	21.1	29.9	23.5	23.8
Education: secondary (%)	44.8	47.7	59.6	48.4
Education: tertiary (%)	34.1	22.3	16.8	27.8
Hungary				
Age (years, mean)	27.4	35.6	34.2	31.5
Length of the first union (years, mean)	4.2	12.1	11.2	8.3
1st union was marriage (%)	44.9	93.7	90.4	70.8
1st partner died (%)	4.1	21.4	2.3	7.6
Number of children (mean)	–	1.78	1.52	1.63
Age of the youngest child (mean)	–	7.7	8.0	7.8
Education: primary (%)	13.5	23.6	18.9	17.6
Education: secondary (%)	65.5	57.5	65.6	63.6
Education: tertiary (%)	21.1	19.0	15.5	18.8
Norway				
Age (years, mean)	27.6	35.0	36.4	31.0
Length of the first union (years, mean)	3.9	11.7	12.2	7.4
1st union was marriage (%)	13.7	73.6	72.9	41.5
1st partner died (%)	1.2	5.0	0.6	2.6
Number of children (mean)	–	1.76	1.60	1.73
Age of the youngest child (mean)	–	6.5	8.8	6.9
Education: primary (%)	26.4	25.4	26.3	26.0
Education: secondary (%)	35.3	42.7	43.6	38.8
Education: tertiary (%)	38.3	31.9	30.1	35.1

Source: Generations and Gender Survey, Wave 1, data for France (2005), Norway (2007–2008) and Hungary (2004–2005), authors' calculations.

only 42 per cent of men married their first stable partners in France and Norway. Due to the low mortality of women in this age group, very few first unions ended with the death of the female partner (3–8 per cent). Among fathers who live with their child(ren) on a part- or full-time basis, this figure is higher, especially in Hungary (21 per cent). Hungarian fathers are more likely to live with their children because of the death of the mother than French or Hungarian fathers are. This difference may also mean that Hungarian men are less likely to take (or to be allowed) partial or full responsibility of their children if the mother is also available.

Fathers have 1.6–1.8 children on average. In all three countries about half of the fathers have one child, one-third have two children and only every fifth father has three or more children. The mean number of children is highest among fathers who live with at least one child full-time or part-time. The youngest child of the men was around 6–8 years old when the relationship of the parents dissolved.

The educational background of fathers with part- or full-time co-resident and non-resident children also differ from each other to some extent in France and Hungary: men with primary and tertiary education are similarly over-represented among fathers with co-resident children, compared to all fathers.

About half of the men in our sample found a new partner before they turned 50. Re-partnering was the most likely in Norway (55.4 per cent) and less likely in France (43.7 per cent) and Hungary (46.3 per cent). Tables 8.5–8.7 show the results of the three sets of event history models for the three countries.

Regarding the likelihood of re-partnering of men in general (Table 8.5), there has been no significant change in France and Hungary. Contrastingly, the chances of finding a new partner increased significantly between the 1980s and the 1990s in Norway but have not changed thereafter.

If we look at the difference between fathers and childless men (Table 8.6), we can see that the likelihood of re-partnering has not changed for men without children in any of the countries since the 1980s. In France there has been no change in either group and fatherhood in general does not influence re-partnering. In Norway fathers have become more likely to enter a new union. Hungarian fathers experienced a temporary drop in their chances of re-partnering in the 1990s. (This finding should be treated with caution due to the small number of cases.)

If we compare fathers with and without co-resident children (Table 8.7), there is no difference between the two groups regarding their chances of re-partnering in Norway: both groups have experienced increasing probabilities, especially in the latest period. This finding indicates that the two groups of fathers are the most similar to each other in Norway. In Hungary

Table 8.5 Determinants of the re-partnering of men after the dissolution of their first relationship: general change

	France		Hungary		Norway	
Period at the end of the first union						
1980–1989	(ref.)		(ref.)		(ref.)	
1990–1999	1.134		0.858		1.300	**
2000–2008	0.952		0.776		1.298	*
Parenthood status						
Had no children	(ref.)		(ref.)		(ref.)	
Had child(ren)	0.969		0.873		1.242	*
Age at the end of the first union						
<25	1.901	**	2.052	***	1.368	*
25–29	1.818	**	1.671	**	1.273	*
30–34	(ref.)		(ref.)		(ref.)	
35–39	0.759		1.288		0.682	**
40–49	0.739		0.658	†	0.705	*
Time since the end of the first union						
<1 year	(ref.)		(ref.)		(ref.)	
1–2 years	1.022		0.706	*	1.389	**
2–3 years	0.663	*	0.377	***	1.181	
3–5 years	0.616	**	0.319	***	0.993	
5+ years	0.152	***	0.090	***	0.370	***

Length of first partnership			
0–6 years	(ref.)	(ref.)	(ref.)
7+ years	1.709 **	1.032	1.081
Type of first partnership			
Cohabitation	0.891	0.946	0.852
Cohabitation then marriage	1.050	0.991	0.976
Direct marriage	(ref.)	(ref.)	(ref.)
First partner died	1.097	1.340	0.641
Level of education			
Primary	0.826	0.891	0.841
Secondary	(ref.)	(ref.)	(ref.)
Tertiary	1.100	1.163	1.011
Intercept	0.006 ***	0.013 ***	0.007 ***
Log likelihood	−1016.8	−1071.9	−2080.4

Notes: Regression results, discrete-time event history analyses; relative risks. Significance levels: *** p <0.001, ** p <0.01, * p <0.05, † p <0.1.

Source: Generations and Gender Survey, Wave 1, data for France (2005), Norway (2007–2008) and Hungary (2004–2005), authors' calculations.

199

Table 8.6   Determinants of the re-partnering of men after the dissolution of their first relationship: difference in change between fathers and childless men

	France		Hungary		Norway	
Period at the end of the first union (no children)						
1980–1989	(ref.)		(ref.)		(ref.)	
1990–1999	1.105		1.092		1.127	
2000–2008	0.893		0.818		0.985	
Parenthood status (in 1980–1989)						
Had no children	(ref.)		(ref.)		(ref.)	
Had child(ren)	0.918		1.067		0.962	
Parenthood status & period (interaction effects)						
Had child(ren) & 1990–1999	1.058		0.599	†	1.336	†
Had child(ren) & 2000–2008	1.179		0.977		1.915	**
Age at the end of the first union						
<25	1.912	**	2.073	***	1.402	*
25–29	1.832	**	1.665	**	1.306	*
30–34	(ref.)		(ref.)		(ref.)	
35–39	0.759		1.349		0.698	*
40–49	0.737		0.670		0.704	*
Time since the end of the first union						
<1 year	(ref.)		(ref.)		(ref.)	
1–2 years	1.021		0.707	*	1.389	**
2–3 years	0.662	*	0.379	***	1.179	
3–5 years	0.616	**	0.321	***	0.989	
5+ years	0.152	***	0.092	***	0.367	***

Variable			
Length of first partnership			
0–6 years	(ref.)	(ref.)	(ref.)
7+ years	1.718 **	1.038	1.060
Type of first partnership			
Cohabitation	0.884	0.931	0.827
Cohabitation then marriage	1.041	1.020	0.953
Direct marriage	(ref.)	(ref.)	(ref.)
First partner died	1.102	1.360	0.623
Level of education			
Primary	0.821	0.872	0.834
Secondary	(ref.)	(ref.)	(ref.)
Tertiary	1.102	1.165	0.996
Intercept	0.007 ***	0.011 ***	0.008 ***
Log likelihood	−1016.7	−1069.2	−2075.1

Notes: Regression results, discrete-time event history analyses; relative risks. Significance levels: *** p <0.001, ** p <0.01, * p <0.05, † p <0.1.

Source: Generations and Gender Survey, Wave 1, data for France (2005), Norway (2007–2008) and Hungary (2004–2005), authors' calculations.

Table 8.7 Determinants of the re-partnering of men after the dissolution of their first relationship: difference in change between fathers with co-resident and non-resident children

	France		Hungary		Norway	
Period at the end of the first union (only non-resident children)						
1980–1989	(ref.)		(ref.)		(ref.)	
1990–1999	1.023		0.754		1.455	†
2000–2008	0.700		0.595		2.038	*
Parenthood status (in 1980–1989)						
No children	0.932		1.078		1.065	
At least one co-resident child	0.707		1.419		1.051	
Only non-resident child(ren)	(ref.)		(ref.)		(ref.)	
Parenthood status & period (interaction effects)						
No child & 1990–1999	1.077		1.439		0.775	
No child & 2000–2008	1.268		1.364		0.484	*
Co-resident children & 1990–1999	1.300		0.744		1.040	
Co-resident children & 2000–2008	2.720	†	2.291	†	0.883	
Age at the end of the first union						
<25	1.933	**	2.042	***	1.405	*
25–29	1.832	**	1.700	**	1.310	*
30–34	(ref.)		(ref.)		(ref.)	
35–39	0.755		1.319		0.704	*
40–49	0.744		0.694		0.708	*

Time since the end of the first union

<1 year	(ref.)		(ref.)		(ref.)	
1–2 years	1.022		0.708	*	1.390	**
2–3 years	0.665	*	0.380	***	1.180	
3–5 years	0.616	**	0.324	***	0.991	
5+ years	0.149	***	0.094	***	0.369	***
Length of first partnership						
0–6 years	(ref.)		(ref.)		(ref.)	
7+ years	1.726	**	0.997		1.059	
Type of first partnership						
Cohabitation	0.892		0.927		0.831	
Cohabitation then marriage	1.066		1.003		0.956	
Direct marriage	(ref.)		(ref.)		(ref.)	
First partner died	1.108		1.237		0.614	
Level of education						
Primary	0.823		0.843		0.835	
Secondary	(ref.)		(ref.)		(ref.)	
Tertiary	1.110		1.154		0.992	
Intercept	0.007	***	0.011	***	0.008	***
Log likelihood	−1014.8		−1064.9		−2074.8	

Notes: Regression results, discrete-time event history analyses; relative risks. Significance levels: *** p <0.001, ** p <0.01, * p <0.05, † p <0.1.

Source: Generations and Gender Survey, Wave 1, data for France (2005), Norway (2007–2008) and Hungary (2004–2005), authors' calculations.

the drop in the 1990s affected both groups of fathers; afterwards, the likelihood of re-partnering increased among Hungarian men with co-resident children. In France there has been a non-significant but visible decrease for men with non-resident children, and the effect of having co-resident children became positive by the 2000s, suggesting that the probability of re-partnering has diverged for the two groups of men. To put it differently, fathers with full- or part-time co-resident children find a new partner more easily in the new millennium than before in all three countries. Norwegian fathers with only non-resident children have also increased their chances of re-partnering. Non-residential fatherhood has become an obstacle to re-partnering in France and Hungary, even though the differences are not significant.

Results regarding the control variables are similar in the three models. The younger the respondents, the faster they find a new partner, especially if they are still in their twenties. The probability of re-partnering usually decreases as more time passes since the end of the first relationship. The characteristics of the first relationship have almost no effect on establishing a subsequent union. The only exception is France, where men are more likely to re-partner after a relatively long (seven years or more) first relationship. Only one socio-economic background variable was available in the dataset, the highest level of education, and it has no effect on re-partnering in any of the three countries.

DISCUSSION

In this chapter we have analysed how fatherhood status affects re-partnering after the dissolution of the first union of men, and how this effect has changed since the 1980s in France, Norway and Hungary. Examining this process among men in more than one country has been rare in this field of research, especially using a perspective of three decades. Our findings also shed light on the importance of distinguishing between different groups of men in the re-partnering process. We used data from the Generations and Gender Survey and performed event history regression analyses.

We formulated five hypotheses for the changing probability of re-partnering and the effect of fatherhood status. These hypotheses were based on the three general considerations of need, attractiveness and opportunity. However, we did not (and could not) test the effect and importance of these three dimensions directly. Instead, we looked at the overall picture and used the three considerations to explain unexpected results and country differences.

The results of the empirical analysis confirmed some of our hypotheses. Hypothesis 1 was confirmed for France and Hungary, where the probability of re-partnering has not changed among men in general; while there was an increase among Norwegian men between the 1980s and the 1990s. Their increasing opportunities (the growing instability of unions, the increasing number of potential partners, developments of the father-friendly welfare state) and the growing attractiveness of involved Norwegian fathers may have made it more likely for these men to re-partner in the new millennium than one or two decades earlier.

The results confirmed Hypothesis 2 for all three countries: there has been no change in childless men's probability to re-partner. Their chances of re-partnering probably depend on factors that are stable over time, or changes in one dimension may have been counterbalanced by changes in another one.

Hypothesis 3 concerned the unchanged probability of re-partnering for fathers, and it was confirmed only for France. Contrary to our expectations, the likelihood of re-partnering has changed in Norway and Hungary: it has increased in the former country, and it temporarily decreased in the latter society in the 1990s. Changes in Norway may be explained by the trends that we summarized above (in relation to Hypothesis 1). The temporarily decreasing re-partnering probability of Hungarian men in the 1990s was probably due to the abrupt and drastic social, economic and policy changes that took place after the transition of 1989. One possible explanation is that the life circumstances (income, material deprivation, well-being, social networks, physical and mental health) of divorced fathers greatly deteriorated after the transition of 1989, while men with families have experienced improving conditions (Vukovich 2006). The coverage of formal childcare for pre-school children also dropped sharply during the early 1990s in Hungary (Blaskó and Gábos 2012). These changes probably influenced custodial fathers more than non-custodial ones.

We found a weak negative effect of non-residential fatherhood in France and Hungary in the 2000s, and a significant negative impact in Hungary in the 1990s (Hypothesis 4). For Norwegian fathers it has become easier to find a new partner, regardless of the residential situation of the children. One possible explanation concerns the high involvement of Norwegian fathers in the upbringing and everyday life of their children that may seem especially attractive for prospective partners in a gender-egalitarian society like Norway, where expectations for fathers go beyond being a good provider for the family and also include fathers as carers (Skevik 2006). Even though parenting takes time and energy, the availability of state-subsidized high-quality childcare leaves parents with more free time and they can focus on spending more 'quality time' with their children (Rønsen 2004).

Previous research found that re-partnering does not necessarily reduce non-resident fathers' contact with their children from the previous relationship (Manning and Smock 1999). Moreover, fathers in shared parenting may feel less stressed and more satisfied than fathers whose children live with the mother (Neoh and Mellor 2010).

Hypothesis 5 was confirmed: having full- or part-time co-resident children has an increasingly positive influence on the re-partnering of fathers. This positive affect appeared earliest in Norway, followed by the other two countries in the new millennium. Fatherhood had a significant negative effect on re-partnering only in Hungary and only in the 1990s, and the effect of co-residential fatherhood has even become positive in the new millennium. This lack of negative impact contrasts with findings regarding the re-partnering of lone mothers and also some of the results on men (e.g. de Graaf and Kalmijn 2003; Poortman 2007; Sweeney 1997), but it is in line with some other results (e.g. Wu 1994; Ivanova et al. 2013 – except for Norway). The 'good father' effect (Goldscheider and Sassler 2006; Prioux 2006; Wu and Schimmele 2005) and changing attitudes towards divorce and separation (Liefbroer and Fokkema 2008) may play an important role in this trend.

The finding that the rate of re-partnering of men with co-resident children has increased coincides with the result of Bernhardt and Goldscheider (2002), the only other study that has examined the changing effect of fatherhood status on re-partnering. As they put it, '[t]his increase may reflect the greater willingness of some women to care for "someone else's" children; men's lack of increase, in contrast, suggests men's continued resistance to having to support them' (Bernhardt and Goldscheider 2002, p. 295).

Our results underline that more targeted research would be needed on single or joint custodial fathers, preferably in a comparative perspective, in order to better understand who these fathers are, how their families live their everyday lives, and what the consequences are of this arrangement for the well-being of the parents and the children. This research area would bridge the gap between studies on fatherhood and fathering – that most often focus on partnered or non-resident separated fathers – on the one hand, and studies of single mothers on the other hand. The questions of how single fatherhood and joint physical custody affect the life course of men and their children, which fathers live with their children either full-time or part-time after parental separation, how custodial decisions are made, and why more and more women are willing to take on the potentially problematic role of the stepmother, clearly require more scholarly attention.

The present chapter shows that fathers' involvement and co-residence with children after parental separation make it easier for men to re-partner. There are a few other studies that show the beneficial effects of joint physical custody. For example, joint physical custody also makes re-partnering easier for mothers (Schnor and Pasteels 2015). Moreover, recent custody law reforms in the United States were proved to have unintended positive consequences on the family behaviour of men (Halla 2013). Among others, it seems likely that men are willing to invest more in children under joint custody, since they can expect to spend a substantial amount of time with their children even after potential divorce or separation. If this relationship is also true for European countries, high father involvement in childcare, egalitarian gender attitudes and a growing preference for joint physical custody may mutually affect and strengthen each other, thus benefiting society on the whole.

Finally, we have to acknowledge the limitations of our study. Firstly, couples with (small) children are less likely to separate than childless ones (Andersson 1997; Waite and Lillard 1991), so fathers are probably under-represented among divorced and separated men. Secondly, some potentially important variables were not available in the data, such as non-resident fathers' contact with their children after separation, and the amount and nature of their involvement in childcare. In the future it would be important for panel surveys to include these kinds of questions because such factors can have important implications not only for the re-partnering process but also for the well-being of children and fathers. Lacking these questions, we also cannot differentiate between co-resident fathers who have sole physical custody and those who share custody, which may be a crucial factor to consider in the future due to the increasing number of shared physical custody decisions in most European countries. No data were available on the employment status of the fathers, although we are aware of the fact that men with better positions on the labour market have a higher probability of re-partnering, especially in less gender-egalitarian societies such as Hungary. We also have no information on a possibly important factor that men and women likely consider when they re-partner: fertility intentions. People who want (more) children, people who are satisfied with their current number of children, or intentionally childless people may select a partner with complementary intentions.

Despite its limitations, however, this study can contribute to a better understanding of the re-partnering process of men and fathers in particular. Such analyses are important because they can make it clearer for policy makers and the general public that policies which foster fathers' involvement with their children are important and beneficial. Fathers' involvement not only can increase the quality of the relationship between fathers and children and decrease the burden of childcare on women, but may also help fathers to find a new partner.

NOTES

*   Acknowledgement: the research was partially supported by the project 'Mapping Family Transitions: Causes, Consequences, Complexities, and Context' (no. K109397) of the Hungarian Scientific Research Fund (OTKA).
1. Here we only consider heterosexual relationships.
2. All dependent children who are younger than 25 years and live with only one parent are included in this calculation.
3. Data were obtained from the Generations and Gender Programme Data Archive and were created by Statistics Norway, the Institut national d'études démographiques (INED) and the Hungarian Demographic Research Institute.
4. We use this age limit because we are mainly interested in re-partnering while the man has children under 18. We are aware that having children of any age may affect re-partnering but we believe that the mechanisms are different in the case of adult children and minors. Studying the effect of having adult children (or even grandchildren) would require a different study.
5. We regard cohabitations that lasted for at least three months as significant for the individual's life. Since most couples have separate households at the start of the partnership and start cohabiting only later (e.g. Ermisch and Siedler 2008), partnerships actually start before the couple moves in together. Moreover, only 4 per cent of the first cohabiting relationships or marriages lasted for less than 12 months in our sample. As a sensitivity check we run the regression models only on those respondents whose first union lasted for at least one year. Omitting men with a shorter first relationship did not change our results.
6. Several alternatives for the parenthood status variables have been tested. The simplest approach is to use a dummy variable (whether someone has any children or not), and there are several other possibilities that previous research has found to be useful predictors. We may make a distinction by the number of children, their residential status or age. The variables may either refer to the start of the risk period (time-constant) or they may be dynamic. Moreover, these criteria may be combined. We had to make a compromise between maximizing information and minimizing complexity. Different regression models (results not shown) indicate that the major distinctions are between having any children or not, and whether any of the children live with the respondent. The age of the children only marginally matters, and moreover, only few people with children above 18 are included in the two subsamples.
7. Joint physical custody (shared residence) presumes approximately equal division of time with children between the parents in all three countries (Boele-Woelki et al. 2005; Kitterød and Lyngstad 2012). The dataset does not include information on what custody decision was made after separation or divorce (and the initial arrangement may later be changed), and on how much time the children actually spend with each parent. In our data the percentages of father–child co-residence are similar to what other studies found, thus it seems reasonable to assume that reports of co-residence in fact mean that the child spends a considerable amount of time in the father's dwelling, and not only a few times a month.
8. We differentiated between the following categories: primary (International Standard Classification of Education, ISCED 1–2), secondary (ISCED 3–4) and tertiary (ISCED 5–6) education. College or university students were assigned tertiary education (around 5 per cent of all the cases in each country).

REFERENCES

Andersson, G. (1997), 'The impact of children on divorce risks of Swedish women', *European Journal of Population*, 13 (2), 109–145.

Barre, C. (2003), '1,6 million d'enfants vivent dans une famille recomposée', INSEE Première No. 901.

Bauserman, R. (2002), 'Child adjustment in joint-custody versus sole-custody arrangements: a meta-analytic review', *Journal of Family Psychology*, 16 (1), 91–102.

Beaujouan, É. (2011), 'Second-union fertility in France: partners' age and other factors', *Population-E*, 66 (2), 239–274.

Beaujouan, É. (2012), 'Repartnering in France: the role of gender, age and past fertility', *Advances in Life Course Research*, 17 (2), 69–80.

Beaujouan, É., A. Regnier-Loilier and C. Villeneueve-Gokalp (2009), 'Neither single, nor in a couple: a study of living apart together in France', *Demographic Research*, 21 (4), 75–108.

Becker, G.S. (1981), *A Treatise on the Family*, Cambridge, MA: Harvard University Press.

Bernhardt, E. and F. Goldscheider (2002), 'Children and union formation in Sweden', *European Sociological Review*, 18 (3), 289–299.

Bianchi, S.M., M. Milkie, L. Sayer and J. Robinson (2000), 'Is anyone doing the housework? Trends in the gender division of household labor', *Social Forces*, 79 (1), 191–228.

Bjarnason, T. and A.M. Arnarsson (2011), 'Joint physical custody and communication with parents: a cross-national study of children in 36 Western countries', *Journal of Comparative Family Studies*, 42 (6), 871–890.

Blaskó, Zs. and A. Gábos (2012), 'Redistribution effects of the childcare system in Hungary: who is cared for?', Budapest: Budapest Institute, accessed 25 September 2014 at http://www.budapestinstitute.eu/uploads/V4_child_care_enrolment_HU1.pdf.

Boele-Woelki, K., B. Braat and I. Curry-Sumner (eds) (2005), *European Family Law in Action: Parental Responsibilities*, Vol. III, Antwerp, Belgium and Oxford, UK: Intersentia.

Breton, D. and F. Prioux (2009), 'The one-child family: France in the European context', *Demographic Research*, 20 (27), 657–692.

Cabrera, N.J., C.S. Tamis-LeMonda, R.H. Bradley, S. Hofferth and M.L. Lamb (2000), 'Fatherhood in the twenty-first century', *Child Development*, 71 (1), 127–136.

Chzhen, Y. and J. Bradshaw (2012), 'Lone parents, poverty and policy in the European Union', *Journal of European Social Policy*, 22 (5), 487–506.

Council of Europe (2014), 'Council of Europe Family Policy Database', accessed 28 August 2014 at www.coe.int/familypolicy/database.

de Graaf, P.M. and M. Kalmijn (2003), 'Alternative routes in the remarriage market: competing-risk analyses of union formation after divorce', *Social Forces*, 81 (4), 1459–1498.

Di Nallo, A. (2015), 'Gender gap in repartnering: the role of children: evidence from the UK', paper presented at the Annual Meeting of the Population Association of America, San Diego, CA, 30 April–2 May.

Ellingsæter, A.L., A-M. Jensen and M. Lie (2013), 'The social meaning of children embedded in institutions and personal relations', in A.L. Ellingsæter, A-M. Jensen and M. Lie (eds), *The Social Meaning of Children and Fertility Change in Europe*, London: Routledge, pp. 170–179.

Elrod, L.D. and M.D. Dale (2008), 'Paradigm shifts and pendulum swings in child custody: the interests of children in the balance', *Family Law Quarterly*, 42 (3), 381–418.

Ermisch, J. and T. Siedler (2008), 'Living apart together', in M. Brynin and J. Ermisch (eds), *Changing Relationships*, New York: Taylor & Francis, pp. 29–43.

European Commission (2009), *The Provision of Childcare Services: A Comparative Review of 30 European Countries*, Luxembourg: European Commission's Expert Group on Gender and Employment.

Eurostat (2012), 'At-risk-of-poverty rate by poverty threshold and household type', accessed 28 February 2015 at http://appsso.eurostat.ec.europa.eu/nui/show.do?dataset=ilc_li03&lang=en.

Földházi, E. (2010), 'New partnership after first divorce: an event history analysis', *Demográfia English Edition*, 53 (5), 78–101.

Gauthier, A.H. and J. Hatzius (1997), 'Family benefits and fertility: an econometric analysis', *Population Studies*, 51 (3), 295–306.

Goldscheider, F. and S. Sassler (2006), 'Creating stepfamilies: integrating children into the study of union formation', *Journal of Marriage and Family*, 68 (2), 275–291.

Goldscheider, F. and L.J. Waite (1986), 'Sex differences in the entry into marriage', *American Journal of Sociology*, 9 (2), 91–109.

Halla, M. (2013), 'The effect of joint custody on family outcomes', *Journal of the European Economic Association*, 11 (2), 278–315.

Hobson, B. and S. Fahlén (2009), 'Competing scenarios for European fathers: applying Sen's capabilities and agency framework to work–family balance', *Annals of the American Academy of Political and Social Science*, 624 (1), 214–233.

IMF (2015), 'World Economic Outlook Database', accessed 2 June 2015 at http://www.imf.org/external/pubs/ft/weo/2015/01/weodata/index.aspx.

Ivanova, K., M. Kalmijn and W. Uunk (2013), 'The effect of children on men's and women's chances of re-partnering in a European context', *European Journal of Population*, 29 (4), 417–444.

Kalmijn, M. and W. Uunk (2007), 'Regional value differences in Europe and the social consequences of divorce: a test of the stigmatization hypothesis', *Social Science Research*, 36 (2), 447–468.

Kitterød, R.H. and J. Lyngstad (2012), 'Untraditional caring arrangements among parents living apart: the case of Norway', *Demographic Research*, 27 (5), 121–152.

Lampard, R. and K. Peggs (1999), 'Repartnering: the relevance of parenthood and gender to cohabitation and remarriage among the formerly married', *British Journal of Sociology*, 50 (3), 443–465.

Lesthaeghe, R. (2010), 'The unfolding story of the second demographic transition', *Population and Development Review*, 36 (2), 211–251.

Letablier, M. (2013), 'The politics of parenting', in A.L. Ellingsæter, A.M. Jensen and M. Lie (eds), *The Social Meaning of Children and Fertility Change in Europe*, London: Routledge, pp. 12–30.

Levin, I. (2004), 'Living apart together: a new family form', *Current Sociology*, 52 (2), 223–240.

Liefbroer, A.C. and T. Fokkema (2008), 'Recent trends in demographic attitudes and behavior: is the second demographic transition moving to Southern and Eastern Europe?', in J. Surkyn, P. Deboosere and J. Van Bavel (eds), *Demographic Challenges for the 21st Century: A State of the Art in Demography*, Brussels: Brussels University Press, pp. 115–141.

Maccoby, E.E. and R.H. Mnookin (1992), *Dividing the Child: Social and Legal Dilemmas of Custody*, Cambridge, MA: Harvard University Press.

Manning, W.D. and P.J. Smock (1999), 'New families and non-resident father-child visitation', *Social Forces*, 78 (1), 87–116.

Martin, C. and I. Théry (2001), 'The PACS and marriage and cohabitation in France', *Journal of Law, Policy and the Family*, 15 (1), 135–158.

Meggiolaro, S. and F. Ongaro (2008), 'Repartnering after marital dissolution: does context play a role?', *Demographic Research*, 19 (57), 1913–1933.

Meggiolaro, S. and F. Ongaro (2010), 'The implications of marital instability for a woman's fertility: empirical evidence from Italy', *Demographic Research*, 23 (34), 963–996.

Merz, E.M. and A.C. Liefbroer (2012), 'The attitude toward voluntary childlessness in Europe: cultural and institutional explanations', *Journal of Marriage and Family*, 74 (3), 587–600.

Munch, A., J.M. McPherson and L. Smith-Lovin (1997), 'Gender, children, and social contact: the effects of childrearing for men and women', *American Sociological Review*, 62 (4), 509–520.

Murinkó, L. (2014), 'A nemi szerepekkel és a családdal kapcsolatos attitűdök európai kitekintésben: Értékek és gyermekgondozás' (Attitudes towards gender roles and family in a European perspective: values and child care), *Szociológiai Szemle*, 24 (1), 67–101.

Neilson, J. and M. Stanfors (2014), 'It's about time! Gender, parenthood and household division of labour under different welfare regimes', *Journal of Family Issues*, 35 (8), 1066–1088.

Neoh, J. and D. Mellor (2010), 'Shared parenting: adding children's voices and their measures of adjustment to the evaluation', *Journal of Child Custody*, 7 (3), 155–175.

Nielsen, L. (2011), 'Shared parenting after divorce: a review of shared residential parenting research', *Journal of Divorce and Remarriage*, 52 (8), 586–609.

Noack, T. (2001), 'Cohabitation in Norway: an accepted and gradually more regulated way of living', *International Journal of Law, Policy and the Family*, 15 (1), 102–117.

OECD (2011a), *Doing Better for Families*, Paris: OECD Publishing, accessed 8 December 2014 at http://dx.doi.org/10.1787/9789264098732-en.

OECD (2011b), 'OECD Family Database', Paris: OECD Publishing, accessed 17 September 2013 at www.oecd.org/social/family/database.

Oláh, L.Sz. (2011), 'Should governments in Europe be more aggressive in pushing for gender equality to raise fertility? The second "YES"', *Demographic Research*, 24 (9), 217–224.

Ongaro, F., S. Mazzuco and S. Meggiolaro (2009), 'Economic consequences of union dissolution in Italy: findings from the European Community Household Panel', *European Journal of Population*, 25 (1), 45–65.

Oppenheimer, V.K. (1988), 'A theory of marriage timing', *American Journal of Sociology*, 94 (3), 563–591.

Poortman, A.R. (2007), 'The first cut is the deepest? The role of the relationship career for union formation', *European Sociological Review*, 23 (5), 585–598.

Prioux, F. (2006), 'Cohabitation, marriage and separation: contrasts in Europe', *Population and Societies*, 422, 1–4.

Reimondos, A., A. Evans and E. Gray (2011), 'Living-apart-together (LAT) relationships in Australia', *Family Matters*, 87, 43–55.

Róbert, P., E. Bukodi and R. Luijkx (2001), 'Employment patterns in Hungarian couples', in H.-P. Blossfeld and S. Drobnic (eds), *Careers of Couples in Contemporary Society: From Male Breadwinner to Dual-earner Families*, Oxford: Oxford University Press, pp. 307–331.

Rønsen, M. (2004), 'Fertility and family policy in Norway: a reflection on trends and possible connections', *Demographic Research*, 10 (10), 265–286.

Rosenfeld, M.J. and R.J. Thomas (2012), 'Searching for a mate: the rise of the internet as a social intermediary', *American Sociological Review*, 77 (4) 523–547.

Saxonberg, S. and T. Sirovatka (2006), 'Failing family policy in post-communist Central Europe', *Journal of Comparative Policy Analysis*, 8 (2), 185–202.

Schnor, C. and I. Pasteels (2015), 'The effect of custody arrangement on repartnering after divorce: evidence from a policy reform promoting joint physical custody', paper presented at the Annual Meeting of the Population Association of America, San Diego, CA, 30 April–2 May.

Scott, J. (2006), 'Families and gender roles: how attitudes are changing', *Arxius de Sociologica*, 15, 143–154.

Skevik, A. (2006), '"Absent fathers" or "reorganized families"? Variations in father-child contact after parental break-up in Norway', *Sociological Review*, 54 (1), 114–132.

Skinner, C., J. Bradshaw and J. Davidson (2007), 'Child support policy: an international perspective', Research Report No. 405, University of York, Department for Work and Pensions.

South, S.J. (1991), 'Sociodemographic differentials in mate selection preferences', *Journal of Marriage and the Family*, 53 (4), 928–940.

Spéder, Zs. (2005), 'Az élettársi kapcsolat térhódítása Magyarországon és néhány szempont a demográfiai átalakulás értelmezéséhez' (The rise of cohabitation as first union in Hungary and some reflections on recent demographic transition), *Demográfia*, 48 (3–4), 187–217.

Spéder, Zs. (2011), 'Ellentmondó elvárások között . . . családi férfiszerepek, apaképek a mai Magyarországon' (Between contradicting expectations . . . male roles in the family, image of fathers in contemporary Hungary), in I. Nagy and M. Pongrácz (eds), *Szerepváltozások: Jelentés a nők és férfiak helyzetéről 2011*, Budapest: TÁRKI and Nemzeti Erőforrás Minisztérium, pp. 207–228.

Spijker, J. and M. Solsona (2012), 'Atlas of divorce and post-divorce indicators in Europe', Papers de Demografia 412, Centre d'Estudis Demogràfics, Universitat Autònoma de Barcelona.

Stewart, S.D., W.D. Manning and P.J. Smock (2003), 'Union formation among men in the US: does having prior children matter?', *Journal of Marriage and Family*, 6 (1), 90–104.

Sullivan, O., F.C. Billari and E. Altintas (2014), 'Father's changing contributions to child care and domestic work in very low-fertility countries: the effect of education', *Journal of Family Issues*, 35 (8), 1048–1065.

Sweeney, M.M. (1997), 'Remarriage of women and men after divorce: the role of socioeconomic prospects', *Journal of Family Issues*, 18 (5), 479–502.

Sweeney, M.M. (2010), 'Remarriage and stepfamilies: strategic sites for family scholarship in the 21st century', *Journal of Marriage and Family*, 72 (3), 667–684.

Szalma, I. (2010), 'Attitűdök a házasságról és a gyermekvállalásról' (Attitudes on marriage and childbearing), *Demográfia*, 53 (1), 38–66.

Thompson, R.A. and D.J. Laible (1999), 'Noncustodial parents', in M.E. Lamb (ed.), *Parenting and Child Development in "Nontraditional" Families*, Mahwah, NJ, USA and London, UK: Lawrence Erlbaum, pp. 103–123.

Toulemon, L. and S. Pennec (2010), 'Multi-residence in France and Australia: why count them? What is at stake? Double counting and actual family situation', *Demographic Research*, 23 (1), 1–40.

UNDP (2014), *Human Development Report 2014. Sustaining Human Progress: Reducing Vulnerabilities and Building Resilience*, New York: United Nations Development Programme.

UNECE (2005), *Generations & Gender Programme: Survey Instruments*, New York, USA and Geneva, Switzerland: United Nations.

Vukovich, G. (2006), 'Az elvált apák helyzetének néhány aspektusa' (Some aspects of the situation of divorced fathers), in T. Kolosi, I. Gy. Tóth and Gy. Vukovich (eds), *Társadalmi riport 2006*, Budapest: TÁRKI, pp. 267–283.

Waite, L.J. and L.A. Lillard (1991), 'Children and marital disruption', *American Journal of Sociology*, 96 (4), 930–953.

Weiss, E. and O. Szeibert (2014), *Parental Responsibilities: Hungary, National Report*, Utrecht: Commission on European Family Law, accessed 30 May 2014 at http://ceflonline.net/wp-content/uploads/Hungary-Parental-Responsibilities. pdf.

Williams, S. (2008), 'What is fatherhood? Searching for a reflexive father', *Sociology*, 42 (3), 487–502.

Wu, Z. (1994), 'Remarriage in Canada: a social exchange perspective', *Journal of Divorce and Remarriage*, 2 (1), 191–224.

Wu, Z. and C.M. Schimmele (2005), 'Repartnering after first union disruption', *Journal of Marriage and Family*, 67 (1), 27–36.

Zagheni, E. and M. Zannella (2013), 'The life cycle dimension of time transfers in Europe', *Demographic Research*, 29 (35), 937–948.

PART IV

Looking forward

9. Why demography needs (new) theories

Wendy Sigle

INTRODUCTION

In his 1995 plenary to the European Population Conference entitled 'God has chosen to give the easy problems to the physicists: or why demographers need theory', Guillaume Wunsch observed that 'Demography has never had a grand explanatory paradigm, such as the postulate of rationality and the concept of utility in microeconomics' (Wunsch 1995, section 3, para. 1). He went on to argue that '[t]he lack of a grand unified approach is not necessarily a disadvantage' (para. 3) but it does mean that 'demographers have to cannibalize other fields of inquiry, in order to found their explanations' (para. 4). I appreciate Wunsch's carefully chosen and evocative turn of phrase, even if, from a different vantage point, and one which benefits from an additional two decades' hindsight, it is not exactly the imagery I would choose: I have tended to think of demographers less as a tribe of cannibals and more as a colonized people,[1] but will set that distinction aside, at least for now. Whether they have been ingested, plundered or thrust upon us, the theoretical perspectives that inform demographic inquiry have often come from elsewhere. Few would deny, I think, that economics has played a particularly prominent role in the theoretical and methodological orientation of some areas of study, including family demography.

Just a few years before Wunsch delivered his plenary, Eileen Crimmins (1993) surveyed three decades of work published in the journal *Demography* and outlined intellectual developments in the field. She cites the 'growing influence of economists and economic modelling' (p. 585) as one of the explanations for changes in 'the theoretical models guiding demographic analysis' (p. 585). As new theoretical priorities gained influence, so too, did their associated methodological priorities and techniques. Crimmins observes that, in the early years of the journal, a relatively large share of studies involved the analysis of vital statistics and census data, with groups rather than individuals as the unit of analysis. By the early 1990s, she describes nothing short of a sea change in the methodology of social demography:[2] 'We have moved from descriptive methods and data to analysis that is based largely on the application of causal models. The availability of certain types of data and the power to easily apply complex statistical techniques have encouraged the development of methods appropriate to this emphasis on causal models' (Crimmins 1993, p. 585). We entered what she called the 'era of the independent variable' (p. 585), a development marked by the rapid increase in the number of studies making use of multivariate regression techniques, with a trend towards increasingly long lists of control variables. This latter development, in particular, meant that the empirical models presented in social demographic research came to look far less distinct from the reduced form models that were being estimated by many applied microeconomists (Sigle-Rushton 2014). In previous work, I have argued that the way demographers responded to new data and computing opportunties had important and enduring implications for the way we understand and produce knowledge (see, e.g., Sigle-Rushton 2012). I find it noteworthy that the transformation Crimmins describes coincided with theoretical developments in the social sciences, such as the elaboration of intersectionality which, if contemplated, could at the very least have motivated a critical pause.

It is not so much the incorporation of theories and methods from economics that troubles me, but rather their predominance. I will not pretend that I do not have some particular concerns about its 'grand explanatory paradigm' and (even more so) its methodological preoccupation with issues of selection and causation (Sigle-Rushton 2012), but I would be just as concerned about the hegemonic rise of any particular discipline or theoretical perspective. As we become increasingly comfortable with particular tools and methods, it is all too easy to start to apply them as a matter of routine, to stop questioning whether and why they are appropriate for our particular purposes. When this happens, the value of utilizing an explicit theoretical or conceptual framework – the self-reflection and the outside scrutiny that it invites and facilitates – is compromised. We might, for example, fail to notice the way a particular perspective lends legitimacy to biases and chauvinism. Arland Thornton's (2001) incisive critique of developmental idealism and the methodology of reading history sideways that it legitimates is a salutary reminder that, even without an explicit theoretical frame, we impose meaning in ways that determine how we describe, interpret and seek to effect change in the world around us. The solution is not to abandon theory but to use it reflexively.

This is why I think it is important to ask why mainstream (and quantitative) demography has remained remarkably impervious to the theoretical interventions of feminism and other critical perspectives (Riley and McCarthy 2003). Previous writers have suggested this might have been a conscious decision: 'demography is highly invested in deflecting critical theories, including feminism, that highlight the political nature of science precisely because its theories, research questions, and applications are so very political' (Williams 2010, p. 200). However, if that is the case, I wonder why social policy has not been equally resistant. Scholars in social policy (as well as political science, sociology and family studies) study demographic processes and ask some of the same research questions that demographers do. As a field rather than a discipline in its own right, social policy has also had to look to other disciplines for much of its theory. Like demography, the influence of economics has figured prominently. In the past quarter of a century, however, feminist theoretical perspectives and methodologies have shaped the intellectual trajectory of mainstream social policy (Orloff 1996, 2009). Even if some authors suggest that the integration of feminist concerns has been partial and incomplete (Brush 2002; Orloff 2009), critical and feminist perspectives have left a more discernible mark on mainstream social policy research than can be observed in mainstream social demography. This puzzles me.

In this chapter, my aim is to demonstrate how demographic research would benefit from a more conscious consideration of a wider range of theoretical perspectives. To illustrate what I mean, I focus primarily on one particular (broad and flexible) critical analytic concept – intersectionality – and I draw examples from my own particular area of demographic inquiry: the study of families and family policy. Intersectionality, which Leslie McCall (2005, p. 1771) described as 'one of the most important theoretical contributions of Women's Studies, along with racial and ethnic studies, so far', has been a fleet-footed traveller in the past couple of decades, but for some reason it has not crossed over into the discipline of demography. It is noteworthy that we see virtually no references to 'intersectionality' on the pages of demography journals.[3] For this reason, I think it is sensible to begin in the next section with a brief introduction to the concept of intersectionality, focusing on the issues that I see as being most relevant to quantitative research in demography. I outline its theoretical premise and then trace out some of the methodological implications. By illustrating some of the ways in which intersectionality could contribute to the study of particular topics or questions, my aim is to initiate a discussion amongst the demographic community about the productive potential of adopting a more critical and interdisciplinary theoretical perspective.

THEORETICAL OVERVIEW AND METHODOLOGICAL IMPLICATIONS

Intersectionality: Its Intellectual Development and Premise[4]

Intersectionality is a concept, or perhaps even a research paradigm[5] (Hancock 2007b), which developed over many decades. It encompasses a number of ideas about the complex multidimensionality of subjectivity and social stratification and the consequences of its misspecification. Its origins can be traced back to an 'internal critique and self-reflection of the imagined community of feminism' (Knapp 2005, p. 260). A number of interventions, some of the most prominent of which came from black feminist scholars and activists (Nash 2008), illustrated how the same exclusionary practices that allowed (some privileged groups of) men to lay claim to the term 'humanity' could also be identified in the way some privileged (white, able-bodied, middle-class, heterosexual) feminists made use of the term 'woman'. These assessments, which rely on an understanding of analytic categories as socially defined, draw attention to the process of categorization as an act of power and exclusion. It follows that the meanings attached to categories cannot be taken as given but must be understood as reflecting a particular (dominant) perspective (Zinn and Dill 1996). Categorical boundaries reflect and reify social hierarchies in a given time and place. However, once particular categorical boundaries are established, it is the experiences and political priorities of the more powerful members that determine how a particular group understands and represents itself, effectively occluding those of the less powerful, multiply marginalized, constituents. Spelman (1988) cites the dominance of a racially privileged perspective in feminist scholarship in the United States as an illustration of this kind of exclusionary process:

> Much of feminist theory has reflected and contributed to what Adrienne Rich calls 'white solipsism': the tendency to 'think, imagine, and speak as if whiteness defined the world'. White solipsism is 'not the consciously held belief that one race is inherently superior to all others, but a tunnel-vision which simply does not see non-white experience or existence as precious or significant, unless in spasmodic, impotent guilt-reflexes, which have little or no long-term continuing momentum or usefulness'. (Ibid., p. 116)

She argues that 'white solipsism' has, in turn, shaped 'habits of thought about the source of women's oppression and the possibility for our liberation' in a way that has limited the 'explanatory and descriptive scope' (ibid., p. 116) of feminist interventions. Although it was not the central focus of her analysis, Spelman (1988) noted that class contributes another form of solipsism. In the context of social and demographic research, I think the influence of class, as well as geopolitical location, merits careful considera-tion since these divisions so often set the feminist demographer (or social researcher more generally) apart from the subject of their analysis.

As these reflections were articulated and refined, some scholars turned their attention to how multiple social dimensions were conceptualized in academic studies, when they were considered at all. The simplifying – but erroneous – assumption that various axes of difference could be treated as separable and additive was extensively critiqued. Spelman's (1988) *Inessential Woman* provided one of the earliest and most comprehensive assessments of this exclusionary practice. The assumption of separability implies that experiences of sexism and racism can be meaningful when examined in isolation.[6] It suggests that we can somehow isolate 'sexism' by focusing on the experiences of (white) women who are otherwise privileged. Similarly, we can isolate 'racism' by focusing the experiences of ethnic minority men. This 'but for' (Crenshaw 1989) strategy becomes especially problematic when comparisons of the most privileged with the otherwise privileged are brought together, in the manner of 'pop-beads' (children's necklace beads), to represent multiple oppressions (Spelman 1988). This additive and separable conceptualization ignores and then potentially misrepresents the distinct experiences of the multiply-marginalized. In the case of black women, the possibility that the gendered experiences differ from those of white women or that their racial oppression differs from that experienced by black men is simply assumed away. The same logic – that there is a pure 'all else equal' sex effect that can be identified and examined in isolation – underpins the specification of linear regression models which include a separate 'sex' indicator and a separate 'ethnicity' categorical vari-able, but no interaction term (Sigle-Rushton 2014). With statistical models and methods, the largest groups tend to have the largest impact on the parameter estimates, and it is the small subgroups (often the multiply mar-ginalized) whose experiences may be misrepresented and misunderstood.

The additive-separable logic and its associated methodology is not merely a convenient (if potentially problematic) academic invention or idiosyncrasy; it is a widespread but often implicit schema that organ-izes representations of and responses to social issues (Crenshaw 1991). It makes it possible to ask, as many did during the Obama–Clinton race for the Democratic presidential nomination in the United States, whether America is more racist or sexist (Hancock 2007a). It is a way of thinking that is reflected in and supported by social structures and institutions. For example, Crenshaw (1989) demonstrates how African American women seeking redress for discrimination were forced to base their claim on either sex discrimination or race discrimination, a constraint which determined the comparator that would be used as evidence. Citing the case of *DeGraffenreid v General Motors*, she shows how the court refused to allow the plaintiffs to argue that they faced a combination of sex and race discrimination. Such a claim, the court stated, went beyond what the drafters of the legislation intended. The implications of this reasoning are significant. As Crenshaw (1989) suggests, it:

> implies that the boundaries of sex and race discrimination doctrine are defined respectively by white women's and Black men's [sic] experiences. Under this view, Black women are protected only to the extent that their experiences coincide with those of either of the two groups. Where their experiences are distinct, Black women can expect little protection. (Ibid., p. 59)

Crenshaw's contribution has the added distinction of providing 'intersectionality' with its name. Developed and deployed over most of its history without a label or name attached, the term 'provided a much-needed frame of reference for the comparison and negotiation of various endeavours, opening up space for critical dialogue' (Sigle-Rushton and Lindstrom 2013, p. 130). Although it remains a rather loosely defined concept or set of ideas, its main theoretical premise, as I have come to understand it in my own work (Sigle-Rushton 2014; Sigle-Rushton and Lindstrom 2013), is that analytic categories and concepts (hierarchies, axes of differentiation, axes of oppression, social structures, normativities) are socially constructed and mutually modifying. If we accept that basic premise, we immediately encounter a number of methodological dilemmas that, while potentially productive, cannot be completely resolved.

Methodological Implications

Intersectionality is a methodologically demanding research paradigm that lacks a clearly specified methodology (Nash 2008). This, I think, is more or less inevitable. As a demographer who uses large-scale secondary data to study families and family policy, I struggle to envision just what it would mean for me to do a quantitative intersectional study. It is telling, I think, that McCall's (2005) careful methodological reflection focuses not on a methodology of intersectionality, but rather on approaches for dealing with the (inevitable and enormous) complexity it evokes. When multiple social dimensions are understood as mutually modifying (and so, in statistical parlance, fully interacted), the amount of information that we must collect and interpret (and without resorting to any exclusionary overgeneralization) quickly becomes intractable. Taken to its logical limit, we would end up splitting our samples into increasingly detailed groups until there is nothing left to study (Young 1994). Nonetheless, we can be more or less intersectional in our thinking and approach.

Accepting the basic premise of intersectionality means acknowledging that it is (potentially) problematic to conceptualize individuals, or any broad category of individuals such as 'women', as a homogenous group. Applied to quantitative analysis, it underscores the need to exercise care when extrapolating from what we observe on average, at the population or group level, to particular subgroups. Because it is concerned with the exclusions and loss of information involved when a diversity of subjects are treated as similar, or as similarly situated, intersectionality directs our attention both towards the wider social and economic context and to individual-level heterogeneity within any particular context (Bose 2012). A consideration of intersectionality's basic tenets, therefore, directs our attention towards the specification, interpretation and use of categories as well as the explicit and implicit assumptions we make about how they relate to one another. It is through its application as a critical lens – a 'frame checker' and 'method checker' (Garry 2011, p. 830) – that I have come to think that intersectionality has the most to contribute to the way research is designed and conducted in quantitative disciplines such as demography.

METHODOLOGICAL IMPLICATIONS: DILEMMAS, OPPORTUNITIES AND INSIGHTS

In this section, I consider how a more conscious consideration of critical theoretical perspectives such as intersectionality could extend and enrich demographic enquiry. Put simply, intersectionality asks us to consider the consequences of what happens when heterogeneity is ignored versus made visible. This requires a (renewed) effort to assess patterns of difference which might otherwise be hidden, and to remain attentive to issues of diversity and exclusion at all stages of the research process. If demographers took these commitments seriously, the primacy of economic models, priorities and methodologies might be disrupted, which would in turn open up space for the development of a more varied, creative and critical approach to research.

Assessing Difference

Intersectionality reminds us to remain ever vigilant to the fact that categorization and assumptions of additive-separability are strategies for managing difference. Decisions we make about how to manage difference have consequences for what we see and how we understand and interpret social phenomena. At the same time, it is also important to stress that its contribution as a critical methodological lens should guide the search for additional complexity rather than impose or stipulate it. The art of model building and theory will always require some amount of simplification. We should decide which combined characteristics to consider with some care, and we should remove unnecessary complexity when there is not substantive or substantial loss of meaning (Hobcraft and Sigle-Rushton 2012; Sigle-Rushton 2014). However, such decision-making requires a detailed descriptive foundation so that the conceptual and methodological implications of any simplifying assumption can be carefully considered. It calls for doing more than simply acknowledging heterogeneity. We must attempt to locate, understand and explain it as an integral and early stage of the research process and with reference to the particular research aims and objectives.

McCall (2005) describes two methodological approaches which can be used strategically and pragmatically to guide this sort of exploration: the inter-categorical approach and the intra-categorical approach.[7] She uses the term 'inter-categorical' to refer to a largely descriptive endeavour that examines how analytical categories – gender, ethnicity, social class and age – interact to produce particular patterns of inequality. In an effort to document complex inequalities, some researchers have estimated standard linear regression models with high-order interaction terms (see, e.g., McCall 2000, 2001). In a study that used this approach to examine the relationship between motherhood and employment in the United Kingdom (UK), Diane Perrons and I (Sigle-Rushton and Perrons 2006) showed how ethnic differentials in the employment rates of mothers of young children are not uniform across educational groups. We were also able to document variation within broad categories – such as Asian or black – that are commonly used in British social research. The findings from such descriptive efforts can be used in a number of ways; however, the results of models with a large number of interactions can be difficult to interpret and present to readers, which, as McCall (2005) cautions, can be an impediment to publication. In previous work, I have suggested that a wider range of methodologies could be considered (Sigle-Rushton 2014). Nonetheless, in a discipline where the identification of causal relationships has become a priority and where the contribution of studies which are 'merely descriptive' is often called into question, it may be difficult to captivate readers with a detailed discussion of inter-categorical complexity, regardless of how well the results are distilled and presented. For this reason, it may be strategic to frame the discussion around the implications for the study of particular research questions. Collins (1999) suggests an incremental approach where the researcher will take as their starting point 'a concrete topic that is already the subject of investigation and . . . find the combined effects of race, class, gender, sexuality and nation, where before only one or two interpretive categories were used' (ibid., p. 278). The approach she advocates would complement and refine existing research efforts rather than challenge them.

The intra-categorical approach, which draws on the epistemological contributions of standpoint feminisms, involves a narrow and intensive analysis of an outlier. At the macro level, this outlier could be a particular country that appears 'puzzling' in some way. At the micro level it would involve, as Crenshaw (1989) advocated, a focus on a particular, multiply marginalized group whose experiences may have been previously oversimplified or overlooked. Case studies are often the methodology of choice (Few-Demo 2014): comparison with some more broadly defined category to which an outlier belongs provides opportunities to identify differences that may be theoretically (outliers) or substantively (the multiply-marginalized) relevant (Sigle-Rushton and Lindstrom 2013). When this approach involves close scrutiny of small and rare groups, those with combinations of characteristics not (well) represented in secondary survey data, more narrative and qualitative approaches have been employed with positive effects (Few-Demo 2014).

The intra-categorical approach (McCall 2005) stands in stark contrast to the *ceteris paribus* approach characteristic of linear regression modelling, where the distinctive experiences of special groups or outliers are seen as something to be expunged or controlled as a confounding effect. However, it represents a way of thinking and an approach to research that has the potential to make a significant theoretical contribution. At a macro level, we see it reflected, for example, in Caldwell's (1986) classic exploration of the relationship between gross domestic product and health, a study focused intensively on high achievers: those countries with better than expected health, given their national income. A similar logic might inspire a close consideration of groups such as non-white migrants from poorer countries who have settled within a particular destination country, such as the UK. This group, which is often observed to have better than average health and health behaviour than the more advantaged, native population, could provide meaningful information as high achievers at the micro level. As a small group, however, their experiences – a limited marital status differential, for example – are occluded when estimation methods that rely on population averages are utilized (Sigle-Rushton and Goisis 2013).

To illustrate the utility of thinking carefully about both inter- and intra-categorical difference, consider the following example from my own research. Suppose we consider that the moderate fertility, high employment[8] group of European countries includes the Scandinavian countries,

England and Wales in its ranks. Although in recent years entitlements to paid leave have been extended and improved, the British family policy model remains far less generous and so much less expensive, than the family policy packages that characterize the Scandinavian countries. If we think that generous family policy and fertility rates are (or should be) associated, England and Wales could be characterized, to use Caldwell's terminology, as high achievers. In a case study of England and Wales that I carried out a few years ago (Sigle-Rushton 2008, 2009), extrapolated to the UK, I suggested that the UK exhibits a qualitatively different version of 'moderately high fertility' than what is observed in the Scandinavian countries. The use of an inter-categorical lens directed my attention to the 'fertility-relevant structuring effects' (Neyer and Andersson 2008, p. 707) of family policy on particular groups of individuals. I described a moderately high but relatively disadvantaged (as measured by education level) fertility profile (as measured by the total fertility rate, TFR) compared to other moderately high fertility countries (see also Rendall et al. 2010). If the pattern of moderately high fertility is qualitatively different across countries, there might be multiple paths to the same fertility level, which are shaped by the wider social and institutional context. My analysis suggested that the 'highest-low' (Andersson 2008) fertility in England and Wales might well depend on their flexible, low-wage labour market (with easy entry and exit), high levels of inequality, and an income support system with benefits that are not generally categorized as family policy but that make it easier for low earners to become mothers at young ages even if they have not built up entitlements to maternity leave benefits (Sigle-Rushton 2009). In contrast, high earners have strong incentives to postpone childbearing and rates of childlessness are higher than what is observed in Scandinavian countries.

If meaningful diversity can be masked within the boundaries of broad categories, and if the wider institutional context represents a potentially important modifying factor (see also, Shalev 2008), there are both practical and theoretical implications. The sudden adoption of the Swedish parental leave model – as happened recently in Germany (Geisler and Kreyenfeld 2012) – might actually reduce fertility in England and Wales, at least in the short term, by increasing incentives for low earners to postpone childbearing. Similarly, tax relief for paid domestic work and childcare – available in Sweden since 2007 – is only feasible if it is affordable, meaning that it requires that the purchaser earn (far) more than the provider of care (Donath 2000; Himmelweit 2007). In labour markets with fairly compressed wages – typical of Scandinavian countries – the option will be feasible for only a small segment of the population. The take-up and impact of this new Swedish policy (which has been rather low) might be far greater if exported to the UK setting where there is far more wage inequality.

While the implications for issues of policy sharing are readily apparent, a consideration of intra- and inter-categorical complexity has implications for the specification of statistical models. If the pattern of moderately high fertility is qualitatively different across countries, does it make sense to estimate cross-national regressions of the TFR on the indicators of the generosity of family policies? Aggregate measures like the TFR may mask substantively relevant cross-national variations in the underlying behaviour we are seeking to model. Indeed, a number of demographers have concluded that individual-level analyses are better suited to the study of how fertility outcomes respond to family policy (e.g. Neyer and Andersson 2008; Rønsen 2014). By focusing attention on the data-generating process, a consideration of intersectionality problematizes individual-level analyses, which rely on average levels of social expenditure (Kalwij 2010) or an indicator of the average (or some other 'representative'). Measures of average social expenditure, which do not account for the details of how that expenditure is accessed (the details of entitlement) and allocated, fail to capture variations in the design and delivery of policies as they are experienced by individual decision makers. These concerns have been well articulated in other disciplines. Welfare regimes were developed, in part, as a response to concerns about the use of crude social expenditure measures, and represent an effort to develop theoretically grounded conceptual measures which reflect 'more fine-grained distinctions among patterns of social provision' (Pierson 1996, p. 150) that vary across national contexts. This sort of variation is a particular concern in the case of family policy which involves a vast array of policies, each complex in their design and delivery (Gauthier 2002; Thévenon 2011). Even if we could easily identify and separate out what is 'family policy' from other policy, which my analysis of England and Wales suggests is not entirely straightforward, it is not clear that the average level of expenditure is in any way a valid indicator of the reduction in the direct costs of childbearing that the average person could anticipate. Moreover, the extent to which it falls short of this interpretation may vary across countries depending on the way their policies are designed.

Recognizing Power

Drawing more generally on critical and feminist perspectives, feminist demographers have challenged the belief that demography is conducted by value-free researchers who engage with hard facts to arrive at objective conclusions (Riley 1998; Williams 2010). Once we concede that objectivity is neither realistic nor attainable, we must consider the role of the researcher in the production of knowledge. For example, in a recent debate on low fertility in Europe, Gerda Neyer (2011) pointed out that:

it is demographers, politicians, the media, or other groups of people or public institutions who produce the perception that fertility levels are too 'low' or too 'high' or 'normal'. Likewise, it is they who construct the social, economic, and political consequences of fertility levels by transforming demographic measures into ostensibly negative outcomes for the future. (Ibid., p. 237)

This suggests that the interests and perceptions of the demographer merit close consideration. Intersectionality provides a reflexive tool that can direct and focus those efforts.

Accepting the basic premise of intersectionality means acknowledging not only that power hierarchies stratify two supposedly homogenous groups – 'women' and 'men' – but also that power hierarchies are involved in determining whose experiences count and who gets to speak on behalf of 'women' (Spelman 1988, pp. 77–79). For example, with insufficient reflection, it becomes easy to use descriptive terms like 'woman-friendly' to refer to policies that (predominantly) benefit particular groups of women (most likely those that resemble the person uttering the phrase). Many feminist researchers who would not otherwise support regressive redistributive measures strongly endorse high levels of wage replacement in parental leave policies which, by their very nature, provide more resources to (already) well-resourced families.

Similar biases and 'solipsisms' can shape the way explanatory variables are deployed and interpreted. For example, it might not be immediately obvious to a white, well-educated and otherwise privileged researcher that the socio-economic benefits that accompany fertility postponement could be greater for some women than others. Education and career opportunities, discrimination and rapidly declining health might modify the net benefits of delay for some ethnic minority groups and, as a consequence, the meaning attached to measures of early or late motherhood may be qualitatively different for particular subpopulations (Goisis and Sigle-Rushton 2014). Informed only with summary statistics or parameter estimates that reflect the average experiences of the wider (larger) population, and viewing the phenomenon through the lens of their own (often privileged) experience, the researcher might conclude that some groups of women are behaving 'irrationally' and should be encouraged to delay parenthood (or to marry; Sigle-Rushton and McLanahan 2002), without asking whether they are likely to benefit in the same way from the processes thought to be attached to that behavioural change. The result of such errors of representation could be unhelpful or even harmful policy innovations.

CONCLUSIONS

In the past decades, intersectionality has transformed feminist theory and politics which, as part of a larger theoretical movement, has influenced the way research is conducted in most of the social sciences. Although demographic research relies to a great extent on the theoretical perspectives of other disciplines, there is little evidence that these critical perspectives have been embraced or integrated in any meaningful way. Instead, demography appears to have embraced the methods and methodological priorities of economics in a way that has limited its scope, its methodological range and, as a consequence, its potential contribution to knowledge.

While demographers have paid increasingly careful attention to important issues of causality, selection and unobserved heterogeneity, I would maintain that it is equally important to consider what those findings mean and how they can be put to use. When applied as critical methodological lenses, critical and feminist perspectives could add some much-needed breadth and depth to demographic scholarship. They might inspire a new appreciation for previous demographic methodologies – descriptive and group-focused – which were increasingly set aside as we moved into the era of the independent variable. Similarly, case study approaches which delve more into both the social context and the detail of policies, and which seek to understand any differential treatment and incentive effects, can be used to build theory and to inform the design and interpretation of subsequent studies. Neither approach provides solid evidence of causality, but both could help to generate testable hypotheses, which would help us to tease out meaningful causal relationships in creative ways. We can and should make use of findings from studies in other disciplines which apply these approaches, but I would like to see more work of this kind carried out by demographers, guided by our own research interests and questions, and published in the pages of top demography journals.

To be clear, I am not calling for a rejection of what I see as the dominant economic perspective and approach that characterizes much of the extant literature in demography, but for a rejection of an uncritical, almost internalized acceptance of some aspects of it. It is time to worry when certain ways of thinking, certain approaches and certain priorities are internalized to the point of being utilized without considering the question, the underlying motivation for asking it, and however many additional complexities we acknowledge might be relevant. If and when this happens, a more interdisciplinary critical perspective can be a valuable, if somewhat disruptive and importunate friend.

Of course, many of the critiques I discuss could be identified and developed without making any explicit reference to intersectionality or to critical theoretical perspectives more generally. In an excellent methodological reflection which was described as 'Drawing on sociological and political science research, [to] outline how studies of the effects of policies are best designed conceptually and methodologically in order to measure potential effects or non-effects of the policies' (p. 700), Neyer and Andersson (2008) touch on many of the same issues as I identify in my analysis.[9] My core argument is not that everyone should adopt and apply the particular conceptual tool that I utilize here, but rather that demography would benefit, in one way or another, from (more) critical reflection. It is possible, without the (explicit) assistance or prompt of a theoretical tool, to think critically about our motivations, methods and the extent to which they are aligned (e.g. Kravdal 2010; Neyer 2011). While not strictly necessary, good theory can help to organize and direct that endeavour.

NOTES

1. This imagery is far from original. See, for example, Loriaux and Vishnievskaia (2006, p. 871).
2. Crimmins distinguishes between social and formal demography in her discussion, and I adopt her terminology here.
3. Not a single study turned up when I searched (on the publishers' web pages) the online content of *Demography*, *Demographic Research*, *Population and Development Review* and the *European Journal for Population Studies* for the term 'intersectionality'.
4. The presentation and discussion of intersectionality and its methodology draws heavily upon Sigle-Rushton (2014) and Sigle-Rushton and Lindstrom (2013). See Brah and Phoenix (2004) for a detailed and comprehensive intellectual history.
5. According to Hancock (2007a, p. 64), a paradigm comprises 'a set of basic beliefs or a worldview that precedes any questions of empirical investigation'.
6. This way of thinking, while erroneous, is nonetheless widespread and taken for granted. We see it reflected in the way academic studies are carried out but also in the meta-data that are used to classify studies. For example, the JEL subcodes for demographic economics (J1) include separate categories for studies of age (J12), gender (J13) and ethnicity (J14), reinforcing the perception that it is valid, and indeed possible, to examine any one of these in isolation (Sigle-Rushton 2014).
7. She also outlines a third approach to the complexity of intersectionality which she calls 'anti-categorical'. This approach aims to deconstruct categories and so strip them of their power and meaning. While this approach can offer useful insights into the way we attach meaning to or interpret categories, this approach has less to offer researchers interested in identifying meaningful interactions.
8. France and Ireland have relatively high fertility as well (Sobotka 2004), but their female employment rates are closer to the European Union average.
9. This is to be expected because, compared to demography, sociology and political science have been rather more influenced by critical race and feminist perspectives, which in turn draw upon the criticisms that comprise intersectionality.

REFERENCES

Andersson, G. (2008), 'A review of policies and practices related to the "highest-low" fertility of Sweden', *Vienna Yearbook of Population Research*, pp. 89–102, available at http://www.oeaw.ac.at/vid/publications/VYPR2008/abstract_Andersson_Policies.html.

Bose, C.E. (2012), 'Intersectionality and global inequality', *Gender and Society*, 26 (1), 67–72.

Brah, A. and A. Phoenix (2004), 'Ain't I a woman? revisiting intersectionality', *Journal of International Women's Studies*, 5 (3), 75–86.

Brush, L.D. (2002), 'Changing the subject: gender and welfare regime studies', *Social Politics*, 9 (2), 161–186.

Caldwell, J.G.C. (1986), 'Routes to low mortality in poor countries', *Population and Development Review*, 12 (2), 171–220.

Collins, P.H. (1999), 'Moving beyond gender: intersectionality and scientific knowledge', in M.M. Ferree, J. Lorber and B.B. Hess (eds), *Revisioning Gender*, Thousand Oaks, CA: Sage Publications, pp. 261–284.

Crenshaw, K. (1989), 'Demarginalizing the intersection of race and sex: a black feminist critique of antidiscrimination doctrine, feminist theory, and antiracist politics', *University of Chicago Legal Forum*, 1989, 139–167, available at https://legal-forum.uchicago.edu/page/issues.

Crenshaw, K. (1991), 'Mapping the margins: intersectionality, identity politics and violence against women of color', *Stanford Law Review*, 43 (6), 1241–1299.

Crimmins, E.M. (1993), 'Demography: the past 30 years, the present, and the future', *Demography*, 30 (4), 579–591.

Donath, S. (2000), 'The other economy: a suggestion for a distinctively feminist economics', *Feminist Economics*, 6 (1), 115–123.

Few-Demo, A.L. (2014), 'Intersectionality as the "new" critical approach', *Journal of Family Theory and Review*, 6 (2), 169–183.

Garry, A. (2011), 'Intersectionality, metaphors and the multiplicity of gender', *Hypatia*, 26 (4), 826–850.

Gauthier, A.H. (2002), 'Family policies in industrialized countries: is there convergence?', *Population*, 57 (2), 447–474.

Geisler, E. and M. Kreyenfeld (2012), 'How policy matters: Germany's parental leave benefit reform and fathers' behavior 1999–2009', MPIDR Working Paper 2012-021, Max Planck Institute for Demographic Research (MPIDR), Rostock.

Goisis, A. and W. Sigle-Rushton (2014), 'Childbearing postponement and child wellbeing: a complex and varied relationship?', *Demography*, 51 (5), 1821–1841.

Hancock, A-M. (2007a), 'Intersectionality as a normative and empirical paradigm', *Politics and Gender*, 3 (2), 248–254.

Hancock, A-M. (2007b), 'When multiplication doesn't equal quick addition: examining intersectionality as a research paradigm', *Perspectives on Politics*, 5 (1), 63–79.

Himmelweit, S. (2007), 'The prospects for caring: economic theory and policy analysis', *Cambridge Journal of Economics*, 31 (4), 581–599.

Hobcraft, J. and W. Sigle-Rushton (2012), 'The childhood origins of adult socio-economic disadvantage: do cohort and gender matter?', in J. Scott, S. Dex and A. Plagnol (eds), *Gendered Lives*, Cheltenham, UK and Northampton, MA, USA: Edward Elgar Publishing, pp. 23–47.

Kalwij, A. (2010), 'The impact of family policy expenditure on fertility in Western Europe', *Demography*, 47 (2), 503–519.

Knapp, G.-A. (2005), 'Race, class, gender: reclaiming baggage in fast travelling theories', *European Journal of Women's Studies*, 12 (3), 249–265.

Kravdal, Ø. (2010), 'Demographers' interest in fertility trends and determinants in developed countries: is it warranted?', *Demographic Research*, 22, 663–690.

Loriaux, M. and T. Vishnievskaia (2006), 'Demography viewed by demographers', in G. Caselli, J. Vallin and G. Wunsch (eds), *Demography: Analysis and Synthesis. A Treatise in Population Studies, Volume 4*, San Diego, CA: Academic Press, pp. 871–891.

McCall, L. (2000), 'Explaining levels of with-in group wage inequality in US labor markets', *Demography*, 37 (4), 415–430.

McCall, L. (2001), 'Sources of racial inequality in metropolitan labor markets', *American Sociological Review*, 66, 520–541.

McCall, L. (2005), 'The complexity of intersectionality', *Signs: Journal of Women in Culture and Society*, 30 (3), 1771–1800.

Nash, J.C. (2008), 'Re-thinking intersectionality', *Feminist Review*, 89, 1–15.

Neyer, G. (2011), 'Should governments in Europe be more aggressive in pushing for gender equality to raise fertility? The second NO', *Demographic Research*, 24 (10), 225–250.

Neyer, G. and G. Andersson (2008), 'Consequences of family policies on childbearing behavior: effects or artefacts?', *Population and Development Review*, 34 (4), 699–724.

Orloff, A.S. (1996), 'Gender in the welfare state', *Annual Review of Sociology*, 22, 51–78.

Orloff, A.S. (2009), 'Gendering the comparative analysis of welfare states: an unfinished agenda', *Sociological Theory*, 27 (3), 317–343.

Pierson, P. (1996), 'The new politics of the welfare state', *World Politics*, 48 (January), 141–179.

Rendall, M.S., E. Aracil, C. Bagavos, C. Couvet, A. DeRose, P. DiGiulio, T. Lappegard, I. Robert-Bobée, M. Rønsen, S. Smallwood and G. Veropoulou (2010), 'Increasingly heterogenous ages at first birth by education in Southern-European and Anglo-American family-policy regimes: a seven country comparison', *Population Studies*, 64 (3), 209–227.

Riley, N.E. (1998), 'Research on gender and demography: limitations and constraints', *Population Research and Policy Review*, 17 (6), 521–538.

Riley, N.E. and J. McCarthy (2003), *Demography in the Age of the Postmodern*, Cambridge: Cambridge University Press.

Rønsen, M. (2014), 'Fertility and family policy in Norway – a reflection on trends and possible connections', *Demographic Research*, 10 (10), 265–286.

Shalev, M. (2008), 'Class divisions among women', *Politics and Society*, 36 (3), 421–444.

Sigle-Rushton, W. (2008), 'England and Wales: stable fertility and pronounced social status differences', *Demographic Research*, 19 (15), 459–502.

Sigle-Rushton, W. (2009), 'Fertility in England and Wales: a policy puzzle?', *Demografie*, 51 (4), 258–265.

Sigle-Rushton, W. (2012), 'Family structure and well-being: (re)framing the question', paper presented at the Annual Meeting of the International Association for Feminist Economics, Barcelona, June.

Sigle-Rushton, W. (2014), 'Essentially quantified: towards a more feminist modeling strategy', in M. Evans et al. (eds), *Sage Handbook of Feminist Theory*, London: Sage Publications, pp. 431–445.

Sigle-Rushton, W. and A. Goisis (2013), 'Family structure, maternal nativity and childhood overweight and obesity: evidence from the UK', paper presented at the Annual Meeting of the Population Association of America, New Orleans, LA, April.

Sigle-Rushton, W. and E. Lindstrom (2013), 'Intersectionality', in M. Evans and C. Williams (eds), *Gender: Key Concepts*, London: Routledge, pp. 129–135.

Sigle-Rushton, W. and S. McLanahan (2002), 'For richer or poorer? Marriage as an anti-poverty strategy in the United States', *Population*, 57 (3), 509–526.

Sigle-Rushton, W. and D. Perrons (2006), *Employment Transitions over the Life Cycle: A Statistical Analysis*, Manchester: Equal Opportunities Commission.

Sobotka, T. (2004), 'Is lowest-low fertility explained by the postponement of childbearing?', *Population and Development Review*, 30 (2), 195–220.

Spelman, E.V. (1988), *Inessential Woman: Problems of Exclusion in Feminist Thought*, Boston, MA: Beacon Press.

Thévenon, O. (2011), 'Family policies in OECD countries: a comparative analysis', *Population and Development Review*, 37 (1), 57–87.

Thornton, A. (2001), 'The developmental paradigm, reading history sideways, and family change', *Demography*, 38 (4), 449–465.

Williams, J.R. (2010), 'Doing feminist demography', *International Journal of Social Research Methodology*, 13 (3), 197–210.

Wunsch, G. (1995), 'God has chosen to give the easy problems to the physicists: or why demographers need theory', Plenary Talk at the Meeting of European Population Conference, Milan, 4–8 September.

Young, I.M. (1994), 'Gender as seriality: thinking about women as a social collective', *Signs: Journal of Women in Culture and Society*, 19 (3), 713–738.

Zinn, M.B. and B.T. Dill (1996), 'Theorizing difference from multiracial feminism', *Feminist Studies*, 22 (2), 321–331.

10. Conflicting family interests: a challenge for family policy

Jacqueline Scott

INTRODUCTION

In this chapter, I bring together two of my long-standing interests in family research which are often not joined up in research, despite some clear inter-connections. One is concerned with the sociology of children and taking the child-centred perspective seriously in family sociology. The second is concerned with gender inequalities, which has been a burgeoning field of social and economic research, as researchers seek to understand how and why the gender revolution has stalled and what can be done, if anything, about the ongoing gendered nature of care and concerns about the 'care deficit'.

These two spheres of research need to be joined up, if family policy is to get a grip on conflicting family interests. Let us take, for example, the question 'Who stands to gain or lose from the traditional gender role order that leads to male specialization in paid work and female specialization in the unpaid work of housework and family care?' If we consider this in terms of the different policy approaches to work–family balance we can begin to unpack the different and sometimes conflicting interests of men, women and children. Going one step further, we can ask whether it is possible for policy to influence the gender divide in unpaid work and enhance fathers' contribution to childcare and other domestic activities. Or to take another example, should policy attempt to equalize men's and women's invest-ment in paid work in order to reduce the gender pay gap and help tackle high rates of poverty, particularly in households headed by lone mothers? Who would this benefit? Children's interests, family interests and societal interests may well be different. For example, policies that aim to increase maternal employment and thus enhance family income may well conflict with desires to strengthen family ties and prioritize parental care of young children.

In this chapter I do not seek to provide answers concerning 'best family policy'. My aim is more modest. I examine some of the social processes that underpin children's experiences of families; I also look at the way the transition to parenthood exacerbates gender inequalities, and examine the different gender equality visions that inform the very different policies for reconciling family and work life in Europe. Research on the effects for children of family disruption, family diversity, changing work–family balance and different care cultures is often contentious. In the family domain, people often have such strong convictions that their claims far exceed knowledge. My conclusion is simple but often ignored: we need family policy that invokes evidence, not ideology.

CHILDREN'S FAMILIES: A CHILD-CENTRED PERSPECTIVE

Unlike both psychology and education, sociology has tended to be an adult-centric discipline. Even nationally representative socio-economic household surveys have, until recently, tended to exclude children. Survey researchers, when investigating aspects of childhood, have preferred to ask adult respondents such as parents or teachers to report on children's lives, rather than to ask children themselves. In part this has been because of concerns about the cognitive ability of children to process and respond to structured questions about behaviour, perceptions, opinions and beliefs. Yet children can be reliable respondents if asked questions that they are willing and able to answer (Scott 2008). By including children as respondents, particularly in longitudinal surveys, social science can shed light on how social inclusion and exclusion affect childhood experiences and children's life course trajectories. Moreover, it is very clear that children and parents often have quite different perceptions on matters like the importance of a child's schooling. The different perspectives of the adult and child matter. For example, if we want to understand how aspirations shape educational outcomes then we need information from both the parent and the child.

Every parent knows that children are wilful beings who, from a very early age, play an active role in shaping their family and household environment. However, this view of the active child is a relatively 'modern' viewpoint. One of the founding fathers of sociology, Emile Durkheim, wrote in 1911: 'Childhood is a period of growth, that is to say the period in which the individual, in both the physical and moral sense does not yet exist, the period in which he is made, develops and is formed' (Durkheim 1979 [1911], p. 150).

Leaving aside current perceptions that referring to the child as 'he' is sexist, the quote is a revealing insight into the limited perspective on children in the early twentieth century. Contrast this with 80 years later when Frances Waksler writes in 1991:

> Children can be viewed as fully social beings, capable of acting in the social world and of creating and sustaining their own culture . . . If we see children as actors . . . we can ask how their actions constrain, facilitate and encourage and in a myriad of ways have implications for others, adults in particular. (Waksler 1991, pp. 23, 68)

This transformation in thinking about children had pronounced effects on both sociology and developmental psychology. Yet, interestingly, sociology was initially somewhat wary of developmental psychology because sociologists insisted that the issue is not just about whom children become, it is also about who children are. As Qvortrup notes: 'Children are "human beings" not only "human becomings", they not only have needs, a fact which is recognised, they also have interests that may or may not be compatible with the interests of other social groups or categories' (Qvortrup 1994, p. 4).

This distinction has led to some unfortunate outcomes. It makes no sense for sociology to distance itself from developmental psychology. It is not a matter of understanding children as beings or as becomings: we need both. Moreover, this difference in emphasis has also led to a strong divide between the mainly quantitative study of children's families that use the life course perspective, on the one hand, and the mainly qualitative research exploring children's perceptions and experiences, on the other. The study of children's families not only crosses disciplinary divides, but it also necessitates the use of different methodologies for different purposes (Scott 2014).

The emergence of the new sociological thinking about childhood and children has gone hand in hand with new political and policy concerns about children's rights and well-being. Policy interests invariably help to shape research agendas; if only because the public purse is an important funder of social research. There are several interrelated public concerns about children and families at national and international levels. One theme relates to concerns about the 'break-up' of family life, parental responsibility when marriage and childbirth are separated, and how children fare in the face of marital stability and family change. A second theme relates to concerns about growing levels of child poverty and its consequences. Another concern involves the changing work–life balance that has put a time squeeze on families and has led to increasing pressures on family care. There are also concerns about the way demographic shifts have changed the balance of generations and the ratio of children to elderly, which has far-reaching implications for the future of welfare. Encompassing these themes is a focus on children's rights and how rights can best be translated into law and practice in an increasingly globalized world.

These areas of policy concern are all bound up with the changing contexts of children's family lives. Childhood experience is intrinsically linked to change in the lives of women and the shifting boundaries of the public and private sphere. In the early twentieth century, the creation of a 'family wage' cemented the notion of women and children as dependents. The traditional gender division of labour went unquestioned. 'Family' consisted of the male breadwinner and his female partner, who would be responsible for the housework and care of children.

How times have changed. Families are becoming ever more diverse. For example, the number of children living with single mothers has increased markedly throughout the world. Moreover, certain types of family structure – particularly single mother families – are disproportionately represented in lower-income households. The 'feminization of poverty' is therefore something of a misnomer. The women who are over-represented among the poor are women with children. As I show in the next sections, it is the feminization and pauperization of childhood that go hand in hand.

Children's Family Structure

The changes in demographic behaviour have been so dramatic that they have been termed by some the 'second demographic transition' (Lesthaeghe 1995). This term contrasts the changes that have occurred since 1960 with those in the first half of the century. Underlying the more recent demographic shifts is an increased value placed on individual autonomy, and the associated shifts in ideas concerning gender equality. These changes have been the subject of heated debate, with 'traditionalists' believing that the family is collapsing, while 'modernists' welcome the new opportunities for women and the wider choices for both sexes. However, among both camps, there are those who suggest that the greater choice for parents, and equality gains for women, may be at the expense of their children (Clarke 1996; Parreñas 2005). Whatever the truth in the judgements about the relative benefits for adults and children, these changes are unlikely to reverse.

Patterns of family formation and dissolution have become markedly more frequent, less strictly patterned and more complex, since the 1960s. But to a great extent it is adults, not children, who trigger these family changes. The evidence is beginning to be assembled on the relative (in) stability of different household forms, the frequency of household compositional change and the amount of time, contact and resources that flow between different family members, as they form, leave and reform house-hold groups. But what has happened to the children?

By the turn of the twenty-first century, children in Northern Europe and the United States (US) were more likely to be born into populations where increasing numbers chose not to have children. Children were also more likely to be born outside marriage, to experience family shifts, to have few siblings and to live either in a dual earner or one parent family (Jensen 2009). An unmarried mother used to be synonymous with a single mother. This is no longer the case. Many children are born to mothers in consensual unions and this proportion is increasing. The disconnect between marriage and childbirth was a first step on the road to the pluralization of children's family forms.

However, it is not just that family forms are plural; they are also more fragile, and children are more likely to spend part of their childhood in different family arrangements and living apart from one of their biological parents (usually the father). Figure 10.1 shows the percentage of young adolescents (aged 11–15) currently living either in a step-family or single parent household. The majority of children still live with both parents but, as the figure shows, a substantial proportion of children in some countries do not. Percentages of children living with both parents range from 87 per cent in Italy to 61 per cent in the US; with the United Kingdom (UK) in the mid-range (73 per cent), with just

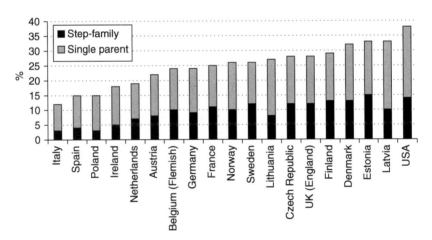

Source: Data from the Health Behaviour in School-aged Children Survey 2005/6 (Chapple 2009).

Figure 10.1   Living arrangements of young adolescents (aged 11–15) in Europe, 2005–2006

over a quarter of children living in single parent or step-parent families. The ramifications of the greater diversity and fragility of family forms for children include the enhanced risk of material deprivation in single parent families, the potential loss of contact with fathers, and the greater likelihood of children having to move between parental homes, as a result of parental splits.

Does it matter that an increasing proportion of children experience a variety of family settings as they pass through childhood and adolescence? The current consensus is that it does, although as I discuss below, the evidence is more complex to evaluate than the media headlines acknowledge. To understand the very different experiences of children as they negotiate the complex family settings that can follow family disruption, qualitative methods can be invaluable. Large-scale, longitudinal surveys, however, are also crucial for following the lives of children over time, and unpacking the complex relationship between family structure and process and between antecedents and consequences of family change. Great Britain has a number of large birth cohort studies, consisting of cohorts born in 1946, 1958 and 1970. More recent cohort studies include the 2001 New Millennium Study and the 2014–2018 'Life Study'.

Researchers using the 1946, 1958 and 1970 cohort data have been able to examine the secular trends since the Second World War, in the overall association of parental divorce or separation and children's educational attainment at school-leaving age and subsequent adult well-being (Ely et al. 1999; Sigle-Rushton et al. 2005). The results refute the commonly held view that the effects of divorce on children would have attenuated with the increasing prevalence of divorce. These results were indeed surprising, as divorce has become less stigmatized than it was for earlier generations and, in addition, the selection hypothesis would suggest that as divorce rates increase, the average child of divorce would come from a less troubled family. Instead, researchers have established that disadvantage has remained remarkably stable over time. In one study 'early disadvantage' was measured by children's temperament and academic success at age 11; and indicators of subsequent disadvantage included lack of educational qualifications, receipt of means-tested benefits and mental health at age 30 (Sigle-Rushton et al. 2005). The robustness of the negative association found between parental divorce, children's well-being at 11 and subsequent adult disadvantage raises an intriguing question for future research: why is it that the associations are so stable across a time period that saw such dramatic change in the frequency of divorce and the acceptance of alternative family structures?

In order to begin to answer this question, researchers need to unpack what really matters about parental divorce for children. Is it a fall in economic status? A loss of a father figure? An erosion of social contacts? A reduction in parental care? Do all of them matter? And is what matters different for different children? We can glean some evidence from studies that go into greater detail about the context of childhood experiences and the process through to later outcomes. For example, a qualitative study of Scottish children unpacks the complex perspectives and choices that accompany parental splits, as well as other family changes such as re-partnering and family migration (Highet and Jamieson 2007). Their findings suggest that even relatively commonplace family changes do not feel ordinary to the child. From the child's perspective such upheavals disrupt what they regard as normal life.

Child Poverty and Children's Well-being

The size and structure of children's families are important in determining child poverty. In Great Britain, despite a fall in the number of families with children and declining family size, the number of children living in households with below half the average income has risen rapidly over the last decades. This rise in child poverty reflected a growth in the number of children living in families without work. In the mid-1990s, 61 per cent of all poor children lived in a household with no one employed. Half of all poor children lived in a lone-parent household. Three-quarters of poor children were white, but the risk of child poverty was higher in all minority ethnic groups, especially households of Bangladeshi or Pakistani origin (Bradshaw 2002). According to Organisation for Economic Co-operation and Development (OECD) statistics (OECD 2009), there is some evidence that the policy targets to reduce UK child poverty, set by the former New Labour governments led by Tony Blair and Gordon Brown, had some success.

As can be seen in Figure 10.2, by the mid-2000s, child poverty in the UK was slightly below the OECD average, with one-tenth of children living in households with below 50 per cent of the median equivalized income (the OECD average being 12.4 per cent). Before the financial crisis, UK child poverty fell by the largest proportion out of all OECD countries (OECD 2011). However, the 2011 OECD report also notes that progress in child poverty reduction in the UK has stalled and is now predicted to increase. One area of concern that the report highlights is the relatively high childcare costs, which remain a barrier to work for many families.

By contrast, child poverty rates remain very high in the United States, with one-fifth of children in the mid-2000s living in poor households with less than half the median equivalized income. Moreover, child poverty is forecast to increase still further. The OECD analysis suggests that the US

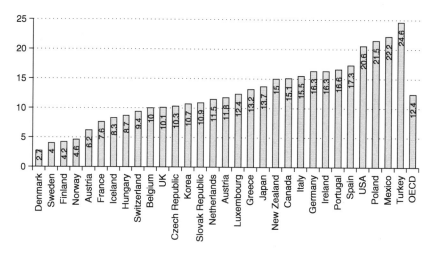

Source: OECD (2009); Income Distribution database (Scott 2014).

Figure 10.2 *Percentage of children (aged 0–17) living in poor households (below 50% of median equivalized income), c.2005*

could do much to reduce children's poverty rates by strengthening early childhood services and benefits, including legislating for paid parental leave and building on the successes of child education and care services, such as the Headstart programme. The US is the only OECD country without a national paid parental leave policy, although some states provide leave payments.

There has also been a great deal of work analysing the complexity of social processes involved in 'growing up poor'. As family structure, parental characteristics and household poverty are so interlinked, sorting out what is causing what, and with what consequences, is no easy task (Duncan et al. 1998; Mayer 2010). However, as we can see in Figure 10.3, children's poverty is particularly associated with growing up in a female-headed household. The vast majority of single parent families are headed by women (92 per cent in the UK, according to ONS 2012) and single mother families are exposed to greater poverty risks, because of the inevitable trade-offs between earning and childcare.

In both the United States and Great Britain, there has been an extraordinary output of work on the causes and consequences of child poverty. Much of the research is directly relevant to policy interventions and is couched in terms of 'What works for children?' (e.g. Chase-Lansdale and Brooks-Gunn 1995; Waldfogel 2006). However, it must be recognized that children's interests, family interests and societal interests may well be

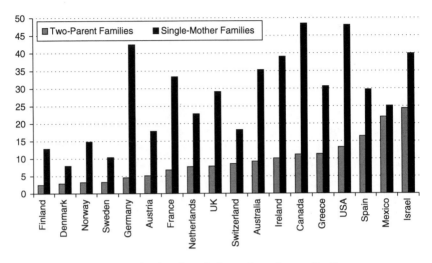

Source: Farthing (2014) using data from the Luxembourg Income Studies.

Figure 10.3   The percentage of children growing up in households below the 50% of median household income by family type, mid-2000s

different (Glass 2001). While there is much discussion of intergenerational conflict at the societal level, particularly in terms of material resources (Willetts 2010), at the family level the well-being of different generations is likely to be interconnected.

In Figure 10.4 we can see how poverty rates are linked to age in many countries across the world. The figure highlights the poverty rates for children and for the elderly, which both tend to be higher than the overall poverty figures. Some countries such as Sweden have not only managed to reduce overall poverty rates but have also broken the pervasive link between poverty and age. A further category of interests at play in policy-making decisions are politicians' own interests, which tend to be directed to policies that will help them get re-elected. This matters when trade-offs between different priorities for poverty reduction are considered, as the power of the 'grey vote' does not go unnoticed. In the UK, for example, the Conservative Party leader (David Cameron) – in the run-up to the 2015 general election – has made promises about protecting the value of the state pension against future inflation. This comes at a time when child benefits are being slashed. It is hard to see this as anything other than a politically motivated trade-off.

Despite the enormous amount of work on the causes and conse-quences of children's poverty, there has been much less work devoted to

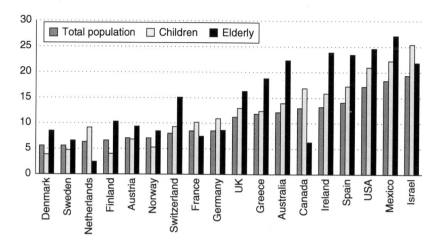

Source: Farthing (2014) using data from the Luxembourg Income Studies.

Figure 10.4 Percentage of people, pre-tax and transfer and post-tax and transfer, having below 50% of median income across the developed world, mid-2000s

understanding children's own experiences and reactions. Child poverty is measured in terms of household income, but we know from a number of influential feminist studies that the household allocation of resources is often structured along gender and generational lines. The 'black box' of household finances is very difficult to prize open. One of the few studies in the UK to look at growing up in poverty from a child's perspective illustrates how children from lower-income families miss out on taken-for-granted aspects of childhood such as celebrating special occasions or owning a bicycle (DWP 2011). While such deprivation may seem trivial compared to the high child mortality rates in parts of the developing world, growing up with these relative deprivations can make children feel excluded, as this study of English children revealed (Ridge 2002): 'I would like to be able to do more things with my friends, when they go down the town and that. But we can't always afford it. So I got to stay in and that, and just in here it's just boring – I can't do anything' (Mike, aged 12).

Policy makers tend to show more of an interest in a household's total income than in how that income is made up, or in how it is received or by whom. This may be particularly the case in the UK, because of the welfare state's traditional reliance on means-tested benefits and more recent reliance on tax credits (Bennett et al. 2012). However, it is also recognized by policy makers that, in some instances, it matters who receives the household income. For example, there is evidence for the UK showing that money is more likely to be spent on children if it is directed via 'the purse' rather than 'the wallet'; in other words, if it is given to the woman, rather than the man (Goode et al. 1998). In paying child benefit to the mothers by default and insisting that child tax credit is paid to the 'main carer', the UK government implicitly recognizes that factors other than income level may make household income more or less effective in contributing to the well-being of children. International evidence has also shown over many years that there is a good reason for this: that how and by whom a household's financial resources are received affects what they can achieve (Bennett et al. 2012; Chant 2006).

Income inequalities within households matter for understanding what Sen (1990) calls 'entitlements': the legitimate access to resources that give rise to an individual's set of opportunities. Sen makes the point that members of a household will often have a shared view of a household's best interests. However, structural factors, internal and external to the household, may mean that pursuing these collective interests may increase one person's access to resources more than another's. For example, a couple's decision that the woman rather than the man should give up employment when they have small children may be a joint decision. It may reduce the consequent loss of household earnings, if she is the lower earner. However, this 'choice' may, in practice, de-legitimize her access to the household income he now earns and thus limit her access to financial resources, especially when couples break up (Bennett et al. 2012).

If policy makers want to further not only children's well-being but also gender equality in its own right, then the impact of within-household gender inequalities on access to resources and to the life chances they facilitate should be of central concern. Within-household gender inequalities are intrinsically bound up with societal gendered patterns of paid and unpaid work, and to what has been termed the 'incomplete revolution' in gender roles (Esping-Andersen 2009).

GENDER INEQUALITIES

In this section, I consider two related aspects of gender inequalities. First, I examine time trends in the gendered division of labour in paid and unpaid work, across Europe and the US. I then consider the thorny issue of work–family balance, where policies are often expressed in gender-neutral terms despite the reality being very different for mothers and fathers.

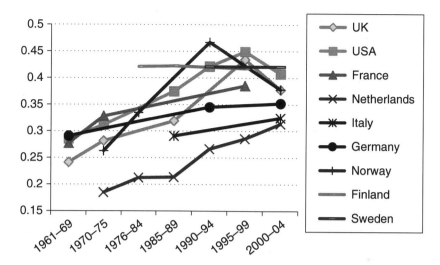

Source: Gershuny and Kan (2012).

Figure 10.5 Trends in women's share of paid employment time (men and women, aged 20–59 irrespective of marital or parental status)

Gender Differences in Paid and Unpaid Work

One of the dominant examples of the gender equality gap in the developed Western world is the pronounced difference in the contribution of men and women to paid and unpaid work. Time-use data across different countries in Europe and the US suggest that the gender gap in paid work time and unpaid work time is closing slowly. Data from the Multiple Time Use Studies show that if we look at trend data in the gender division of labour across countries and time, we see some interesting patterns that have some pronounced implications for men, women and children.

Figure 10.5 illustrates the well-known increase in the share of paid work that is done by women from the 1960s through to the 2000s. The female share of paid work is defined as women's average paid work time divided by the total of paid work time done by both women and men. It can be seen that women's time spent on paid work is less than that of men. In all countries, women's share of paid work is less than half of the total paid work time. However, across all nine countries, the trend is generally upwards (Gershuny and Kan 2012).

What are the implications of these trends in paid work, for the division of unpaid labour? Figure 10.6 illustrates the share in unpaid labour done by

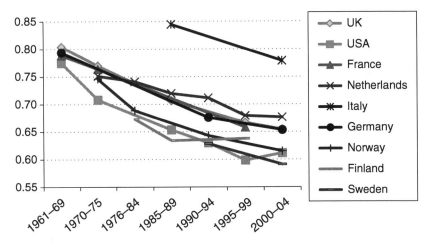

Source: Gershuny and Kan (2012).

Figure 10.6   Trends in women's share of unpaid work time

women over the decades. While there is an outlier here – Italy, with Italian women doing much more of the domestic labour than women in any of the other eight countries shown – the trend is still downwards. Italy, like other countries in Southern Europe, has minimal state provision for work–family balance and, although there has been an increase in female employment, there has been a marked fertility decline, which partly reflects the poorly paid maternity leave and limited childcare provision outside of the family. In Germany, the Netherlands and France the decline is somewhat less pronounced than in other countries, with women still doing more than 65 per cent of the unpaid work; presumably because of the emphasis on tra-ditional family roles that underlies the policy design and implementation in these countries. Overall, there is almost a 20 per cent shift in women's share of unpaid work over this period, which is a substantial decline and shows a remarkable change in family life (Gershuny and Kan 2012).

It is necessary to break down these trends into their component parts in order to interpret what is going on. Unpaid work time includes core domestic work (such as cleaning, doing the laundry and cooking), caring for family members (including childcare) and non-core domestic unpaid work (such as shopping, gardening and household repairs). If we look separately at men's and women's efforts in core and non-core domestic tasks and caring, then we find considerable differences. For example, women's contribution to care time in absolute terms in the 2000s is almost three times that of men. In core domestic work, women are doing about twice the amount of men. Only in non-core work is there less of a gender divide in overall amounts, although tasks remain highly gender segregated.

Does it matter if women and men specialize? Isn't this what a sensible division of labour is about? Moreover, surely it is only fair that if men, on average, work more paid work hours than women, then women should do more of the unpaid work than men. In overall work time, men's and women's hours are not dissimilar, so why should policy makers be concerned about the gender difference in paid and unpaid work?

In modern societies, paid and unpaid work have very dissimilar consequences. Participation in paid labour is crucial for acquiring human capital, which strongly helps to determine subsequent life opportunities. Paid work provides not just income, but also access to social networks, insurance and pension schemes, and monetary credit, all of which help to improve the paid worker's bargaining power within the family (Gershuny and Kan 2012).

The existing gender division of labour is firmly embedded in institutional practices and cultural norms that reinforce the status quo. The gender divide becomes much more marked with the birth of the first child. Using household panel data, following people across time, research has clearly shown a marked divergence in the way that childbirth affects men and women, with the man maintaining or increasing his share of paid work, while the woman markedly increases her domestic work and childcare (Gershuny 2004). As a consequence, the woman is accumulating human capital at a slower rate than the man, further increasing the pressure for gendered specialization. Moreover, parental caring and routine domestic labour has to be done at times which fit around the needs of the child(ren), and this may well conflict with the long and unsocial work hours which tend to be associated particularly with fathers' employment.

As Gershuny and Kan point out, persistent traditional gender ideologies and traditional work practices interact with the rise in 'family breakdown'. The high rates of partnership dissolution, when coupled with gendered specialization in paid and unpaid work, are associated with gendered differences in life course prospects for financial well-being and life opportunities. This means that when a man leaves a marriage, he takes with him his relatively enhanced human capital. In contrast, a woman who specialized in unpaid work is left not just with the child(ren) to raise, but also with her earning capacity relatively diminished by her disproportionate responsibilities for unpaid work.

It is tempting to surmise that if more active efforts were made on the part of the state and society to mobilize greater involvement of fathers in domestic life, this could be beneficial for both gender equality and the well-being of children. This is, in part, because greater father involvement might help to increase the 'entitlements' of women and children, giving them greater access to resources and enhancing their life opportunities. I discuss in more detail below the 'culture of care', in general, and fathers' involvement in family life, in particular. First, however, it is important to examine more closely how gender inequalities and work–family balance interrelate.

Work–Family Balance

In recent years public interest in work–family balance policies has expanded significantly. The issue for policy makers is the extent to which the state can and should intervene to help men and women reconcile work and family responsibilities. One important concern is how working mothers and fathers can provide good care for their children while at the same time performing paid work effectively. Different policy regimes take different approaches. In Nordic countries in particular, policies have been based on the assumption that men and women will be fully engaged in the labour market. The Nordic model treats women as workers, but then allows for gender difference by grafting on transfers and services in respect of care work for partnered and unpartnered mothers alike. The Swedish variant has been described as the 'gender participation model', focusing on promoting gender equality in employment and providing cash support for parental leave and services of family care. As a result of this 'supported adult worker model' a high proportion of mothers work part-time hours, exercising their right to work a six-hour day when they have a pre-school child (Lewis 2012).

In many European countries, including the UK, Germany and the Netherlands, part-time work remains the main way for women to reconcile work and family demands. Interestingly, in the Netherlands, part-time work has received considerable support from the state in a deliberate attempt to create a one-and-a-half breadwinner family, rather than a full-time dual-earner family.

Is part-time work a panacea for reconciling work and family life? This question was examined by Scott and Plagnol (2012), using data from the European Social Survey (ESS) to explore people's own perceptions of work–family conflict. The ESS included a module on work, family and well-being in 2004 and 2010. Perceptions of work–family conflict were tapped using four questions:

1. How often do you keep worrying about work problems when you are not working?
2. How often do you feel too tired after work to enjoy the things you would like to do at home?

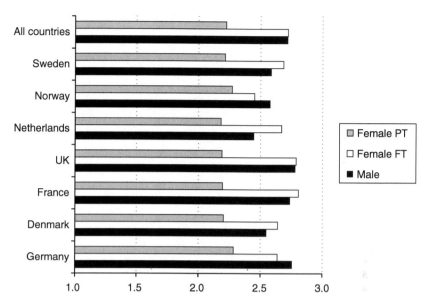

Source: European Social Survey 2004 (Scott and Plagnol 2012).

Figure 10.7   Work–family conflict by country, work status and gender

3. How often do you find that your job prevents you from giving the time
    you want to your partner or family?
4. How often do you find that your partner or family gets fed up with the
    pressure of your job?

The range of responses runs from 1 to 5, where 1 is the lowest possible
work–family conflict and 5 is the highest.

Figure 10.7 shows the perceptions of work–family conflict for men and
women aged 18–65 in heterosexual partnerships. Most responses are positioned between 2 and 3, which indicates that they experience work–family
conflict either 'hardly ever' or ' sometimes'. Interestingly, the perceptions
of work–family conflict for men and women who work full-time are very
similar. However, women who work part-time report significantly lower
levels of work–family conflict than women in full-time employment.

In further analysis, using multivariate models that include possible predictors of work–family conflict, it was found that people's perceptions of
work–family conflict are driven more by their work conditions than by
their family circumstances (Scott and Plagnol 2012). However, family circumstances show some interesting gender differences in the way they affect

people's perception of work–family conflict. Not surprisingly, the presence of young children increased the work–family conflict for women but not for men. However, what is surprising is that in couples where there was a traditional gender divide of domestic labour – with the woman doing all the housework chores – then it was his work–family conflict that increased, rather than hers. The fact that doing most of the housework chores does not increase women's perceived work–family conflict presumably indicates that women find nothing unusual about doing a 'double shift', with responsibility for both a job and the bulk of the housework. Men's increase in work–family conflict might arise because of the dissonance caused by behaviour being at odds with equality beliefs. Alternatively, it may be that men's heightened work–family conflict reflects their partner's dissatisfaction, as one of the questions asks, 'How often do you find that your partner gets fed up with the pressures of your job?'

This evidence suggesting that men can benefit in terms of reduced work–family conflict if they take up their share of the domestic chores hopefully bodes well for the uptake of more equitable gender roles in the future. The interpretation that there is more harmony in couples who divide up domestic work more evenly has received some additional support from a recent study based on the 1970s Great British birth cohort data. This shows that a more equitable divide of housework offsets the enhanced risk of divorce associated with female employment (Sigle-Rushton 2010). This is an intriguing finding because it suggests that tackling gender inequalities in domestic work might help to increase the stability of couples, which would also benefit children.

On the whole, the task policy makers face to improve work–family balance is a minefield of competing interests (Lewis 2012). This is in part because there are many different policy goals. First, there is the concern of addressing the challenges of an ageing society, by enabling women to work and thereby improving the dependency ratio. Second, there is the concern of tackling falling fertility rates, which are thought to be exacerbated by lack of support for women as workers. Third, in some countries, work–family balance policies have been seen as a good way of tackling child poverty. In the UK, for example, there have been explicit attempts to encourage lone mothers to return to work, by limiting welfare benefits. Another goal, in both the UK and Germany, has been to raise children's educational achievement by promoting high-quality care in nursery settings.

Unfortunately, the issues around care in and of itself have often figured less prominently on the agendas of governments. This may change, because one of the most striking new social risks is the matter of care for dependents, both young and old. We need a better basis of evidence in order to guide how best to compensate and organize care, and also to ensure greater equality between men and women, as well as greater benefits for children.

Culture of Care

Formal childcare provision has increased in all Western European countries as policies designed to provide time to work have become more central to the trajectory of social policy. However, in the UK childcare provision, although expanding, remains fragmented, expensive and intended more to enable mothers to work at least part-time than to benefit the child, in terms of the child's own needs. A recent example of this was an attempt to raise the number of children that childminders can legally care for, in order to reduce care costs.

So what about the children? How do children view the complex 'culture of care' that is necessary when both parents go out to work? One interesting qualitative study in the US suggests that young children have very different responses to their care situations (Hochschild 2001). One child clearly resented the parents' absence and was angry and difficult when they returned home. Another child did not seem to feel any resentment and had ceased to look to the parents as exclusive caregivers. What explains this difference? Hochschild suggests that children are sophisticated observers of their social world and they pick up on what parents never say to them directly. They learn about the 'problems' parents experience in finding care, the 'conflicts' that result from different expectations. Moreover, children know whether carers are doing the childcare for love, or money, or both. The point is worth reiterating that what is 'good care' from the adult perspective may not appear the same to the eyes of the child. Children's interests, mothers' interests and societal interests do not necessarily coincide. Since the family is not a monolith, it is necessary to differentiate between the different family members whose acceptance, responses and contributions to change will vary. Children's perspectives and their contributions to family life (and many children themselves are active caregivers) must be taken seriously.

Increasing Fathers' Involvement in Childcare

There is an increasing amount of evidence to show the clear benefits of greater father involvement for children. Most studies agree that high-quality involvement, support and communication from any type of father, whether biological or social, residential or non-residential, can improve the well-being of the child (Carr et al. 2014). Change is slow and, on average, fathers still play a somewhat minimal role in caring and core domestic labour compared to mothers. However, men today play a far greater role in domestic work than did their fathers or grandfathers. Further change may come faster if the benefits of a more equitable divide of unpaid work became more widely known. Policies can help to 'nudge' a more equitable gender divide. Even a largely symbolic step, such as making it possible for parents to choose how to divide up parental leave, is a step in the right direction. In law, parental leave is a 'family right' to be divided between parents as they see fit in Austria, Denmark, Finland and Luxembourg; and an individual entitlement in Belgium, France, Germany, Greece, Italy, Ireland, Portugal, Spain, the Netherlands and the UK (Lewis 2012). But this is fast-changing territory and country approaches are shifting. Iceland, Norway and Sweden offer a mixed entitlement, part family and part individual; these countries have a specific 'daddy leave', which is an entitlement for the father that is lost if he fails to take it up. The uptake of parental leave by men is universally low. Interestingly, however, in Iceland, where one-third of the nine-month parental leave is allocated to the father alone, the uptake figure rose to 80 per cent after the introduction of the three-month quota.

There are considerable institutional, structural and cultural changes needed before we can make gender equality a reality, and change takes time. Perhaps both setting an example and educating our children and grandchildren in the balance of time-to-work and time-to-care is a useful start. One important element in addressing the care deficit is to find ways, at both family and societal levels, to value domestic work and care work more highly, regardless of whether the carer is a child, woman or man.

CONCLUSION

It is worth reiterating that debates about whether we are in the midst of 'family change' or 'family decline' are unhelpful. Research on the effects on children of family disruption, family diversity, changing work–family balance and different care cultures is often contentious. Ideology frequently colours interpretations, and claims far exceed knowledge. Examples of ideology masking interpretation come from both liberal and conservative viewpoints. To use currently fashionable jargon, we need to deconstruct the literature on children's families and gender inequalities to examine how ideas of childhood, gender roles and family life shape not only what questions are asked but also what answers are found. The stakes could not be higher, because to be effective, family policy must be informed by evidence, not ideology.

REFERENCES

Bennett, F., J. De Henau, S. Himmelweit and S. Sung (2012), 'Financial togetherness and autonomy within couples', in J. Scott, S. Dex and A. Plagnol (eds), *Gendered Lives: Gender Inequalities in Production and Reproduction*. Cheltenham, UK and Northampton, MA, USA: Edward Elgar Publishing, pp. 97–122.

Bradshaw, J. (2002), 'Child poverty and child outcomes', *Children and Society*, 16, 131–140.

Carr, D., K. Springer and K. Williams (2014), 'Health and families', in J. Treas, J. Scott and M. Richards, *The Wiley Blackwell Companion to Sociology of Families*, Oxford: Wiley–Blackwell, pp. 255–276.

Chant, S. (2006), 'Poverty begins at home? Questioning some (mis)conceptions about children, poverty and privation in female-headed households', UNICEF Report on the State of the World's Children, accessed 7 April 2015 at http://www.unicef.org/sowc07/docs/chant.pdf.

Chapple, S. (2009), 'Child well-being and sole-parent family structure in the OECD: an analysis', OECD Social, Employment and Migration Working Paper, no. 82, Paris: OECD.

Chase-Lansdale, P.L. and J. Brooks-Gunn (1995), *Escape from Poverty: What Makes a Difference for Children?* Cambridge: Cambridge University Press.

Clarke, L. (1996), 'Demographic change and the family situation of children', in J. Brannen and M. O'Brien (eds), *Children in Families: Research and Policy*, London: Falmer Press, pp. 66–83.

Duncan, G., W.J. Yeung, J. Brooks-Gunn and J. Smith (1998), 'The effects of childhood poverty on the life chances of children', *American Sociological Review*, 63, 406–423.

Durkheim, E. (1979 [1911]), 'Childhood', reprinted in W.F. Pickering (ed.) (1979), *Durkheim: Essays on Morals and Education*, London: Routledge, pp. 149–154.

DWP (2011), 'Households below average income', accessed 10 February 2012 at http://research.dwp.gov.uk/asd/index.php?page=hbai.

Ely, M., M.P.M. Richards, M.E.J. Wadsworth and B.J. Eliott (1999), 'Secular changes in the association of parental divorce and children's educational attainment – evidence from three British birth cohorts', *International Journal of Social Policy*, 28 (3), 437–455.

Esping-Andersen, G. (2009), *The Incomplete Revolution: Adapting to Women's New Roles*, Cambridge: Polity Press.

Farthing, R. (2014), 'Family poverty', in J. Treas, J. Scott and M. Richards (eds), *The Wiley–Blackwell Companion to the Sociology of Families*, Oxford: Wiley–Blackwell.

Gershuny, J. (2004), 'Time through the life course, in the family', in J. Scott, J. Treas and M. Richards (eds.), *The Blackwell Companion to the Sociology of Families*, Oxford: Blackwell, pp. 158–178.

Gershuny, J. and M.Y. Kan (2012), 'Half-way to gender equality in paid and unpaid work', in J. Scott, S. Dex and A. Plagnol, *Gendered Lives: Gender Inequalities in Production and Reproduction*, Cheltenham, UK and Northampton, MA, USA: Edward Elgar Publishing, pp. 74–94.

Glass, N. (2001), 'What works for children? The political issues', *Children and Society*, 15, 14–20.

Goode, J., C. Callender and R. Lister (1998), *Purse or Wallet? Gender Inequalities and Income Distribution within Families on Benefits*, London: Policy Studies Institute.

Highet, G. and L. Jamieson (2007), 'Cool with change: young people and family change', accessed 7 January 2013 at http://www.crfr.ac.uk/reports/CWC%20 final%20report%202007.pdf.

Hochschild, A. (2001), 'Eavesdropping children, adult deals, and cultures of care', in R. Hertz and N. Marshall (eds), *Working Families*, Berkeley, CA: University of California Press, pp. 340–353.

Jensen, A.-M. (2009), 'Pluralisation of family forms', in J. Qvortrup, W. Corsaro and M.-S. Honig (eds), *The Palgrave Handbook of Childhood Studies*, London: Palgrave Macmillan, pp. 140–156.

Lesthaeghe, R. (1995), 'The second demographic transition in Western countries: an interpretation', in K. Mason and A.-M. Jensen (eds), *Gender and Family Change in Industrialized Countries*, Oxford: Clarendon, pp. 17–62.

Lewis, J. (2012), 'Gender equality and work–family balance in a cross-national perspective', in J. Scott, S. Dex and A. Plagnol (eds), *Gendered Lives: Gender Inequalities in Production and Reproduction*, Cheltenham, UK and Northampton, MA, USA: Edward Elgar Publishing, pp. 206–224.

Mayer, S. (2010), 'Revisiting an old question: how much does parental income affect child outcomes?', *Focus*, 27 (2), 21–26.

OECD (2009), 'Doing better for children', accessed 7 January 2013 at http://www.oecd.org/els/familiesandchildren/doingbetterforchildren.htm.

OECD (2011), 'Doing better for families', accessed 7 January 2013 at http://www.oecd.org/els/familiesandchildren/doingbetterforfamilies.htm.

Office for National Statistics (ONS) (2012), *Statistical Bulletin: Family and Households, 2012*, accessed 16 March 2016 at http://webarchive.nationalarchives.gov.uk/20160105160709/http://www.ons.gov.uk/ons/dcp171778_284823.pdf.

Parreñas, R.S. (2005), *Children of Global Migration*, Stanford, CA: Stanford University Press.

Qvortrup, J. (1994), 'Childhood matters: an introduction', in J. Qvortrop, M. Bardy, G. Sgritta and H. Wintersberger (eds), *Childhood Matters: Social Theory, Practice and Policy*, Aldershot: Avebury, pp. 1–23.

Ridge, T. (2002), *Childhood Poverty and Social Exclusion: From a Child's Perspective*, Bristol: Policy Press.

Scott, J. (2008), 'Children as respondents: the challenge for quantitative methods', in P. Christensen and A. James (eds), *Research with Children*, 2nd edn, London: Falmer Press, pp. 87–108.

Scott, J. (2014), 'Children's families: a child-centred perspective', in J. Treas, J. Scott and M. Richards (eds), *The Wiley–Blackwell Companion to the Sociology of Families*, Oxford: Wiley–Blackwell, pp. 404–423.

Scott, J. and A. Plagnol (2012), 'Work–family conflict and well-being in Northern Europe', in J. Scott, S. Dex and A. Plagnol (eds), *Gendered Lives: Gender Inequalities in Production and Reproduction*, Cheltenham, UK and Northampton, MA, USA: Edward Elgar Publishing, pp. 174–205.

Sen, A. (1990), 'Gender and cooperative conflicts', in I. Tinker (ed.), *Persistent Inequalities: Women and World Development*, New York, USA and Oxford, UK: Oxford University Press, pp. 123–149.

Sigle-Rushton, W. (2010), 'Men's unpaid work and divorce: reassessing specialisation and trade in British families', *Feminist Economics*, 16 (2), 1–26.

Sigle-Rushton, W., J. Hobcraft and K. Kiernan (2005), 'Parental divorce and subsequent disadvantage', *Demography*, 42 (3), 427–446.

Waksler, F. (1991), *Studying the Social Worlds of Children: Sociological Readings*, London: Falmer Press.

Waldfogel, J. (2006), *What Children Need*, Cambridge, MA: Harvard University Press.

Willetts, D. (2010), *The Pinch: How the Baby Boomers Took Their Children's Future and Why They Should Give It Back*, London: Atlantic Books.

Index

abortion 15, 17
  recourse to 35, 40
adolescence 6, 81, 238–9
adoption 14
  transnational 122
Amato, P. 44–5
American Panel Study of Income
  Dynamics 54
Andersson, G. 230
anthropology 121–2
Anxo, D.
  research on household division of
    labour 52, 54
assistive reproductive technologies
  122–3
Australia 21, 54, 149
Austria 149, 151
  family policies in
    parental leave 146, 252
  female employment in 153, 156,
    171
    full-time 164
    part-time 148
    role of childcare in 166
  rate of marriage in event of
    pregnancy in 34
  unmarried cohabitation in 32–3

Baby Boomer 25
Baltimore Study 18–19, 22
Barre, C.
  association between non-resident
    children and formation of non-
    marital unions 181
Becker, Gary
  theory of
    division of housework 53
    new home economics 2, 142
Belgium 57, 82, 85, 149, 151
  cohabitation contract (*cohabitation
    légale*) 37

divorce rates in 32
family policies in 145
  parental leave 146, 252
female employment in 156–7, 170
  full-time 156, 162
  maternal employment patterns
    148
  role of childcare in 166
Flanders
  Antwerp 103, 113
  Ghent 103
intersectionality in 90, 92
part-time employment in 148
undocumented mothers in 103–4,
  109, 111, 113
Bernhardt, E.
  association between re-partnering of
    men and fatherhood in 206
Billari, F.C. 5
biotechnologies 122
Blair, Tony
  child poverty policies of 240
Bolivia 105, 113
  Santa Cruz 113
Breiman, L. 89
Brown, Gordon
  child poverty policies of 240
Buhlmann, F. 76
  view of role of social context in
    parenthood for division of
    housework 56
Bulgaria 57, 149
  average age at first marriages for
    women in 28
  divorce rates in 32
  female employment in 156–7
Butler, J. 109

Caldwell, J.G.C. 226
Cameron, David 242
Cameroon 115